Studies of Video Practices

A unique and insightful collection of essays, carefully crafted video-based studies of video practice, that reveal how visual media increasingly inform and enable everyday social interaction, be it interaction between friends and family, collaborative video games, or the production of highly complex, organisational activities. This book is an important and original contribution to contemporary studies of technology in action and our understanding of language use and social interaction.

—*Christian Heath, King's College London*

The last two decades have seen a rapid increase in the production and consumption of video by both professionals and amateurs. The near ubiquity of devices with video cameras and the rise of sites like YouTube have lead to the growth and transformation of the practices of producing, circulating, and viewing video, whether it be in households, workplaces, or research laboratories.

This volume builds a foundation for studies of activities based in and around video production and consumption. It contributes to the interdisciplinary field of visual methodology, investigating how video functions as a resource for a variety of actors and professions.

Mathias Broth is Associate Professor of Language and Culture at Linköping University, Sweden.

Eric Laurier is Senior Lecturer in Geography and Interaction at Edinburgh University, UK.

Lorenza Mondada is Professor in General Linguistics and French Linguistics at the University of Basel, Switzerland.

Routledge Research in Cultural and Media Studies

Studies of Video Practices
Video at Work

**Edited by Mathias Broth, Eric Laurier,
and Lorenza Mondada**

 Routledge
Taylor & Francis Group

NEW YORK AND LONDON

First published 2014
by Routledge
711 Third Avenue, New York, NY 10017

and by Routledge
2 Park Square, Milton Park, Abingdon, Oxon OX14 4RN

*Routledge is an imprint of the Taylor & Francis Group,
an informa business*

© 2014 Taylor & Francis

Library of Congress Cataloging-in-Publication Data
Studies of video practices : video at work / edited by Mathias Broth, Eric
   Laurier, and Lorenza Mondada.
      pages cm — (Routledge research in cultural and media studies)
   Includes bibliographical references and index.
   1. Industrial cinematography.   2. Audio-visual materials.   3. Motion
pictures—Production and direction.   I. Broth, Mathias, editor of
compilation.   II. Laurier, Eric, editor of compilation.   III. Mondada,
Lorenza, editor of compilation.
   TR894.S78 2014
   777—dc23
   2013049675
ISBN: 978-0-415-72839-3 (hbk)
ISBN: 978-1-315-85170-9 (ebk)

Typeset in Sabon
by Apex CoVantage, LLC

Contents

PART III
Assembling

Introducing Video at Work

Mathias Broth (Linköping University)
Eric Laurier (University of Edinburgh)
Lorenza Mondada (University of Basel)

1. INTRODUCTION

Although film has been available for research, leisure, and commercial purposes since the end of the 19th century, and even though the television and
the VCR have been with us for more than a generation, the last decade has
seen a new and quite distinct proliferation, transformation, and redistri-
bution of video. Indeed, video, in this loose definition, is now at work in
consumer smartphones, car seats, desktop computers, children's toys, traffic
warden's shoulders, the tools of dentistry, sports coaching, probes for sewer
systems, and, of course, film production (where more films are now shot in
digital video than in film stock). It is this very proliferation and transformation of video as it traverses settings from the everyday to highly specialized
workplaces that provides the motive for this collection.

Part of the reason for the steady dispersal and integration of video into a
profusion of expected and unexpected places has been the reduction in the
cost of screens, lenses, and storage technologies, as well as the miniaturization and usability of devices. Once prohibitively expensive and technically
intimidating, the editing and manipulation of video are built into phones,
photographic cameras, tablets, and almost all current computers. Of equal
import has been the rise of new networks for the distribution of video such
as Youtube, Facebook, and online newspaper reporting, in tandem with the
long promised video telephony of Skype and other systems. Video has come
to a point of ubiquity and commonplaceness in the more affluent regions
of the world, reminiscent of the spread of paper and pens. And, like pen
and paper, it is becoming enfolded into the routine documentation, communication, and reception of all manner of human (and more than human)
practices. The point of comparison is worth pursuing further because, if we
begin to think about how we might want to study pen and paper, it becomes
apparent that we could say only limited things about them as media in and
of themselves. A richer line of inquiry is around what we *do* with paper
and pens. What they are used for could take us to the desks of international
aid organizations, shoppers making lists of groceries, pharmacists annotat-
ing prescriptions, state officials marrying individuals, architects adjusting a

wall length, teenagers writing song lyrics, and so on and so on. In fact, the sheer diversity of what is done with paper and pens would make such a collection seem foolhardy. Perhaps, though, we have caught a moment a little earlier in the spread of video where its uses are not yet so common as to go unnoticed and the skills required to shoot it, edit it, and show it remain arcane enough to be restricted in their distribution.

The aim of this collection, then, is to begin to capture what different groups *do* with video in everyday, leisure, and workplace *practices*. In other words, the collection aims at focusing on a selection of social, cultural, and professional activities that involve video practices and on how the shooting, assembling, viewing, editing, and showing of video are now also involved in the organization of those practices. In some cases, such as endoscopy, the activities could not be undertaken without video.

A long and complex tradition of studying video practices in media studies has ranged from encoding/decoding (Hall, 1973), via the interplay between new media (Jenkins, 2006), the integration of video into various everyday settings (Buckingham and Willett, 2010) and, more recently, the cultures of video production (Mayer, Miranda & Caldwell 2009; Caldwell 2008). As a disciplinary field in itself with a long history of approaches (see Scannell, 2007), we cannot hope to summarize the broad field of media studies here, even though the studies in this chapter have been influenced by it in particular ways. What we would like to compare media studies with is the approaches to video that have grown out of ethnomethodology and conversation analysis (EMCA) (Garfinkel, 1967; Sacks, 1992). It is a body of interdisciplinary work that has utilized video for the purposes of the close analysis of ordinary practices. In other words, on the one hand, we have the changing traditions of approaching video in media studies that have those media as their object, and, on the other hand, we have studies in, for example, sociology, anthropology, and linguistics that utilize video to analyse other practices as their object. Until recently, these two bodies of video research, one *on* video and the other *using* video, had little to do with one another. As the first of its kind, this collection marks a point where there is now a body of studies that *both* analyse video practices and use video to analyse those practices. This collection offers, in short, *video analyses of video practices*. What is distinctive to this new approach is that, taking video practices as its object of research, it is based in the detailed description of the step-by-step, moment-by-moment organization of these practices allied with the explication of their situated organization. This type of organization routinely brings together talk, gestures, facial expressions, camera operation, and orientation towards screens in the concerted and ongoing production of video practices, such as the live-editing of a TV broadcast, video game playing, or endoscopic surgery.

In this chapter, we would like to set the scene for the studies in this book by sketching out the extensive fields in which both the topic of the book and its approach are situated. This will involve traversing some of the fields that have long had video as their object and our own approach that has video as its equipment, empirical material, and analytic medium.

2. BACKGROUND

In this section, we will provide a sketch of the two broad areas of existing research that have inspired this book. The first area is concerned with the emergence of the analysis of video recordings in the social sciences and, in particular, EMCA. The second is a growing interest in EMCA in using video recordings to study other practices involving video, directly and indirectly.

In these historical notes, we describe first how film has been used in the social sciences since its discovery and then how film has been gradually supplanted by video and its new potentialities (miniaturization, digital formats, storability, cheap prices, etc.). Meaningful distinctions can be drawn between film and video, not least between different technologies (e.g. cameras, editing machines, projectors, etc.) but also in terms of indexing histories, genres, academic disciplines, and so on. When the differences between video and film are relevant in what follows, we will draw upon them, but in general we will use the term "video" to encompass a wide variety of media practices, some of which would usually be referenced by "film" (also taking into account the fact that many "films" are today, in fact, produced by video technology).

2.1. Video Analysis

Since its introduction at the end of the 19th century, film has been used for anthropological and sociological research. For instance, Felix-Louis Regnault, visiting the Exposition Ethnographique de l'Afrique Occidentale in Paris in 1895, used Marey's chronophotography to capture the movements of a Wolof woman. This early form of motion picture was employed only six months before the Lumière brothers made their first public projection of cinematograph films. Film was also used for ethnographic purposes by Alfred Cort Haddon, who trained Malinowski and was influential in developing the sense of fieldwork of his student. During the Cambridge Anthropological Expedition to Torres Strait in 1898, Haddon shot various films of natives dancing, performing ceremonies, and living their everyday lives. These early uses of film in anthropological studies for the first time documented the duration and flow of embodied human practices.

But later on, after a series of other major attempts (such as those of Mead and Bateson in Bali [Mead & Bateson, 1977] and after the advent of synchronized sound recording), film made available, for detailed study, talk, and embodied conduct in naturally occurring social interactions. In this respect, the *Natural History of an Interview,* a project initiated by Bateson in 1955 (see McQuown, 1971), is an important landmark. It consists of a film recording of an entire therapy session in which Bateson himself talks with a patient, Doris. It was a landmark in using film to record naturalistic rather than experimental settings and in using film to investigate the details of embodied communication in real time (Leeds-Hurwitz, 1987). The film also led to the development of transcription techniques and in-depth analyses from a variety of disciplinary perspectives. Over the long term, Bateson's project led to new studies on kinesics (Birdwhistell, 1970), context analysis (Scheflen, 1972), and gesture studies (Kendon, 1990, 2004).

Although not a direct development from the use of film in anthropology, EMCA analyses have pursued parallel and sometimes divergent analyses of the details of social interactions (Sacks, 1984). Although audio recordings of telephone calls characterized the beginning of conversation analysis in Sacks' work on calls to a suicide prevention centre (1966) and Schegloff's work on calls to the police (1967), video was also used early on. As early as the 1960s, David Sudnow was experimenting with film recordings (Hill & Crittenden, 1968), and at the beginning of the 1970s, Charles and Candy Goodwin began videotaping everyday encounters (Goodwin, 1979, 1981) and making their videotaped recordings available to others for research. They were used at a series of seminars at Penn University, where the Goodwins were joined by, among others, Harvey Sacks, Emmanuel Schegloff, Gail Jefferson, Erving Goffman, William Labov, and Dell Hymes. Their recordings were also used at the Linguistic Institute held in 1973, where the Goodwins worked with Sacks and Schegloff, who later presented a paper on the "home position" of body movements based on these tapes (Sacks & Schegloff, 2002). Further, Charles Goodwin's doctoral dissertation (Goodwin, 1981) was based upon these same tapes. Goodwin has subsequently developed and inspired a rich tradition of studies of embodied conduct in EMCA (Goodwin, 1996, 2000, 2007, etc.).

Although there are other traditions of work on embodiment, especially within gesture studies (see Kendon [2004] for a historical account), EMCA has provided one of the most extensive literatures reliant on video recordings of interaction. Its inquiry into embodied practices is characterized by a number of aspects. First, video is used to record "naturally occurring" social interactions. Given that interaction is treated by EMCA as being accomplished in a locally situated way by the participants, central to capturing any social phenomenon is recording activities that are not orchestrated or elicited by the researcher but rather unfolding as they would whether the researcher is present or not (Potter, 2002). It is a form of video-recording-as-fieldwork that follows rather than directs the action (Heath, Hindmarsh, & Luff, 2010). It is aimed at identifying the relevant settings of action to be recorded and using the relevant devices for capturing situated, embodied, material, and environmental features. Second, aspects of the action recorded on video are then rendered in detailed transcripts of talk and of visual conduct that carefully represent the temporal unfolding of talk and other conduct. These fine-grained specificities of emergent trajectories of action are vital because these details are considered in and as the interactional resources that participants actively mobilize, arrange, and adjust for the production of the shared intelligibility (the "accountability," Garfinkel, 1967) of what they are doing together. Third, the produced video recordings are examined—together with their transcripts, for the analysis of the ways in which talk, gesture, body movement, the handling of objects and so on—and are collectively mobilized to achieve recognizable actions in situated social interaction.

These three characteristics—recording, transcription, and analysis of recorded and transcribed data—reflect the importance of locally situated, endogenous orders of action in EMCA. The constant return to recordings and transcripts is motivated by a desire to describe the in vivo order of how members of particular settings do the things that they do. Where other social sciences tend towards producing "ironic" descriptions of human practices—in which researchers' reasoning tends to supplant members' reasoning—EMCA analyses prioritize understanding the endogenous perspectives of those practices, from the inside and in members' own terms. It answers the abiding question of social order by showing how the order itself is locally produced at source. Where many other social sciences theorize a world driven by essences or by foundational forces, EMCA has instead demonstrated how it is produced through practice, in an emergent situated way. In so doing, it has been distinctive in using its recordings and transcripts to show both that this is so and how the members of particulars settings make it so. This has generated original and specific techniques for video recording particular social actions, a distinct style for transcribing relevant details, and, of course, original studies arising out of them, in the form of both single case studies and systematic collection-based studies.

This EMCA video-based approach has been developed out of, and for, a variety of settings and topics. On the one hand, everyday conversations—considered as the primordial locus of socialization and achievement of social order as well as of language and grammar (Ochs, Schegloff, & Thompson, 1996)—have been extensively documented, often by videos focusing on mealtimes (Goodwin, 1981). On the other hand, professional activities have also been studied: medical encounters (Heath, 1986), control rooms in airports (Suchman, 1993, 1996, 1997), underground control rooms (Luff & Heath, 1999), operating rooms (Mondada, 2003, 2007), TV studios (Broth, 2004, 2008a), and airplane cockpits (Nevile, 2004). Relatedly, institutional settings have also been investigated, such as care homes (Antaki, Walton, & Finlay, 2007; Lindström & Heinemann, 2009), management meetings (Svennevig, 2012), and educational settings (Lindwall & Lymer, 2005). These studies have produced a rapidly expanding body of findings on both the role of multimodality in the organization of joint action and how action and context are mutually constitutive of one another.

In terms of the former, studies using video have begun to uncover how language, gesture, gaze, body posture, and other forms of embodied conduct are synchronized and coordinated, mutually informing each other. In terms of the latter, video recordings make available for analysis not only embodied conduct but also how it configures and is configured by material environments, technologies, and objects.

EMCA studies themselves use video and thus depend on camera techniques, adaptations of recording devices to site specificities, organization of video data, and, finally, transcriptions of video recordings, but these research techniques have themselves remained largely unstudied. The practices of EMCA video analysis are predominantly transmitted in hands-on seminars and everyday teamwork, though they have also been inscribed in a handful of methodological textbooks and chapters (Goodwin, 1993; Heath & Hindmarsh, 2002; ten Have, 1998; Heath, Hindmarsh, & Luff, 2010; Knoblauch, Schnettler, Raab, & Soeffner, 2006; Mondada, 2006a, 2012a). There are good reasons why EMCA has not formalized its research procedures, given that the heart of EMCA is not about building its own normative and general methodologies but rather about studying the myriad ethnomethods at work in the world (Lynch, 1993). The video practices of EMCA are usually only briefly presented as a precursor to scrutinizing the specific settings and practices that they have recorded (e.g. classrooms, airports, cafes, family mealtimes, business meetings, etc.). Video is treated as a window opened onto social interaction and generally not discussed *per se* in terms of the configuring and reflexive effects they have on the very social order they are supposed to exhibit (Laurier & Philo, 2006). Consequently, the practices in which video plays a part have largely been overlooked.

A prime ambition in this collection then is to turn video analysis towards studying the increasingly varied video practices we find in the contemporary world. In this collection, we have sought out a variety of settings that rely upon video in one way or another to learn more about what video practices might be, how they are accomplished, and what they achieve. The book aims at casting new light upon exactly how video is at work in the world, whether it is as part of ethnomethodologies of the everyday, of workplaces, of media production, of gameplay, or of scientific activities. In pursuing exactly what it is we do with video through studying video recordings of it, we nevertheless also aim to continue to explore social actions such as conversing, arguing, disagreeing, assessing, and so on that video is at work within and without. We do this because a deeper understanding of how video is used contributes to our knowledge of the increasing role of video in the contemporary scene not only in media production but, more importantly, in a growing collection of other situations. Studying the production and consumption of video in detail provides a sense of how enthusiasm, skill, craft, affection, memory, humour, augmented vision, evidence, and the like are achieved in and through video.

2.2.   Video Analysis of Video Practices

The precursors to this book are two classic essays, one by Lena Jayyusi (1988) on the intelligibility of filmic structure and the other by Douglas Macbeth (1999) on the continuous shot in cinema verité. Although neither of these essays used video recordings to analyse other settings where video was a feature, they established the relevance of EMCA for studying film and video. Jayyusi drew upon existing work on sequence organization and category analysis to show how film editing practices drew upon these yet also structured them in its own particular filmic way. Macbeth meantime was concerned with the camera shot as a particular form of looking with a camera, one that is "both a record of the affairs witnessed, and a record of the witnessing too, where the work of looking itself is sometimes especially in view" (Macbeth, 1999: 164). It was not just that these investigations would take EMCA into film and media studies; the reverse was also true. Jayyusi proposed that "sustained empirical-analytic investigation, at least in the area of visual narratives . . . will prove very rich indeed, in diverse ways, for our understanding not only of film, but of accounting and communicative practices and of the informal logic of our culture" (1988: 292).

One of the pioneering studies that brought together both the EMCA perspective and video recordings of video practices was the analysis of "professional vision" offered by Charles Goodwin (1994). It is one of the first studies that focused on video with regard to how it is consequential for a setting's ongoing activity. In the study, the analysis of video recordings of an earlier set of events is relevant for the participants themselves as part of their professional work. Goodwin provides a description of the sharply alternate interpretations offered by the courtroom defence and prosecution of the same video clip shown as evidence in the famous Rodney King trial in 1992. The unedited video footage of the violent arrest of Rodney King had been recorded by a bystander. Invoking different "coding schemes," each party provided a reasonable and yet incompatible set of instructions to see what was recorded on video as either evidence of a group of police officers clearly beating up a defenceless black man or standard police procedure for a suspect visibly resisting arrest. The very possibility of securing such incompatible viewings of the same video clip demonstrates that even unedited video does not just show, in a transparent and straightforward way, "what happened." Instead, it becomes clear that, as Jayyusi had earlier argued, the intelligibility of video is not given but is achieved. However, Goodwin extends and complicates Jayyusi's work in his examination of the incompatible alternate instructions on how to see the recording given by the two sides in the courtroom. Moreover, because he is drawing upon video recordings of the setting, he was also able to examine the practical mobilization of talk, gesture, and artefacts (like the coding scheme itself) within a context of activity and interaction (e.g. a courtroom trial) that locally produce the sense of what the video displays.

Following Goodwin's exemplary analysis, a small number of studies analyse interaction in different settings where video is a relevant aspect of the activity (e.g. Broth, 2008b; Laurier, 2008; Luff & Heath, 1999; Mondada, 2003; Tutt & Hindmarsh, 2011). These studies have, however, been dispersed through a number of journals and edited collections; they have not yet been integrated within a broader and comparative conceptual framework. The main aim of the current book is therefore to bring together, for the first time, a substantial collection of studies of naturally occurring social interactions where video is used. In doing so, the volume provides a demonstration of the use of video recordings to investigate how video practices are organized, accomplished, and made sense of by specific video cultures, be they everyday, professional, artistic, or scientific.

3.   WHOSE PRACTICES? THE SOCIAL WORLDS OF VIDEO

As we have already noted, video is found in an increasing diversity of real-world settings, and research from various disciplinary and interdisciplinary backgrounds is only beginning to catch up with those settings. What we would like to do in this section is mark out a larger terrain of social worlds where video has grown in importance: the everyday, professional workplaces, the arts, and, finally, research itself, treated as an institutional and professional activity among others.

3.1.   The Everyday

It would be easy to forget that video and film have a long-ish history of involvement in a number of everyday practices. Initially through super 8 and other film formats (Zimmerman, 1995) and then through VHS and other video formats, recording was domesticated into the familial practices of weddings, births, sports successes, and graduations (Moran, 2002). Similarly, tourist practices have long drawn upon film and video as resources for both framing sites and sights during travel, while also sharing and recollecting those travels upon return (Crang, 1997). A parallel record of various public events has been ongoingly created by amateur film and video makers, most famously the Zapruder footage of the assassination of JFK and more recently numerous other events recorded by amateurs (such as the Rodney King event). Many of these then go on to circulate in the news media and elsewhere (e.g. the importance of amateur videos in reporting on the shooting of Gadafi and the Japanese tsunami). Although amateur film is not a new phenomenon (Zimmerman, 1995), the recent opening up of broadcast and circulation through Youtube and other video sharing sites has transformed practices still further as individuals and groups have found new and larger audiences and have developed new practices such as video blogging (Burgess, Green, Jenkins, & Hartley, 2009). Video telephony is becoming increasingly common (Koskinen, 2007) and is now augmenting and changing long-standing forms of telephony as voices become accompanied by gestures and visible (and thus show-able and noticeable) environments (Licoppe & Morel, 2012). Similarly, the use of web-based interfaces supporting video, like Skype, has modified visual practices and communication in significant ways (see Keating, Edwards, & Mirus [2008] on the use of such a technology by deaf people).

3.2. The Professional

Today, video is heavily used, and increasingly so, in a range of new and more traditional workplaces. The introduction of video in the workplace has led to new video-based practices alongside existing practices, which are also then being supplemented, augmented, and transformed by video.

The most obvious professional activity that has grown up around, and remains inextricable from, video is television production and related practices in film (Mayer, Miranda & Caldwell, 2009). Here, a particular video sequence (live or pre-edited) is a carefully crafted object in itself. Particular professions have grown up around dedicated tasks—producers, directors, camera operators, floor managers, makeup artists, and the like (see further, for example, Zettl, 2003), whose shared overall objective is to produce the recognisable qualities of broadcast TV and movies. At the same time, these professions remain generally invisible to the audience (this last point being noticeable, for instance, in the common saying among camera operators, "Don't shoot your colleagues"). This means that from an EMCA perspective, documenting practices of film shooting on the set must involve the researcher's own video recording of practices that are otherwise systematically rendered invisible (see the extensive studies developed by Schmitt [2007, 2010] on the basis of his own shooting on a film set).

Another set of workplaces that have emerged through and with video are the different kinds of control rooms that work as "centres of coordination" (Suchman, 1997) not only in TV-production but also in activities as diverse as control of public transport systems, airport control (Goodwin & Goodwin, 1996), and urban surveillance. These technologically complex settings have been extensively studied by Suchman and colleagues (Suchman, 1993, 1996, 1997), as well as by Heath and Luff (2000). Coordination centres are characterized by complex and fragmented ecologies, in which multiple video screens and related technologies allow individuals or teams to collaborate, monitor each other as well as other people, intervene in remote places, and organize distributed work across heterogeneous spaces.

However, video increasingly is also making its way into a vast variety of other professional activities, transforming them to varying degrees. Many professional tasks have thereby become easier, less expensive, and less risky to carry out. Just to take a few examples, the police now use video for disarming planted bombs, documenting evidence for the prosecution of crime, and supporting urban surveillance on the ground; surgeons and dentists use images produced by means of very small cameras for making otherwise hidden parts of the body visually available (see Chapter 5 by Lindwall, Johansson, Rystedt, Ivarsson, & Reit and Chapter 3 by Mondada, this volume) or for observing patients at home; teachers increasingly use podcast video for giving access to a lecture at a distance and at different times; therapists use video as a tool for patient analysis (McIlvenny, 2011); salespeople and real estate brokers use it to display and promote all sorts of products to potential clients locally and globally; architects use it to simulate, model, and present virtual plans to customers; and a wide range of other professionals enhance their collaborative work using videoconferencing technologies that allow them to conduct meetings at a distance (Licoppe & Relieu, 2007; Meier, 1997). All these different uses of video show how deeply this technology has already penetrated professional practices, as well as how largely it has not only supported them but also radically changed them.

3.3.   Artists

Although the edited collection does not have any chapters on artists adopting video, it is too significant an area not to mention in our brief introductory review. Video art emerged in the 1960s as a radical critique of television: from 1959 on, Fluxus artist Wolf Vostell presented a series of work with the title "Television Decollage" in which the TV image is blurred, perturbated, transformed. One of the first exhibitions of Nam June Paik, shown in Düsseldorf in 1963, consisted of 13 screens presenting 13 versions of the same TV program, offering 13 ways of deforming the image ("Exposition of Music-Electronic Television"). Another famous work, "TV Bra for Living Sculpture" (1969), diverted the TV set, transforming it into a bra worn by the cellist Charlotte Moorman. With the engineer Abe, Paik built in 1969 the "Abe/Paik synthesiser," which changes colour and black-and-white images and allows for online editing of video images, in ways similar to the work of Woody and Steina Vasulka, who invented computer programs and synthethizers and generated new dynamic landscapes ("Golden Voyage" [1974], "Reminiscence" [1974]). Nam June Paik was among the first artists to use the new Sony Portapak to shoot images of Pope Paul VI's procession through New York, as well as a taxi drive in Greenwich Village in the early 1960s. In its beginning, video art represented an active, irreverent, critical perspective on the use of the image by TV as well as a creative, innovative, and both artistic and technological attempt to invent new, nonrealistic, video images that were assembled in a way that was more reminiscent of the pictorial technique of collage rather than of TV or mainstream movies images (Meigh-Andrews, 2006).

What is striking is the long delay and relative obscurity of video in the arts scene before the rise in video art over the last decade. The recent success of video in arts practice can be measured by the number of video works taking major art prizes, by the commonality of video installations in galleries and elsewhere, and by the sheer number of students continuing to move into the field (Rush, 2007). As a consequence of the spread of video as a medium into the arts, the long tradition of the so-called white box of the gallery now alternates with the black box for the projection of video installations (Manovich, 2006). In the exhibition spaces for video works of art, the practices of art spectatorship, interpretation, and appreciation have then also been altered (Friedberg, 2006; Mondloch, 2010). Relatedly, the practices of video artists now draw upon the range of production skills that we might previously have expected to find in film and television production, albeit on a smaller and more experimental scale, some reimagining them, some critically subverting and resisting them, and some entirely distinct from them.

In this sense, video art is an important pioneering field that has developed a reflexive use of the medium from its very beginning in artistic practices.

3.4.   Researchers

As previously mentioned, the use of video in the social sciences has grown steadily. Accompanying this growth, video has also been taken up as a recording medium for research in the natural sciences. It has a long-standing role in the recording of insect and animal behaviour (Fleichmanet & Endler, 2000), in zoology (Visser, Smith, Bullock, Green, Carlsson, & Imberti, 2008), and in animal welfare. Equally interesting has been its growth in other natural sciences where its capacity to record movement, time and, to some extent, three-dimensionality has led to its increased use as a further instrument for recording data to be used in combination with other instruments. For example, in nano engineering, it provides real-time images of the effects of different forces on engineered materials and then provides for both their measurement and their visual documentation (Cumings & Zettl, 2000). In geoscience, it has been used for monitoring what happens at shorelines through visual indicators of wave and ocean current conditions (Holman, Stanley, & Ozkan-Haller, 2003; Martinez, Hart, & Ong, 2004).

Although video is used in a wide diversity of scientific programs and paradigms, analytic studies on it are still very scarce. In the social sciences, pioneering work has been done by studies dealing with the history of the use of film and, later, of video, mainly in anthropology. They show that film has been used in the social sciences since its very discovery (Banks & Ruby, 2011; Griffiths, 1996; Kendon, 1979). Despite this historical interest, the actual practices of researchers are still understudied. In most of the social sciences, including EMCA, video has first and foremost been discussed in methodological handbooks and manuals. These texts give insightful recommendations on how researchers *should* (or should not) produce their video data, but they do not offer any analytical insights about how researchers actually *do* video. Only very recently, texts discussing video issues have introduced this latter view (see Büscher, 2005; Mondada, 2006a, 2012a; Heath, Hindmarsh, & Luff, 2010), turning video from a methodological resource for research into a topic of analysis.

4.   OBSERVING VIDEO PRACTICES

These activities could all be studied for the relevance of video practices in and for their ordinary accomplishment by competent members of different communities. Members of each of these communities are accomplishing different things with different logics and criteria for judgement: commemorating a child's first steps, broadcasting a live football match, creating an art installation, monitoring shoreline drift, and so on. Our collection here then begins the work of mapping out these varied video practices in describing how they are locally produced. Here we will turn to briefly discuss two major ways to document and observe how these communities make use of video technologies: video-based reconstruction and video recording of video practices.

4.1.   Reconstruction

Although we have argued for the use of video to record video practices, reconstruction from the video media produced by particular settings can also be used in researching video practices as a topic in its own right. The researcher is able to recover much of the practical reasoning of the participants who are studied, provided that the activity has been recorded in a way that documents the relevant unfolding events. The most obvious research technique is to analyse the recording itself as the result of a recording activity. In his highly influential study, Macbeth (1999) studied anthropological and documentary film to recover how the continuous shot as a camera action is related to the ordinary order that is unfolding in the scene being filmed. The cameraperson looks around with the camera to find the relevant phenomena for the recording. As a result, the recording itself can be considered to be documenting camera operators' understanding of what is relevant in the world around them from within the very recording situation. This important insight has subsequently informed a number of praxeological studies of video work, including surgical settings (Mondada, 2007; Koschmann, LeBaron, Goodwin, & Feltovich, 2011; Sanchez Svensson, Heath, & Luff, 2007), research data (Mondada, 2006a, 2012c), television (Broth, 2004; Engström, Juhlin, Perry, & Broth, 2010; Bovet, 2009), and film production (Laurier, Strebel, & Brown, 2008).

Alongside studying the video produced by other video makers, reconstructive attention has turned towards the EMCA researcher's own videos focusing on their research participants' orientation towards the camera. Their analytical perspective has dealt with camera gaze, not as a bias hindering the scientific use of the record (supporting the famous observer's paradox introduced by Labov, 1972) but instead as a social phenomenon that reveals the constitutive features of the ongoing activity (Heath, 1986; Laurier & Philo, 2006; Lomax & Casey, 1998). Similarly, the ethical issues related to recordings that are usually discussed in a methodological and normative way have also been turned around into analytical phenomena that can be studied for how participants introduce such issues, orient towards them, dispute them, agree with them, and so on (Mondada, 2006b, 2013; Speer & Hutchby, 2003).

We may also note that the reconstruction of video work, and hence the manifest orientation of the person recording with the camera, is now increasingly done not only for the sake of studying researcher's videos *per se* but is also drawn upon for exploring topics other than video practices, related to, for instance, space, mobility, deixis, and turn taking (e.g., Broth & Lundström, 2013; Fele, 2012; Mondada, 2005, 2012c; De Stefani, 2010; Mortensen & Lundsgaard, 2011). These studies show how mobile trajectories, spatial orientation, constitution of interactional space, pointing gestures, and the like do not involve just the local resolution of participants' practical problems but also generate practical challenges for the camera operator documenting them. These studies acknowledge and exploit the fact that the recording activity was part of the recorded event and reconstruct, as an analytic tool, the ways in which the camera was handled—integrating the details of video production into the analysis of the topicalized phenomenon.

Reconstruction is, in fact, already a central feature of all sorts of *watching practices* (see Chapter 7 by Bovet, Sormani, & Terzi, this volume). For instance, a TV director who sees a shot that is moving on a screen in the control room understands that the camera is panning, tilting, or dollying without actually seeing the camera and its operator (Broth, 2009). And seeing a sudden change of perspective in an edited video sequence, we can know that a cut from one shot to another has been made without having to see the person(s) actually involved in making it (Mondada, 2009). Reconstruction can concern phenomena based on what is not actually visible in a piece of video, such as when a London underground supervisor infers the presence of some obstacle based on seeing people on a screen who all take the same kind of curved trajectory, which is then understandable as a detour (Luff, Heath, & Jirotka, 2000: 202–205). This ability of viewers to reconstruct a world beyond the screen is also routinely exploited in editing, where editors count on the fact that viewers will indeed reconstruct (whether this is the case or not) particular aspects that are not actually visible in a current shot, based on what is shown in previous shots (Jayyusi, 1988). Also, researchers in different fields trade heavily on reconstruction based on what some video actually shows, as in the practice of video-stimulated recall in cognitively oriented research about intentions (Kagan, Krathwohl, & Miller, 1963).

However, there are limits to what can be explored by reconstruction based on what the video shows and how it was produced. As Relieu (1999) acknowledges in his reflexion about the use of images in the social sciences, there is a need to shift from the long established study of broadcast television, of film, and, more generally, of video products to capturing the hidden work of how varied forms of video were produced as part of equally varied settings. This brings us to the second way to observe the use of video for practical purposes.

4.2.   Video of Video Practices

Reconstruction is based on the final object produced by video practices; however, the practices that produce the object are indefinitely more complex and rich than, and not recoverable from, the resulting video. The finely tuned ways in which video practices are arranged, coordinated in teams, organized within local ecologies, or adjusted to the contingencies of context escape from analytical scrutiny when only the audiovisual medium resulting from these activities is analysed. As already explained, the collection of papers gathered in this volume aims at taking the step of dealing with video practices *per se* not as a reconstructed phenomenon but as a video-documented phenomenon. Rather than acting like archaeologists who happen to have unearthed some dusty old videos, researchers can engage in doing fieldwork, visit the settings where video is used, witness the lived work of the production of these media (Sharrock & Hughes, 2004), and indeed create their own detailed audiovisual recordings of this lived work for later analysis (Mondada, 2006a). This step involves not only a change of perspectives but also new methodological challenges, not least in gaining access, as a legitimate peripheral participant, to the places where video is used. Turning video practice into a topic of analysis presupposes access to those practices, as well as their video documentation.

Although video often makes the cameras relatively invisible (even in video games; see Chapter 6 by Laurier & Reeves, this volume), studying them means capturing the processes of camera handling, viewing screens, operating editing software, and so on. Recording video practices can be done by researchers but, interestingly, has begun to be carried out by various professions for their own purposes. With the proliferation of video, many workplaces now document their own video practices and critically assess and comment on them. Surgeons video-record themselves evaluating the quality of the light and colour while they set up the endoscopic camera before an operation and discussing the choice of the best optics while engaging in complex anatomical procedures (Aanestad, Røtnes, Edwin, & Buanes, 2002, Mondada, 2003). And for the making of documentaries that accompany films and TV, actors, editors, and directors offer commentary on the shooting and cutting of movie scenes (see Laurier, Strebel, & Brown, 2008). Films in a reflexive mode will also incorporate film audiences (as in *Shirin*, Kiarostami, 2008) and film production into their final product. In these so-called meta-films, joining a long tradition of reflexive novels, the process of making the film is part of its very narrative (see the long tradition going from *Peeping Tom* [Powell, 1960], *8½* [Fellini, 1963], *Le Mépris* [Godard, 1963] to *Living in Oblivion* [DiCillo, 1995]), or it is embedded in the practice of found-footage (such as in *The Last Broadcast* [Avalos & Weiler, 1998] or *The Exorcist Tapes* [Prest, 2011], and so on), in which the events are seen through the camera of one of the characters.

Central to the present collection of studies, though, is researchers' documenting the use of video across a number of everyday settings, workplaces, and leisure spaces. In previous research, the video documentation of other professional video practices has involved recording: a film set (Schmitt, 2007), the control room where a TV programme is assembled (Broth, 2004), other control rooms such as surveillance and coordination units in the underground (Heath & Luff, 2000), or domestic settings or game centres where gamers are playing video games (Mondada, 2011, 2012b, Keating & Sunakawa, 2010; Sjöblom, 2011). The documentation of EMCA researchers' research practices by themselves has taken the simple form of metadata associated with recordings but can also take the form of video footage of the video recording (Mondada, 2012c, this volume) or of a video "data session" (Tutt & Hindmarsh, 2011).

Video documentation is not a straightforward matter and raises methodological challenges. What level of granularity and detail should be documented? How do we deal with both the action recorded and the way it is recorded in its relevant details? How many cameras should be used, and where should they be operated? How do we circumscribe the participation framework and the relevant ecology of these complex video and film activities? Responses to these questions crucially involve screen capture, as well as multiple cameras (often also filming the screen to capture gestures made over it) and the complex coordination and editing of these multiple sources (Heath, Hindmarsh, & Luft, 2010). The collection of studies we present here also aims to provide insights into some of these methodological difficulties, together with the possibilities and limitations they offer for the analytic process.

5. TOWARDS THE EXPLORATION OF THE SITUATED ORDER OF VIDEO PRACTICES

As already described, turning video practice from a resource into a topic involves several methodological challenges as well as new objects of inquiry. Video practices form part of long and complex courses of action, such as programme production, games of combat, urban surveillance, surgical operations, and so on. Key issues become how to establish access to sites where video is being used and how to identify video practices, focus on them, capture them, and understand them. Moreover, it may be that very different video practices intervene at different stages of projects, such as setting up the camera, choosing what to shoot, manoeuvring the camera, assessing recorded images, circulating them, and so on. In what follows, we will consider the complexity and distribution of practices in these longer projects, showing that video involves video actions combined with a diversity of activities. We begin with preparatory and recording practices, move on to editing activities, and end with practices of watching video.

5.1. Setting Up for Video

Video shooting always takes place in some kind of setting and for some kind of purpose—and the setting and purpose may be produced for the video (see Chapter 7 by Bovet, Sormani, & Terzi, this volume). What is shot and just how it is shot, as well as how shooting is prepared, are tightly connected to the reason for shooting and to available recording resources. Setting up will involve quite different elements if the aim is to use video for recording a family event, for examining sports technique or a scene as part of a feature film or, quite differently, for augmenting vision for video surveillance or during surgery.

Before the camera is ever switched on, places are often chosen, built, or reorganized to make them visible to video. Such organization and reorganization can take many forms, from a slight repositioning of a chair in recording a family event to the complete building of a studio or even significant modifications of natural environments in feature film production (as in Danny Boyle's *The Beach,* 2000) The "place" may itself be both solely constructed for video and to be accessible through video (which is the case for virtual reality and computer games). The people who will figure in the recording may prepare themselves to different degrees, from adjusting their hair or facial expression prior to making a home video to spending hours with a make-up artist before shooting in a professional movie production. There also needs to be a place from which the stationary or mobile camera can shoot, with or without a camera operator behind it, because this then creates the perspective of the recording. The location of the camera is sometimes found in the existing environment, or it may be constructed or mobilized using tripods, cranes, rails, or even helicopters. In settings where camera intrusion is to be kept to a minimum, cameras may be built into walls (McIlvenny, 2011) or into particular kinds of objects, such as sunglasses (Zouinar, Relieu, Salembier, & Calvet, 2004) or specialized surgical tools (see Chapter 3 by Mondada and Lindwall, Johansson, Rystedt, Ivarsson, & Reit, this volume).

Broadly, the relationship between the camera and the world that it is viewing and/or recording can be seen in two ways, constituting different directions of reflexivity, depending on the motivation for using video. First, the environment is built and furnished, and agents move within it for the benefit of the camera and microphone. These environments are typically the resources drawn upon for professional television or feature film production, with their standards for broadcast quality, and for video games. Second, the encompassing situated activity is seen as primary, and the camera and microphone are used to see, hear, and in other ways register the relevant aspects of that activity or setting, the devices adapting to the contexts of action rather than the reverse. This holds not only for research recordings of naturalistic settings (versus laboratory settings) but also, to a large extent, for family therapy sessions, sports technique recordings, and, of course, all manner of TV broadcasts of events (e.g. wars, music concerts, courtroom trials, sports matches, etc.), whenever the overall purpose is to document how something "really" happened, as well as for uses of video cameras for augmented vision (e.g. surgery, repair of nuclear plants, bomb disposal, etc.).

From even this broad characterization, we can begin to understand that the set-up of the environment and the camera falls within the logics of everyday settings and workplaces. Moreover, there is a reflexive relationship of the action of video recording and its setting to objects that mutually configure one another. This reflexive organization also characterizes the very action of shooting, when the camera, once it is set up, is then put to work.

5.2. Seeing with a Camera

In the previous section, we focused on the reflexive relationship between video recording devices and their environment. In this section, we deal with camera movements and their detailed local and temporal organization.[1]

The set-up and movements of the camera are designed to capture the relevant events that the camera operator is attempting to document. Following the action is one of the key challenges of camerawork, which offers insights into not only video practices (the actual work of the camera operator) but also the very understanding of those social practices that are being videographed. Following the action with a camera is already a form of "proto-analysis" (Mondada, 2006a; cf. Macbeth, 1999; Branigan 2006), undertaken in vivo by the camera operator as a coparticipant in the setting and in real time. The movements of the camera—and, with it, of the body of the camera operator or the command of the device at a distance—both adjust to the ongoing action and may also reshape that action. The camera adjusts to the action in a reflexive relationship in which camerawork and recorded action mutually configure each other. Although in this book we are more interested in the action of the person controlling the camera (usually termed "secondary movement") than in the action of the co-participants being seen and filmed (the "primary movement"), the latter is of interest too, especially when the responses of the "secondary movement" reflexively re-shape the "primary movement". Moving the camera—panning shots, zooming in and out, and the like—is a powerful sense-making and categorizing device, focusing on details and making them relevant (immediately for the film-maker and the filmed persons, later on for the final recipient of the video).

Mobile cameras try to follow—that is, anticipate—action and sometimes to impose on it. The latter is most obvious in the direction of action in fictional films, scripted dramas, and recordings of staged actions. The locations of immobile camera and microphone set-ups require a preparatory spatial analysis of the visual and acoustic organization of the studio or external set, locations that then anticipate the possible participation framework and ecology of future action. Preinstalled cameras are not always fixed in perspective because certain set-ups allow them to be controlled at a distance, manually or automatically, with a limited range of movements. Examples of this are multiple cameras filming wild animals across wide ranges, bomb disposal, sewer pipe repair, or surveillance cameras. In both cases, the issue is how to capture the action, given the local constraints on the camera set-up and on the camera's possible movements.

Understanding how video is woven into human action is the main focus of this collection of studies. However, the methodical ways in which video is used, for all practical purposes, depends on just what the video practice is (e.g. surgery versus science fiction), on just what is being filmed (wild animals, nano movements, football matches, public demonstrations), on just whose action it is (in the widest sense, from a skilled camera operator to a collective agency of director, director of photography, focus puller, etc.), and on its local and unfolding contingencies. Following wild animals in a park for scientific purposes, shooting a movie scene or a TV debate, surveilling a public space, spying on a person with camera glasses, exploring the anatomy of a patient, and so on are all video activities that involve different and specific skilled uses and moral orders of the camera. Moreover, the purposes of the video camera vary between *seeing with a camera for the current activity* and *documenting and recording the action for later uses.* In other words, while in some cases the main ambition is to record for storing, conserving, and archiving events and actions, in other cases the purpose is to observe, actively look, or surveil, whereas in still other cases the aim is to communicate (see Chapter 2 by Broth, this volume). Whereas in the former cases the camera view favours events that are recordable and storable for further, later viewing, as well as for remembering, objectifying, or proving, in the latter cases the camera view can be used to explore a visual field, to constitute and enhance the visibility of things, and even to discover possible phenomena, or just to refer to its own movement.

5.3.   Editing and Post-Production

By means of the video practices usually called "post-production," the raw media from the video cameras and microphones are carefully assembled into an edited object and served into the circulation of video media. These practices are as fundamental to cinema and television as the practices of editing are to novels, newspapers, and academic articles. They involve the in vivo analysis of what may or may not be intended audiovisual media in order to make intended media. To say that they involve finding where to cut into and out of any video clip or camera shot and/or voice recording and/or music only begins to describe the complexity of work that occurs under the topical heading of "editing."

The live editing studies pioneered by one of the editors (Broth, 2004, 2008a, 2008b) revealed how camera operators collaborate with editing rooms. During the live broadcast of a French TV debating show, camera operators have to find shots of the host, the guests, and studio audience that are broadcastable but also relevant to the ongoing debate between the parties in the studio. Live editing involves selecting amongst the shots offered to the editing team for broadcast. It turns upon the use of a script, knowledge of the host and guests, and a grammar of editing that provides for the intelligibility of the broadcast shots. Most remarkably of all and unlike most forms of editing, it is done in real time. What it relies upon for doing its work is only in part the script, and it is reflexively tied to the courses of action of the participants on the studio floor through monitoring their talk, gesture, and embodied movements. Replay production in sports television is also reflexively tied to events that are unfolding live (Engström, Juhlin, Perry, & Broth, 2010; Chapter 9 by Perry, Juhlin, & Engström, this volume). This work involves at least one replay operator, who, in response to significant game events, plays through very recent video footage (which we may call "tertiary movement"—following the "primary movement," i.e. the recorded action, and the "secondary movement," i.e. the shooting). The operator produces a replay sequence of one or several shots and then negotiates and coordinates the insertion of the replay into the live broadcast with the director. This kind of editing is live inasmuch as it is edited into a live broadcast. At the same time, however, it is also already post-production because it works on recordings of (just) past events, that need to be scrutinized and assembled very quickly.

Less spectacular, yet equally complex, are the varied forms of non–live editing. There is more time in these practices for the viewing, reviewing, assessment, rejection, classification, cataloguing, and selection of video materials (Laurier, Strebel, & Brown, 2008). Editors may be working alone or with large teams, and, as part of that collaboration, the materials that they are working on have to be made visible to one another for these tasks in ways that are distinctive to video technology, through playing, pausing, winding, rewinding, and so on (Chapter 5 by Laurier & Brown, this volume; Laurier & Brown, 2011). These video-specific tasks occur as part of a more familiar ecology of gestures, talk, objects, tools, screens, and indeed furniture.

Accompanying the primary tasks of building videos as sequences of clips are other more arcane post-production tasks, such as special effects, animations, colour correction, subtitling, sound design, and so on. Each of these is open to investigation for the forms of video analysis that they draw upon and for how video materials serve as both resources and topics of their workplaces. Like editing, the result of such post-production work profoundly influences how a viewer or an audience will see and understand a piece of video.

5.4.   Looking at Looking at Video

Videos are made to be seen and sometimes watched. In this collection we also take into consideration the seemingly final destination for video production at its reception point, though videos are always also circulating amongst sites of use. Indeed, we can highlight the diversity of projects, settings, visual practices, and users that we can find even where video is watched. Two basic forms of reception of videos can be distinguished: on the one hand, video can be watched as a unique product, from the beginning to the end, without any intervention on it. This form of watching is reflexively related to the concept of the viewer of broadcast TV. On the other hand, video can be used by viewers in a more active way, by inspecting portions of the medium and by rewinding, going forward, playing fragments again and again, at normal speed or in slow motion. When we think about these more interactive practices, we come upon a heterogeneous collection of practices. In a growing number of other settings, video is part of the background, seen but unnoticed, such as advertising on digital screens in public places, CCTV output in shops, the TV being on during family conversations, and so on. These latter situations are also of interest, though more challenging to study because of the minimal or intermittent orientation to video in these settings.

Watching a video object such as a film or TV programme is a broadly receptive practice, in which the video is analysed as an intelligible final, edited product. Within everyday, domestic settings, videos are routinely made sense of during their consumption by viewers, and this "decoding" work has been heavily researched by media studies (Scannell, 2007). EMCA analyses complicate and extend existing studies in media reception, especially within what has been called the "domestic paradigm" (Morley & Silverstone, 1990). Media reception studies carried out pioneering work using ethnographic methods to recontextualize the reception of television within the household. They helped shift the focus of understanding of how media are consumed by individual watchers, showing how families were involved in different kinds of activities during "watching the TV." These studies were followed by research that documented how viewers play an increasingly active role in the choice and use of various entertainment and informational services across multiple devices (Jenkins, 2006; Hess, Ley, Ogonowski, Wan, & Wulf. 2011). The approach we are advocating expands this body of work by video-documenting these practices and analysing them in the embodied, situated, and online details of the activities of watching a movie or a football game (Gerhardt, 2007).

In post-production work, the analysis of video by picture and sound editors and other production staff is more visible than it is in practices like TV viewing. Videos are used as resources in observing, discovering, studying, working, or playing across a wide area of topics such as human or animal behaviour, illegal activities, sport exploits, and so on. Professional vision is an example of these practices of vernacular video analysis: this is the case of police officers looking at the Rodney King tapes studied by Goodwin (1994); flight controllers looking at screens in their control room (Goodwin, 1996); train controllers inspecting a station's CCTV monitors to check whether all of the passengers are on-board before closing the doors (Heath, Hindmarsh, & Luff, 1999); oceanographers and other naturalists working on a scientific ship and inspecting their screens (Goodwin, 1995); social researchers inspecting, rewinding, replaying again and again portions of tape in data sessions (Tutt & Hindmarsh, 2011). Again, in these cases, a quick glance or an extended study of a sequence can favour either seeing with a camera, such as by exploring in real time a given setting or exploiting the possibilities offered by video-records of the scene. In all cases, however, the use of the video does not concern the entire record but only specific portions of it, which might be seen in various ways and in repeated and modified manners.

Although this section on watching video supposes that a video has been constituted, it is important to recall that video might be watched in the very process of its constitution: in this sense, the linear organization of these last sections has to be relativized as actually constituting a recursive process. Shooting video can be followed by checks of the recorded images, editing supposes active viewing, and viewing impacts the way in which the next images will be produced. Moreover, in the wide net we have cast are video practices that do not have the production–consumption pathways of TV programmes and films. Constructing a video may be an activity undertaken as part of a classroom lesson and the assessment of student learning (Greiffenhagen & Watson, 2009), or, as already noted, watching video provides the visual materials necessary to undertaking the actions that the video is documenting (e.g. surgery (Chapter 3 by Mondada, this volume) or dentistry [Chapter 5 by Lindwall, Johansson, Rystedt, Ivarsson, & Reit, this volume).

6.   CONCLUSION

6.1.   General Conclusion

As we hope has become clear, video studies have developed along two broad avenues, one that is well known in the field of film, television, and media studies and the other, perhaps a little less well known outside of ethnomethodology and conversation analysis and other social sciences using video. Only a scattering of studies have put the two together and used video recordings to analyse video practices. It might have seemed to be only a limited set of situations that these combined studies might inquire into, but what should have become clear in the light of our review is that the ongoing rapid integration of video technologies into a myriad of settings offers multitudinous possibilities for new inquiries. We have signposted some of the domains that video has passed into and transformed: the everyday life of places around the world, an ever growing variety of workplaces, the methods and documentations of the sciences, and the creation and exhibition of video art. It thus appears that whereas video is currently entering into virtually all major activities of humanity, just how it is shot, played, watched, referred to, used as evidence, and so on as part of the accomplishment of these activities and their outcomes is significantly under-researched. As the first of its kind, this book can only aim to begin to fill this gap.

There are, as we have argued, two broad modes of inquiry for video studies of video practices. They can reconstruct elements of video practices from the existing media that already exhibit their orderly properties. Alternatively, researchers can set up for and produce their own recordings of video practices that recover elements of the lived work of video application that are otherwise lost in the final video object. In pursuing either of these modes of inquiry into video at work in the world, we have outlined four broad sets of activities wherein video practices can be found: setting up for video, seeing with and recording with a camera, post-production, and watching video. The different studies in this book are all based on video recordings of video practices, and address one or more of these activities as they play out in a range of everyday and professional settings. We will now end this introduction by briefly presenting the chapters that will follow.

6.2.   The Structure of This Book

This edited collection contributes to the study of video practices from an EMCA perspective by considering a diversity of settings and languages within a shared praxeological approach. The chapters are based on video recordings of video practices and on their detailed analysis. As a whole, the book offers insights into each of the progressive steps that the use of video implies: shooting, manoeuvring the camera, editing the recorded shots, and viewing media. The ambition of the book is to provide a form of grammar that is drawn upon in organizing these practices. In other words, we aim to describe their praxeological order and systematicity by showing their family resemblances and differences, as well as their situated adaptation to a variety of contexts.

The book begins with chapters describing the practices of *shooting* video: it aims at reconstructing the practical problems that participants encounter and ongoingly solve in the lived work of filming. Three workplaces are considered here as exemplary cases. The first chapter (by Mondada) studies researchers recording naturalistic video data for scientific purposes, the other two in turn consider professional camera operators producing communicative camera gestures in interacting with a TV control room (Broth) and camera operators producing shots for the practical purposes of surgical procedures using endoscopic cameras (Mondada). The chapters reveal how shooting video is a collective achievement requiring a finely tuned coordination of all of the participants and a form of constant online monitoring, interpretation, and understanding of the past, current, and future actions.

The second part of the book is centred on a range of practices in which the camera is manoeuvred for seeing and showing details in the environment. It deals with social activities where the video camera is mobilized in order to explore, to discover, and to enhance the vision of the participants. Within mediated conversations, such as through Skype or mobile video communicative technologies, the camera is being used to show participants' local environment (Licoppe and Morel). Within educational settings, the camera is being used to exhibit the relevant details for sophisticated procedures in which participants are being trained, such as dentistry (Lindwall, Johansson, Rystedt, Ivarsson, and Reit). Within video games, the camera is crucial in exploring the environment to prepare the next appropriate move in the game (Laurier and Reeves). Within broadcast TV, the camera is used not only to display but also to actively build the accountability of the event being filmed, establishing the criteria for its assessment amongst the viewers (Bovet, Sormani, and Terzi).

A third fundamental moment characterizing the production of video concerns the methods by which, once shot and recorded, the video is *assembled* as part of the work of editing. Knowledge of transitions and the sequential relations between clips characterize the overlooked skills of film makers (Laurier and Brown), and they also structure other professional practices, such as the work of real-time cutting between shots within live sport programs (Perry, Juhlin, and Engström).

The studies presented in this collection show, through video recordings of a variety of professional and everyday settings, how video is contributing in powerful and distinct ways to the live, situated, communal, online and offline production of the intelligibility, appreciation, and qualities of specialized and routine events. By adopting a shared EMCA perspective on the temporal, sequential, and situated organization of video in and as action, as well as of video-recorded social actions more widely, these studies reveal the complex orderly character of video when it is at work in the world. They begin to reveal the methodical ways in which it is used by a diversity of professional and ordinary actors to archive, to surveil, to exhibit, to play, to build, and, at the heart of these activities, to make sense of the world as they shoot, grasp, see, show, revisit, assess, instruct, assemble, broadcast, watch, and witness video.

Acknowledgements

The editors would like to thank the Freiburg Institute for Advanced Studies (FRIAS) for hosting the Workshop "Video Studies of Video Activities" held on 1–2.7.2010 in Freiburg from which this collection originated.

NOTE

1. We have set aside the work of sound capture here, and it remains a further fascinating possibility for similar consideration in relation to how we hear and listen to social practices with microphones.

REFERENCES

Aanestad, M., Røtnes, J. S., Edwin, B., & Buanes, T. (2002). From operation theatres to operation studios: Visualising surgery in the age of telemedicine. *Journal of Telemedicine and Telecare, 8*(1), 56–60.

Antaki, C., Walton, C., & Finlay, W. (2007). How proposing an activity to a person with an intellectual disability can imply a limited identity. *Discourse and Society, 18*(4), 393–410.

Banks, M., & Ruby, J. (2011). *Made to Be Seen: Historical Perspectives on Visual Anthropology.* Chicago: University of Chicago Press.

Birdwhistell, R. L. (1970). *Kinesics and Context.* Philadelphia: University of Pennsylvania Press.

Bovet, A. (2009). Configuring a television debate: Categorisation, questions and answers. In R. Fitzgerald & W. Housley (Eds.), *Media, Policy and Interaction* (pp. 27–48), Aldershot, UK: Ashgate.

Branigan, E. (2006). *Projecting a Camera.* London: Routledge.

Broth, M. (2004). The production of a live TV-interview through mediated interaction. In *Proceedings of the Sixth International Conference on Logic and Methodology* (August 17–20). Amsterdam: SISWO.

Broth, M. (2008a). The studio interaction as a contextual resource for TV-production. *Journal of Pragmatics, 40*, 904–926.

Broth, M. (2008b). The "listening shot" as a collaborative practice for categorizing studio participants in a live TV-production. *Ethnographic Studies, 10*, 69–88.

Broth, M. (2009). Seeing through screens, hearing through speakers. Managing distant studio space in TV-control room interaction. *Journal of Pragmatics, 41*, 1998–2016.

Broth, M., & Lundström, F. (2013). A walk on the pier. Establishing relevant places in a guided, introductory walk. In P. Haddington, L. Mondada, & M. Nevile (Eds.), *Interaction and Mobility: Language and the Body in Motion* (pp. 91–122). Berlin: Mouton de Gruyter.

Buckingham, D., & Willett, R. (2010). *Video Cultures Media Technology and Everyday Creativity.* London: Houndmills Palgrave Macmillan.

Burgess, J., Green, J., Jenkins, H., & Hartley, J. (2009). *YouTube: Online Video and Participatory Culture.* Cambridge: Polity Press.

Büscher, M. (2005). Social life under the microscope? *Sociological Research Online, 10*(1). www.socresonline.org.uk/10/1/buscher.html

Caldwell, J. T. (2008). *Production Culture: Industrial Reflexivity and the Critical Practices in Film and Television.* Durham, NC: Duke University Press.

Crang, M. (1997). Picturing practices: Research through the tourist gaze. *Progress in Human Geography, 21*(3), 359–373.

Cumings, J., & Zettl, A. (2000). Low-friction nanoscale linear bearing realized from multiwall carbon nanotubes. *Science, 289*(5479), 602–604.

De Stefani, E. (2010). Reference as an interactively and multimodally accomplished practice: Organizing spatial reorientation in guided tours. In M. Pettorino, A. Giannini, I. Chiari, & F. Dovetto (Eds.), *Spoken Communication* (pp. 137–170). Newcastle upon Tyne, UK: Cambridge Scholars Publishing.

Engström, A., Juhlin, O., Perry, M., & Broth, M. (2010). Temporal hybridity: Mixing live video footage with instant replay in real time. In *Proceedings of ACM CHI 2010* (Atlanta, Georgia). New York: ACM.

Fele, G. (2012). The use of video to document tacit participation in an emergency operations centre. *Qualitative Research, 12*, 280–303.

Fleichmanet, L. J., & Endler, J. A. (2000). Some comments on visual perception and the use of video playback in animal behavior sciences. *Acta Ethologica, 3*(1), 15–27.

Friedberg, A. (2006). *The Virtual Window.* London: MIT Press.

Garfinkel, H. (1967). *Studies in Ethnomethodology.* Englewood Cliffs, NJ: Prentice-Hall.

Gerhardt, C. (2007). Moving closer to the audience: Watching football on television. *Revista Alicantina de Estudios Ingleses: Special Issue on Linguistics and Media Discourse, 19*, 125–148.

Goodwin, C. (1979). The interactive construction of a sentence in natural conversation. In G. Psathas (Ed.), *Everyday Language: Studies in Ethnomethodology* (pp. 97–121). New York: Irvington.

Goodwin, C. (1981). *Conversational Organization: Interaction Between Speakers and Hearers.* New York: Academic Press.

Goodwin, C. (1993). Recording interaction in natural settings. *Pragmatics, 3*(2), 181–209.

Goodwin, C. (1994). Professional vision. *American Anthropologist, 96*(3), 606–633.

Goodwin, C. (1995). Seeing in depth. *Social Studies of Science, 25*(2), 237–274.

Goodwin, C. (1996). Transparent vision. In E. Ochs, E. A. Schegloff, & S. Thompson (Eds.), *Interreaction and Grammar* (pp. 370–404). Cambridge: Cambridge University Press.

Goodwin, C. (2000). Action and embodiment within situated human interaction. *Journal of Pragmatics, 32*, 1489–1522.

Goodwin, C. (2007). Participation, stance and affect in the organization of activities. *Discourse and Society, 18*(1), 53–73.

Goodwin, C., & Goodwin, M. H. (1996). Seeing as a situated activity: Formulating planes. In D. Middleton & Y. Engeström (Eds.), *Cognition and Communication at Work* (pp. 61–95). Cambridge: Cambridge University Press.

Greiffenhagen, C., & Watson, R. (2009). Visual repairables: Analysing the work of repair in human–computer interaction. *Visual Communication, 8*(1), 65–90.

Griffiths, A. (1996). Knowledge and visuality in turn of the century anthropology: The early ethnographic cinema of Alfred Cort Haddon and Walter Baldwin Spencer. *Visual Anthropology Review, 12*(2), 18–43.

Hall, S. (1973). *Encoding and Decoding in the Television Discourse.* Stencilled Paper 7. Birmingham, UK: CCCS.

Heath, C. (1986). *Body Movement and Speech in Medical Interaction.* Cambridge: Cambridge University Press.

Heath, C., & Hindmarsh, J. (2002). Analysing interaction—Video, ethnography and situated conduct. In T. May (Ed.), *Qualitative Research in Practice* (pp. 99–121). London: Sage.

Heath, C., Hindmarsh, J., & Luff, P. (1999). Interaction in isolation: The dislocated world of the London underground train driver. *Sociology, 33*(3), 555–575.

Heath, C., Hindmarsh, J., & Luff, P. (2010). *Video in Qualitative Research, Analysing Social Interaction in Everyday Life.* London: Sage.

Heath, C., & Luff, P. (2000). *Technology in Action.* Cambridge: Cambridge University Press.

Hess, J., Ley, B., Ogonowski, C., Wan, L., & Wulf, V. (2011). Jumping between devices and services: Towards an integrated concept for social TV. In *Proceedings of the 9th International Interactive Conference on Interactive Television* (June) (pp. 11–20). New York: ACM.

Hill, R. J., & Crittenden, K. S. (1968). *Proceedings of the Purdue Symposium on Ethnomethodology.* Lafayette: Institute for the Study of Social Change, Purdue University.

Holman, R., Stanley, J., & Ozkan-Haller, T. (2003). Applying video sensor networks to nearshore environment monitoring. *Pervasive Computing, IEEE, 2*(4), 14–21.

Jayyusi, L. (1988). Towards a socio-logic of the film text. *Semiotica, 68,* 271–296.

Jenkins, H. (2006). *Convergence Culture: Where Old and New Media Collide.* London: New York University Press.

Kagan, N., Krathwohl, D. R., & Miller, R. (1963). Stimulated recall in therapy using video tape: A case study. *Journal of Counseling Psychology, 10*(3), 237–243.

Keating, E., Edwards, T., & Mirus, G. (2008). Cybersign: Impacts of new communication technologies on space and language. *Journal of Pragmatics, 40,* 1067–1081.

Keating, E., & Sunakawa, C. (2010). Participation cues: Coordinating activity and collaboration in complex online gaming worlds. *Language in Society 39,* 331–356.

Kendon, A. (1979). Some methodological and theoretical aspects of the use of film in the study of social interaction. In G. P. Ginsburg (Ed.), *Emerging Strategies in Social Psychological Research* (pp. 67–91). New York: Wiley.

Kendon, A. (1990). *Conducting Interaction: Patterns of Behavior in Focused Encounters.* Cambridge: Cambridge University Press.

Kendon, A. (2004). *Gesture. Visible Action as Utterance.* Cambridge: Cambridge University Press.

Knoblauch, H., Schnettler, B., Raab, J., & H.-G. Soeffner (Eds.) (2006). *Video Analysis: Methodology and Methods. Qualitative Audiovisual Data Analysis in Sociology.* Bern: Lang.

Koschmann, T., LeBaron, C., Goodwin, C., & Feltovich, P. (2011). "Can you see the cystic artery yet?" A simple matter of trust. *Journal of Pragmatics, 43,* 521–541.

Koskinen, I. (2007). *Mobile Multimedia in Action.* Piscataway, NJ: Transaction.

Labov, W. (1972). *Sociolinguistic Patterns.* Philadelphia: University of Pennsylvania Press.

Laurier, E., & Brown, B. (2011). The reservations of the editor: The routine work of showing and knowing the film in the edit suite. *Social Semtioics, 21*(2), 239–257.

Laurier, E., & Philo, C. (2006). Natural problems of naturalistic video data. In H. Knoblauch, B. Schnettler, J. Raav, & H.-G. Soeffner (Eds.), *Video Analysis: Methodology and Methods. Qualitative Audiovisual Data Analysis in Sociology* (pp. 183–192). Bern: Lang.

Laurier, E., Strebel, I., & Brown, B. (2008). Video analysis: Lessons from professional video editing practice. *Forum: Qualitative Social Research, 9*(3).

Leeds Hurwitz, W. (1987). The social history of the natural history of an interview: A multidisciplinary investigation of social communication. *Research on Language & Social Interaction, 20*(1–4), 1–51.

Licoppe, C., & Morel, J. (2012). Video-in-interaction: "Talking heads" and the multimodal organization of mobile and skype video calls. *Research on Language & Social Interaction, 45*(4), 399–429.

Licoppe, C., & Relieu, M. (Eds.) (2007). De la rue au tribunal: Etudes sur la visio-communication [special issue]. *Réseaux, 144*(25).

Lindström, A., & Heinemann, T. (2009) "Good enough": Low-grade assessments in caregiving situations. *Research on Language & Social Interaction, 42*(4), 309–328.

Lindwall, O., & Lymer, G. (2005). Vulgar competence, ethnomethodological indifference and curricular design. In *Proceedings of CSCL'05* (pp. 388–397). Taipei: International Society of the Learning Sciences.

Lomax, H., & Casey, N. (1998). Recording social life: Reflexivity and video methodology. *Sociological Research Online 3,* U3–U32.

Luff, P., & Heath, C. (1999). Surveying the scene: The monitoring practices of staff in control rooms. In *Proceedings of the International Conference on Human Interfaces in Control Rooms, Cockpits and Command Centres, Bath, UK, 21–23*, Bath: IEE Conference Proceedings, Issue CP463.

Luff, P., Heath, C., & Jirotka, M. (2000). Surveying the scene: Technologies for everyday awareness and monitoring in control rooms. *Interacting with Computers*, *13*(2), 193–228.

Lynch, M. (1993). *Scientific Practice and Ordinary Action*. Cambridge: Cambridge University Press.

Mead, M., & Bateson, G. (1977). On the use of the camera in anthropology. *Studies in the Anthropology of Visual Communication*, *4*(2), 78–80.

Meier, C. (1997). *Arbeitsbesprechungen: Interaktionstruktur, Interaktionsdynamik und Konsequenzen einer sozialen Form*. Opladen: Westdeutscher Verlag.

Manovich, L. (2006). The poetics of augmented space. *Visual Communication*, *5*(2), 219–240.

Macbeth, D. (1999). Glances, trances, and their relevance for a visual sociology. In P. L. Jalbert (Ed.), *Media Studies: Ethnomethodological Approaches* (pp. 135–170). Lanham, MD: University Press of America.

Martinez, K., Hart, J.K., & Ong, R. (2004). Environmental sensor networks. *Computer*, *37*(8), 50–56.

Mayer, V., Miranda, J.B., & Caldwell, J.T. (Eds.) (2009). *Production Studies: Cultural Studies of Media Industries*. London: Routledge.

McIlvenny, P. (2011). Video interventions in "everyday life": Semiotic and spatial practices of video as a therapeutic tool in reality TV parenting programmes. *Social Semiotics*, *21*(2), 253–282.

McQuown, N. (Ed.) (1971). *The Natural History of an Interview*. Chicago: Microfilm Collection, Manuscripts on Cultural Anthropology, Joseph Reginstein Library, Department of Photoduplication, University of Chicago.

Meigh-Andrews, C. (2006). *A History of Video Art*. London: Berg.

Miller, T., & McHoul, A.W. (1998). *Popular culture and everyday life*. London: Sage.

Mondada, L. (2003). Working with video: How surgeons produce video records of their actions. *Visual Studies*, *18*(1), 58–72.

Mondada, L. (2005). La constitution de l'origo déictique comme travail interactionnel des participants: Une approche praxéologique de la spatialité. *Intellectica*, *2–3*(41–42), 75–100.

Mondada, L. (2006a). Video recording as the reflexive preservation and configuration of phenomenal features for analysis. In H. Knoblauch, B. Schnettler, J. Raab, & H.-G. Soeffner (Eds.), *Video Analysis: Methodology and Methods. Qualitative Audiovisual Data Analysis in Sociology* (pp. 51–67). Bern: Lang.

Mondada, L. (2006b). La demande d'autorisation comme moment structurant pour l'enregistrement et l'analyse des pratiques bilingues. *Tranel*, *43*, 129–155.

Mondada, L. (2007). Operating together through videoconference: members' procedures accomplishing a common space of action. In S. Hester & D. Francis (Eds.), *Orders of Ordinary Action* (pp. 51–68). Aldershot, UK: Ashgate.

Mondada, L. (2009). Video recording practices and the reflexive constitution of the interactional order: Some systematic uses of the split-screen technique. *Human Studies*, *32*, 67–99.

Mondada, L. (2011). The situated organization of directives in French: Imperatives and action coordination in video games. *Nottingham French Studies*, *50*(2), 19–50.

Mondada, L. (2012a). The conversation analytic approach to data collection. In J. Sidnell & T. Stivers (Eds.), *Handbook of Conversation Analysis* (pp. 32–56). London: Blackwell-Wiley.

Mondada, L. (2012b). Coordinating action and talk-in-interaction in and out of video games. In R. Ayass & C. Gerhardt (Eds.), *The Appropriation of Media in Everyday Life. What People Do with Media* (pp. 231–270). Amsterdam: Benjamins.

Mondada, L. (2012c). The establishment of a common focus of attention: Issues for participants, camera(wo)men and analysts. *Work, Interaction and Technology: A Festschrift for Christian Heath* (pp. 43–56). London: King's College.

Mondada, L. (2013). Ethics in action: Anonymization as a participant's concern and a participant's practice. *Human Studies*, DOI 10.1007/s10746–013–9286–9.

Mondloch, K. (2010). *Screens: Viewing Media Installation Art.* Minneapolis: University of Minnesota Press.

Moran, J. (2002). *There's No Place Like Home Video.* Minneapolis: University of Minnesota Press.

Morley, D., & Silverstone, R. (1990). Domestic communications: Technologies and meanings, *Media, Culture and Society*, 12(1), 31–55.

Mortensen, K., & Lundsgaard, C., (2011). Preliminary notes on "Grooming the Object": The example of an architectural presentation. In J. Buur (Ed.), *Participatory Innovation Conference Proceeding (PINC11)* (pp. 99–104). Sønderborg: University of Southern Denmark.

Nevile, M. (2004). *Beyond the Black Box.* Aldershot, UK: Ashgate.

Ochs, E., Schegloff, E.A., & Thompson, S.A. (Eds.), (1996). *Grammar and Interaction.* Cambridge: Cambridge University Press.

Potter, J. (2002). Two kinds of natural. *Discourse Studies*, 4(4), 539–542.

Relieu, M. (1999). Du tableau statistique à l'image audiovisuelle. Lieux et pratiques de la représentation en sciences sociales. *Réseaux*, 17(94), 49–86.

Rush, M. (2007). *Video Art.* New York: Thames and Hudson.

Sacks, H. (1966). "The Search for Help: No One to Turn To." Unpublished PhD, University of California, Berkeley.

Sacks, H. (1984). Notes on methodology. In J.M. Atkinson & J. Heritage (Eds.), *Structures of Social Action* (pp. 21–27). Cambridge: Cambridge University Press.

Sacks, H. (1992). *Lectures on Conversation [1964–72]* (2 vols.). Oxford: Basil Blackwell.

Sacks, H., & Schegloff, E.A. (2002). Home position. *Gesture*, 2(2), 133–146.

Sanchez Svensson, M., Heath, C., & Luff, P. (2007). Instrumental action: The timely exchange of implements during surgical operations. *ECSCW '07*, 41–60.

Scannell, P. (2007). *Media and Communication.* London: Sage.

Scheflen, A. (1972). *Body Language and Social Order: Communications as Behavioral Control.* Englewood Cliffs, NJ: Prentice Hall.

Schegloff, E.A. (1967). "The First Five Seconds: The Order of Conversational Openings." Unpublished PhD, University of California, Berkeley.

Schmitt, R. (2007). Das Filmset als Arbeitsplatz. Multimodale Grundlagen einer komplexen Kooperationsform. In L. Tiittula, M.-L. Piitulainen, & E. Reuter (Eds.), *Die gemeinsame Herstellung professioneller Interaktion* (pp. 25–66). Tübingen: Narr.

Schmitt, R. (2010). Verfahren der Verstehensdokumentation am Filmset: Antizipatorische Initiativen und probeweise Konzeptrealisierung. In A. Deppermann, U. Reitemeier, R. Schmitt, & T. Spranz-Fogasy (Eds.), *Verstehen in professionnellen Handlungsfeldern* (pp. 209–362). Tübingen: Narr.

Sharrock, W.W., & Hughes, J.A. (2004). Ethnography in the workplace. *Team Ethno Online*, 1(1), 1–21.

Sjöblom, B. (2011). *Gaming interaction: Conversations and competencies in internet cafés.* Linköping, Sweden: Linköping University.

Speer, S., & Hutchby, I. (2003). From ethics to analytics: Aspects of participants' orientations to the presence and relevance of recording devices. *Sociology*, 37(2), 315–337.

Suchman, L. (1993). Technologies of accountability: Of lizards and airplanes. In G. Button (Ed.), *Technology in Working Order: Studies of Work, Interaction and Technology* (pp. 113–126). London: Routledge.

Suchman, L. (1996). Constituting shared workspaces. In D. Middleton & Y. Engeström (Eds.), *Cognition and Communication at Work* (pp. 35–60). Cambridge: Cambridge University Press.

Suchman, L. (1997). Centers of coordination: A case and some themes. *NATO ASI Series F Computer and Systems Sciences, 160,* 41–62.

Svennevig, I. (Ed.). (2012). Multimodal analyses of meetings [special issue]. *Discourse Studies, 14*(1).

ten Have, P. (1998). *Doing Conversation Analysis. A Practical Guide.* London: Sage.

Tutt, D., & Hindmarsh, J. (2011). Reenactments at work: Demonstrating conduct in data sessions. *Research on Language & Social Interaction, 44*(3), 211–236.

Visser, I. N., Smith, T. G., Bullock, I. D., Green, G. D., Carlsson, O. G. L., & Imberti, S. (2008). Antarctic peninsula killer whales (*Orcinus orca*) hunt seals and a penguin on floating ice. *Marine Mammal Science, 24*(1), 225–234.

Zimmermann, P. R. (1995). *Reel Families: A Social History of Amateur film.* Bloomington: Indiana University Press.

Zettl, H. (2003). *Television Production Handbook.* Belmont, CA: Wadsworth.

Zouinar, M., Relieu, M., Salembier, P., & Calvet, G. (2004). Observation et capture de données sur l'interaction multimodale en mobilité. *Mobilité & Ubiquité '04, 1–3 June 2004.* Nice: ACM.

Part I

Shooting

1 Shooting as a Research Activity

The Embodied Production of Video Data

Lorenza Mondada (University of Basel)

1. INTRODUCTION

Video recordings are being increasingly and extensively exploited for research within various disciplines of the social sciences (for an historical sketch, see Mondada, in press a). However, their use is far from homogeneous. Video is used either as raw scientific data or as edited film for popularizing and presenting scientific results. In the former case, which is considered here, it can record semiexperimental tasks given to the participants. It can also record interviews and other elicited discourses, as well as naturalistic recordings of social actions and events (De Stefani, 2007; Erickson, 1982; Goldman, Pea, Barron, & Derry, 2007; Knoblauch, Schnettler, Raab, & Soeffner, 2006; Knoblauch, Baer, Laurier, Petschke, & Schnettler, 2006, 2008; Ruby, 2000). In all these cases, video data are produced in heterogeneous ways, implementing different analytical mentalities and epistemological positions.

In this chapter, I focus on a specific use of video for gathering data, characteristic of ethnomethodology (EM) and conversation analysis (CA). The specificity of this use consists of documenting naturally occurring social interactions (Mondada, 2006, 2012a): EMCA is interested in the endogenous organization of social activities in their ordinary settings; it considers social interaction as collectively organized by coparticipants, in a locally situated way, achieved incrementally through its temporal and sequential unfolding, achieved moreover by mobilizing a large range of vocal, verbal, visual, and embodied resources, which are publicly displayed and monitored in situ. The analysis of these features insists on their indexicality, contingency, and dynamic emergence, all of which have consequences for the way in which data are collected. The importance of audio and video recordings within EMCA emerges from these analytical demands: EMCA insists upon the study of *naturally occurring activities* as they ordinarily unfold in social settings and consequently on the necessity of recording actual situated activities for a detailed analysis of their relevant endogenous order.

Within EMCA, as elsewhere, video for research is discussed either in methodological texts, generally in prescriptive and normative ways (in terms of do's and don'ts) (Goodwin, 1993; Heath & Hindmarsh, 2002;

Heath, Hindmarsh. & Luff, 2010), or in sections presenting the data studied, generally in a post hoc short reconstruction or an ethnographic storytelling of what has been made (as well as in the *metadata* describing the
corpus). Thus, the production of video data has been predominantly treated
as a *resource* for research and seldom as a *topic* of research. Even if some
chapters integrate the camera movements in the analysis of social action
(Broth & Lundström, 2013; Mondada, in press b; Büscher, 2005) or deal
with the effect of the camera and cameraperson on the recorded settings
(Heath, 1986; Laurier & Philo, 2006; Lomax & Casey, 1998), they rely on
the *reconstruction* of how video has been shot, based on the actual video
data, and not on a *direct documentation* of the shot. So the way in which
video data are actually produced through the situated and embodied practices of the researcher remains an unstudied topic. While the use of video
data in research is increasingly exponentially, the video documentation of
the video practices that generate that data is almost inexistent.

This chapter aims at opening up the black box of research video practices
and at offering a first account of some fundamental systematic procedures
through which meaningful and scientifically usable data are manufactured
in a locally situated way. It shows that filming relies on a protoanalytic gaze
and constitutes a case of "professional vision" (Goodwin, 1994), as well
as an embodied exercise of inquiry within a "praxeology of seeing with a
camera" (Macbeth, 1999: 152; cf. Büscher, 2005; Mondada, 2006), orienting in real time to the locally emergent, relevant organizational features of
social action. In this sense, the chapter aims both at treating video scientific
practices as another social practices for study and at analyzing them in order
to make a specific contribution to the social studies of science (Lynch, 1993).

2.   DOCUMENTING MOBILE CAMERAWORK

To uncover the fundamental aspects of the "grammar" of video-making
practices, this chapter explores an exemplary use of the camera: filming
social action with a mobile camera. Although traditionally most of the work
done in EMCA with video data has been realized with fixed cameras, the
use of mobile cameras is more revealing of the challenges of documenting in
vivo naturally occurring social activities.

The use of fixed cameras—most often placed on tripods or other clamps—
has been privileged within EMCA for two reasons. On the one hand, it is the
best way to record static activities, such as family dinners or work meetings,
which have been largely favoured over mobile activities. On the other hand,
it is also a solution for carefully choosing a global frame that consistently
captures the entire participation framework, avoiding irrelevant camera
panning and zooming, which run the risk of missing or excluding relevant
details. Fixed cameras rely on a preliminary protoanalysis of the activity to
be documented, often produced during ethnographic fieldwork, aimed at

choosing the moment and perspective to be recorded. This protoanalysis concerns the participants, the interactional space, and the temporal boundaries of the event to be recorded—the aim being to preserve the participation framework, the relevant ecology of action, and the entire duration of the event (Heath, Hindmarsh, & Luff, 2010; Mondada, 2006, 2012a). This protoanalysis is then implemented in the choice of the number of cameras and microphones to use, their location and direction, the camera angles, field size and focus, and so on. Turning fixed camera use into a topic of research (although not the focus here) is possible, such as by video-recording discussions about the video device to adopt, its installation, the negotiations with the participants concerning the best location of the cameras, and other activities.

The use of mobile cameras is almost inescapable for recording mobile actions (for instance. walking across large environments) and has been increasingly discussed within the "mobile turn" of EMCA and the social sciences (Büscher, Urry, & Witchger, 2010; Haddington, Mondada, & Nevile, 2013; McIlvenny, Broth, & Haddington, 2009). This way of filming, as noted earlier, relies on a protoanalysis of what is happening—which has to be implemented immediately by the embodied movements of the cameraperson. Contrary to staged scenes—for example, in the movie industry where they have been carefully planned and prepared and can be played again if the shot is not good enough—naturalistic activities happen only once and can be documented only in real time, through camerawork relying on improvisation. This implies a constant adjustment to the movements of the participants and, more particularly, an online analysis of the changing participation framework, the dynamic interactional space, the sequential organization of embodied actions, and the observability of their relevant multimodal details. Thus, the mobile camera constantly both *anticipates* and *follows* key sequential features of the interaction being recorded.

This chapter studies the use of the mobile camera in a corpus of guided visits: it considers this activity type as a mobile event that raises, in exemplary ways, practical problems for the researcher documenting it.

3. MANOEUVRING A MOBILE CAMERA IN GUIDED VISITS

Guided visits are a perspicuous setting (Garfinkel & Wieder, 1992) for the study of mobility in social interaction involving the entire body in motion. Guided visits (Birkner & Stukenbrock, 2010; Broth & Lundström, 2013; De Stefani, 2010; Mondada, 2012b, 2012c) involve participants walking together from one point to the other, thus being an exemplary kind of situation for the study of mobile interactions. They involve the guide pointing out details of the environment to the participants, making it an exemplary type of activity for the study of instructed perception and joint attention. Both of those aspects raise challenging questions about video documentation involving one or more mobile cameras trying to capture the movement of the participants and the objects they look at (see also Heath, Hindmarsh, & Luff, 2010).

In this setting, the problems of the participants and the problems of the cameraperson are reflexively bound. The participants coordinate their walking in order to constitute mobile "withs" (Goffman 1971); the camera adjusts to their movements in order to follow or to anticipate them, adapts to their changing participation framework (Goodwin & Goodwin, 2004), mobile formations (Kendon, 1990; Broth, Haddington, & McIlvenny, in press), and mobile interactional spaces (Mondada, 2009), which also include objects they are gazing at. These objects can be closer—such as fruits and plants that can be touched in a garden—or distant—such as architectural landmarks seen at the horizon (Mondada, 2012c). The participants inter-actionally achieve a common focus of attention, coordinating and moni-toring each other's gaze; the camera monitors, follows, and focuses on the dynamic emergence of shared attention, and the collective convergent or divergent orientations to objects gazed at (Mondada, 2012b). Because the interactional space constantly changes during guided visits, it requires closer or wider attention and demands very different degrees of granularity to the video documentation.

More specifically, guided visits are typically organized by moments alter-nating between *stopping* around an object or a place that is looked at and commented upon and *walking* from one spot to another. Stopping and walk-ing are collective mobile achievements that rely on the finely tuned coordi-nation of the participants. They are reflexively related to the organization of sequence openings and closings and thus to the recognizability of the initiation and completion of actions and sequences. In the same way, the work of the cameraperson consists of identifying the beginning and ending of an episode, the completion of a current action and the projection of the next one, and the closing of a sequence and the preparation of the following one—all in order to smoothly document them.

This chapter offers an analysis of these organizational features, paying special attention to transitions between static episodes in which a collective focus of attention is established and mobile episodes in which the partici-pants walk together forward or away. It considers that these key episodes are particularly revealing for the embodied practices of the cameraperson as well as for the form of professional vision (Goodwin, 1994) that is manifest in the online protoanalysis of the participants' motion.

In this context, describing the camera movement of the researcher highlights several issues:

1. it provides for a better understanding of video practice research as a situated practice;
2. it helps to understand the specificities of the filmed activity and the systematic methodical way in which they are achieved by the partici-pants (and seeable by an observer);

3. it contributes to conceptual discussions about the way in which participation, space, and sequence organization are visibly/audibly recognized in situ, thereby offering new insights about the conceptualization of their embodied dimensions.

4. DATA

This chapter is based on original data that have been systematically planned and gathered in order to allow a detailed analysis of the embodied practices of the cameraperson: they are video recordings of video documentations of naturalistic settings. These video recordings have been organized in such a way as to make analytically available the situated practice of recording video for EMCA research purposes.

Several guided visits have been recorded in this way. I have systematically organized the data collection by using two cameras: the first one is focused on the participants; the second one—the metacamera—is focused on the former and the participants. Both cameras have filmed the opening of the activity, with the arrival of the participants and the way in which they have been equipped with microphones and have signed the agreement forms. Throughout the event, the metacamera has continuously documented the work of the first camera. Moreover, in some of the data, some participants were wearing camera glasses, which are not considered here, but see Mondada (2012b) for an analysis integrating these aspects.

The data used for this chapter were recorded during a guided visit video-recorded in 2010 in the garden of a university campus in Lyon. This garden was planned by a renowned landscape architect, Gilles Clément, and is carefully cared for by the gardeners, who embody Clément's principles in their everyday work. Four participants are engaged in the visit: a gardener, Luc; an organizer of cultural events on campus, Jean; and two architects interested in gardens, Yan and Elise. All participants agreed to be video-recorded and signed a written authorization. The visit lasted three hours and unfolds as they follow a small path through the garden, stopping to look at various plants, animals, places, and objects they find on their way.

Other data, coming from three other corpora recorded with the same video installation, have also been analysed, and they support the analyses of this chapter; however, they have not been included here because of space limitations.

The analyses rely both on the camera and the metacamera data; transcripts offer a detailed multimodal annotation of the conduct of the participants, as well as of the cameraperson (cam). Screen shots show both the view recorded by the camera (data) and by the metacamera (metadata).

5. ADJUSTING TO THE SPECIFICITIES OF VISITING
AS A MOBILE ACTIVITY

The guided visit is a mobile activity that raises several issues for the camera-person filming it. Walking with a camera, recording participants who walk, generates practical problems of mobile coordination—concerning both the trajectory of the walk (which can be more or less projectable and expectable, confronted with junctions, as well as sudden changes of direction, etc.) and the ecology of the walk (which can be scattered with diverse obstacles, related to the architecture, the urban/vegetal environment, other people and activities on the way, etc.). The aim of this chapter is not to review these problems in general but to focus analytically on the finely tuned coordination between details of the visit as a verbal and embodied activity and details of the camerawork.

Thus, my analysis focuses on the main stages of both organizing the mobile activity of the visit by the walkers and structuring the video record-ing by the cameraperson: I begin with the systematic description of how participants and the camera stop; then I study the problems generated by the emergence, establishment, and transformation of focuses of attention within the participation framework and the camera field; finally I analyse the practical problems of anticipating and coordinating participants' recom-mencement of their walking.

The first excerpt shows some of the fundamental aspects of the guided visit as a mobile activity. These consist of walking, stopping at a particular spot (about which the guide speaks), and walking forward towards the next spot. (See the Appendix at the end of this chapter for transcript conventions.)

(1)   [moy1_16.11=meta1_14.30]

```
1  LUC    là y a d'la *scabieuse# qui pousse±% par exemple, vo*yez,*
          there you have some scabious growing for example, see,
          >>walks frwd---------------------------------------*stops*
                            *points->
   elya                                          ±look-->
   jea                                           %looks-->
   fig                         #fig.1
2         (0±%.5)±%
   elya   ->±stop±and look--->
   jea      ->%stops%and looks--->
3  LUC    *alors on l'a épargnée avec• la *machine•
          then we have spared it with the lawnmower
          *goes twrd plant pointing-------*leans down pointing----->
   cam    >>walks bckwd--------------•stops-------•
4         mais# regardez comme c'est joli ça
          but look how it's nice this
   fig        #fig.2
5  YAN    ouais ouais
          yeah yeah
6  LUC    ça ça *attire aussi pas mal les insectes* (.) .hh%
          this this attracts quite well the insects (.) .hh
               ->*stands up---------------------*walks frwd--->>
   jea                                          -->%walks-->>
```

```
7          (1.•0)
   cam     ->•walks backwds->
8  LUC     c'est# c'est+ joli
           it's   it's nice
   eli               -->+walks-->>
   fig           #fig.3
9  JEA     c'est bien†
           it's good
   yan               ->†walks-->>
```

Figures 1.1–3   Metacamera views.
Figure 1.1   The participants are, from the left to the right, Elise, Yan, Jean, Luc.

As the group is walking along the footpath, Luc spots a plant—"*la scabieuse*"—names it, points, and stops, inviting the coparticipants to observe it (line 1 of the transcript). This produces a change in the progression of the group: participants slow down and eventually stop; they look at the plant that has been pointed at (lines 1–2). Moreover, Luc provides an account for it, while he approaches, leaning towards it and continuing to point at it (line 3). The visit consists of constituting a common focus of attention around an object—making it observable, identifiable, recognizable, label-able—and this is generally done by stopping in front of the object itself.

These specificities of the visit are consequential for the work of recording it: the cameraperson is walking backward at the beginning of the episode, a few metres from the group (Figure 1.1) and continues to walk until line 3: she stops after the participants have already stopped and while the guide continues with his explanation. In this sense, the camerawork adapts to the conduct of the group: it stops after they have stopped and after it has become clear that the plant is not just being pointed at and mentioned en passant but is established as a topic to be fully developed. The topic is sustained in further explanations and in a pointing gesture transformed into a leaning forward—a kind of pointing with the entire body (Figure 1.2).

This short episode is completed with a series of closing assessments (lines 4, 8) that are responded to by the participants (5, 9) and by Luc standing up and beginning to walk again (6). Jean aligns immediately with this embodied action (6), whereas Elise and Yan continue to look at the plant and walk forward a bit later. The cameraperson responds to the guide's movement, by moving immediately after him (7) (Figure 1.3).

In this way, the camera responds not only to the movements of the participants but to a selective sequential interpretation of their multimodal actions: it orients to the sequential organization of the episode and to the projections of emerging, developing, and closing actions. It captures the movement of the group as a whole, although paying special attention to the guide's action: at the beginning, the camera stops when the entire group has stopped, whereas at the end it moves as soon as the guide stands up and walks again.

In the next sections, I study these relevant sequential steps within the visit: stopping as a new sequence is initiated, focusing on a pointed-at object, walking forward at sequence completion.

6.   STOPPING AT SEQUENCE INITIATION

Stopping is an apparently simple action, which in fact relies on a finely tuned coordination. How does the guide invite the other participants to stop? How do the participants stop together? How does the cameraperson recognize that the participants are going to stop? Does the cameraperson orient to various persons stopping progressively or to the group stopping and achieving a new configuration—both a new formation and a new interactional space?

In the following excerpt, the group is walking forward along the footpath, as Luc attracts their attention on the sophistication of the "*pelouse*," which cannot be reduced to plain grass.

(2)   [Moy1-14.45 = meta1_13.07]

```
((the group walks forwards))
1   LUC    et et voyez donc c'est c'est intéressant parce
            and and see so then it's it's interesting because
    cam    >>walks backwards--------->
2          *que ‡vous# avez% donc‡ une pelouse,* (0.2)* %hein%‡ mais
            you have then a lawn,            (0.2)  right but
    luc    *points to the L------------------*stops-*cont to point->
    elya        ‡look to the L---‡pivot in front of LUC-------‡look->
    jea             %looks to the L-------------%stops%
    fig            #fig.1
3          (0.3)
4   LUC    euh* (0.4) %mais qui a été% traitée diff•éremment, #
            ehm  (0.4)  but that has been treated differently
    luc    ->*
    jea             %aligns with ELYA%
    fig                                                 #fig.2
    cam                              ->•stops
```

Figures 2.1–2   Metacamera views.
In Figure 2.1, the participants are, from the left to the right, Luc, Jean, Elise, Yan.

Luc introduces a new object and focus of attention—"*une pelouse*"—by using a positive assessment ("it's interesting," line 1), followed by a pointing gesture and the nomination of the referent (2). Elise and Yan first, then Jean, look to the left, where Luc is pointing, and they stop. They also progressively constitute a new interactional space: whereas the group was walking forward, occupying the entire width of the footpath (Figure 2.1), when they stop, their bodies pivot, and arrange in a line in front of Luc, looking at him and at the object he is pointing at (Figure 2.2). This new configuration, to which Jean aligns a bit later on (4), recognizes Luc as the guide and the main speaker and the other participants as his audience.

The cameraperson walks backward while the group is walking forward. She continues to walk back until the group has achieved a new interactional space—as Luc has already begun to develop his new topic. Here, the cameraperson seems to orient to the group as a whole and to its new configuration: she stops only when the new formation is recognizable.

As shown by the next segment, this raises some practical problems for the cameraperson: if she stops too early, the risk is to come too close to the group, colliding with it or having one of the participants out of the camera frame. If she stops too late, the risk is to be too distant from the group and to lose relevant details of its conduct.

The next segment occurs as the group is walking while discussing the problem of how to get rid of parasites without using chemical means. We join the discussion as Jean is proposing to cut and burn the sick branches.

(3)   [meta3_10.35=moy3_12.07]

```
((The group is walking, speaking about plants affected by a parasite))
1  JEA    i va falloir couper les branches=
          you will have to cut the branches=
2  LUC    =oui=
          =yes=
3  JEA    =et: (.) [brûler
          =and: (.) [burn
```

```
4   LUC          [c'est ce qu'on a fait. (.) et les# brûler. c'est
                 [that's what we did.    (.) and burn them. it's
    fig                                                    #fig.1
5        c'qu'on a fait déjà, .h mais, on en est pas #venu à bout.
         what we already did, .h but, we didn't succeed.
    fig                                                  #fig.2
```

Figures 3.1–2 Camera views.
In Figure 2, we can see, from the left to the right, Jean, Yan, Luc. Elise is visible in the back.

```
6   YAN    mhm mhm
7   LUC    parce que c'est bien joli, c'est vrai qu'on dit les les les
           because it's quite nice, it's true that people say the the the
8          la* (.) la+ médcine dou:tce%, les *les moyens les •moyens eh*#
           the (.) the soft medicine, the the treatments the treatments eh
    luc        *stops                        *1 more step------------*
    eli            +stops
    yan                          †stops
    jea                          %stops
    cam →                                           •stops
    fig                                             fig.3#
```

Figure 3.3 Camera view.

```
9   ELI    •alternatifs
           alternative
    cam    •fast zoom in->
10  LUC    voilà mais• bon
           that's it but well
    cam            -->•
11  ELI    ouais
           yeah
12  LUC    voyez? (.) ça:. # y a des limites quoi,
           see? (.) that:. there are limits PART
    fig                  #fig.4
```

Figure 3.4   Camera view.

At the beginning, the members of the group are walking one after the other (Figure 3.1). Because the discussion takes place mainly between Jean and Luc (lines 1–5), Luc turns towards Jean, who walks a bit behind him (Figure 3.2). While Luc goes on with a critical note about alternative medicine (7–8), he stops (8), successively followed by the others (8). Immediately after everybody has stopped, the camera stops too (end of line 8) (Figure 3.3).

As it is clearly visible from the frame-grabs in Figures 3.1, 3.2, and 3.3, there is a contrast between the image produced while the camera operator is smoothly walking backward at the same pace as the group (Figures 3.1 and 3.2) and the image produced after the group has stopped (Figure 3.3). Even if the cameraperson stops immediately after the participants, the distance between the group and the camera increases (Figure 3.3). The cameraperson orients to this practical problem by operating a zoom-in immediately after having stopped (9). This zoom permits the cameraperson to reduce the distance accumulated during the delayed stop (as visible in Figure 3.4).

In this case, the practice adopted by the cameraperson consists of a combination of an embodied move (stopping) with a technological move (zooming), producing a frame that is close enough to capture the details of the entire interactional space and far enough to preserve the distance with the participants.

In the next extract, a similar issue is observable, with an interactional space including both the participation framework and the object that the participants are observing.

(4)   [meta3_12.00 = moy3_13.34]

```
((all participants are walking down the footpath))
1  LUC    >vo*yez?<
          >see?<
              *points---->
2         (0.2) *(0.8)
   luc         ->*points and goes closer to a tree->
3  LUC    voyez les:, on pr-* on parlait des+ •des%• des^abris+
          you see the: we ta- we talked about the the the shelters
                          --->*stops, still pointing->
   eli                                    +approaches-------+
   jea                                         %stops
   cam  → >>walks backwards------------------•stops•walks frwd->
```

```
4          pourt les insectes. alors,
           for the insects. so,
   yan        ↑approaches--->
5          (0.2)
6  LUC     vous avez des:↑* (0.3) ces* ces graines•↑ là,
           you have some: (0.3) some some seeds there,
                      -->*picks up fruit*
   cam →                              -->•
   yan                 ->↑                    ↑looks at seeds->
```

The group is walking along the path and Luc introduces a new focus of attention with "look" (line 1) and by pointing at a tree (1–2). He repeats the instruction, projecting the name of the object to be seen (3–4) and stopping. Responding, Elise approaches the tree, and Jean stops (3).

Even before Yan has approached (4), the camera stops (end of line 3). So, in this case, the stop occurs before all participants are positioned again. Moreover, the cameraperson does not only stop her walk backward but walks forward (3). Thus, she orients not only to the new participation framework but also to the new focus—i.e. to the fact that Luc approaches the tree and picks up a fruit, inviting the coparticipants to closely inspect it. The camera does (in fact, anticipates) a movement very similar to the embodied one of the participants by offering a close-up on the group, making available the embodied details of the scrutinizing of the fruit.

Stopping is a methodical practice that relies on a finely tuned coordination for the participants and on a close monitoring of the projected action for the cameraperson. The latter orients to distinctive features of the action of stopping: she differentiates the action of the mobile formation versus the stopping of the group leader, as well as stopping and creating a new interactional space versus stopping and focusing on a new object of attention. When the focus is clearly recognizable and projectable, the camera stops *earlier, anticipating* the participants' movements, whereas when the camera orients to the mobile formation, it stops *later, following* the participant's movements.

7.   FOCUSING

Once stopped, the group engages in various activities and in particular in the achievement of a common focus of attention. Achieving joint attention is also a more general practice, recurrent in many different settings and requiring complex coordination and body arrangements (for guided visits, see Mondada, 2012c; for other settings, see Goodwin, 2000; Heath & Luff, 2000; Hindmarsh, Heath, vom Lehn, & Cleverly, 2005).

The emergence and establishment of participants' shared attention raises practical problems for the cameraperson too. On the one hand, the issue is how to document bodily orientations and participants' gazes in a relevant way; on the other hand, there is the issue of making the referent more or less accessible within the camera frame, depending on the position and distance of the object. Collective attention to objects raises different issues depending on the type of activity and type of referent: objects often introduce a different level of granularity to be documented, much more detailed than the global participation framework filmed by the camera. This is the case, for example, of reading texts and plans or computer screens, for which a global view on the participants is not enough and generally demands extra cameras (for discussion, see Luff & Heath, 2012; Mondada, 2012a). Whereas several cameras are easier to organize when they can be fixed on tripods, in mobile settings the use of several cameras is more problematic (but see Mondada [2012b] about the use of camera glasses in this setting; see Zouinar, Relieu, Salembier, & Calvet [2004] for other settings). Here, I study the way in which focusing is treated and solved as a practical problem when recording with only one mobile camera.

We join the continuation of excerpt 2, in which Luc stopped and focused the attention of the coparticipants on the "*pelouse*," which is situated on his right:

(5)   [Moy1-14.45 = meta1_13.07 *pelouse*]

```
1   LUC    c'est-à-dire* que• (0.3) pour montrer (.) la ri*chesse d'u- d'une•
           that's to say that (0.3) to show (.) the richness of a- of a
                      *points---------------------------*
    cam                 •zoom in-------------------------------------------•
2          *pelouse,• .h ben (0.2) •par# endroits on• la l-• on la laisse viv'
           Lawn, .h well (0.2) at some places we l- we let it live.
           *points------>
    fig                                 #fig. 1
    cam            -->•                 •looks on the L--•moves tw L•
3          on la laisse évoluer. (.) du coup .h rgardez (.) *vous avez #du tref
           we let it evolve. (.) so .h look (.) you get some trefoil,
                                                 -->*points,leans over->
    fig                                                 fig. 2#
4          ça c'est formidable pour les *abeilles, du trèfle rouge, •du trèfle•
           that's great for the bees, some red trefoil, some white trefoil
                             ->*stands up still pointing->
    cam                                                 ->•stops---•
```

Figures 5.1–2   Metacamera views.

```
5           blanc, .h vous avez plein d'choses, .h *et no*tamment des graminées
            .h you get lots of things, .h and in particular grass
                                          --->*,,,,,*comes back to path->
6           qu'on ne trouve* pas ailleurs. .h y a •y en a plein d'autres en plus
            that we don't find elsewhere. .h there are there are plenty of other
                                  -->*points again-------->
   cam                                             •zoom out--->
7           des graminées.• si on avait l'temps •j'vous montrerais, mais y a
            types of grass. if we had time I'dlike to show you, but there are
   cam                     -->•              •zoom in-->
8           +des trucs• ex*traordinaires au niveau des des:# (.) •voyez
            extraordinary things as far as ART ART (.) see
                          ->*leans over and points------>
   eli      +approaches--->
   fig                                            #fig.3
   cam      -->*                                  •zoom in-->
9           celle-ci par exetmple?
            this one for example?
   yan                      †approaches-->
10          (1.7)•
   cam      -->•
11 LUC      ça on la voit jamais,+
            we never see that,
   eli                    ---->+
12          (1.0 %(0.9)†
   yan                 ->†
   jea      %approaches-->
13          alors elle a un n- elle a un nom à coucher% dehors celle-là# aussi,
            then it as a n- it has an impossible name this one too,
   jea                                   -->%
   fig                                              #fig.4
```

Figures 5.3–4 Camera views.

Luc has already stopped, and the participants have aligned on his left, listening to him talking about the "*pelouse*" (see excerpt 2). In this fragment, we join the action as Luc is introducing the idea that grass is not a uniform surface but a complex composition.

As soon as he points at the grass, the camera does a zoom in (line 1), responding to his action. This is a first immediate response. But another kind of response follows too. More extended talk is projected, both by the pointing gesture and by the introductory talk (Luc's turn is characterized by a series of subordinate clauses, projecting a syntactically and discursively complex multiunit turn). Just after the zoom, the cameraperson looks on her left (Figure 5.1), inspecting the environment around her. This inspection prepares the next move, to the left, where another footpath intersects the main path on which the participants are walking, making it easier for the person holding the camera to walk and find a better position for filming the action. Thus, the cameraperson projects and prepares the camera focus on a next extended stretch of action that might occur on the left-hand side of the perspective space she is covering. This preparation includes an exploration of the characteristics of the environment. In this case, the cameraperson exploits a contingently found path for easing her movement to the left.

As a consequence, the camera moves to her left (2), just before Luc not only points but—after having issued an instruction to look (*"regardez,"* 3)—leans over the grass (Figure 5.2), showing the different kinds of plants composing it and listing their names (3–4). At the end of the list, Luc stands up again (4), and the camera stops panning to the left.

As Luc utters a global final comment closing the list (5–6), he moves out of the grass and comes back to the footpath where the coparticipants are still looking at him. The camera responds to that body movement by zooming out (6). But at the same time, Luc introduces further arguments, although alluding to the fact that he does not have enough time to fully develop them (6–8), and he speaks about the "extraordinary things" that can be found in the garden. He does this by pointing again to the grass. The camera responds to the gesture by zooming in (7), just before he leans over again, pointing to the grass and inviting the others to examine it in more detail (*"voyez celles-ci par exemple?,"* 8–9). Thus, the camera anticipates this repeated focus on the grass and is ready to zoom further when not only Luc leans over but the other participants begin to walk closer to him (Figures 5.3 and 5.4).

This zoom anticipates the new interactional space initiated by Luc's last visual instruction (*"voyez,"* 8). The previous interactional space, maintained over except 2 and the beginning of this excerpt, was more like a "lecturing" space, in which Luc was facing the other participants aligned in front of him (Figure 5.3). The new interactional space, however, is shaped by the bodies rearranged circularly around him and looking at the little plant he has picked up (Figure 5.4). For this latter configuration, a zoom-in allows the camera operator to document not only the bodily disposition but also the focus of attention of the participants, all looking at the blade of grass showed by Luc.

Accessing the site on which the participants' attention is refocused is not always easy to perform. It depends on direct visual access, the right distance, and the absence of obstacles between the camera and the group. In the previous fragment, there was an open flat space between the camera and the group; this is not the case in the next fragment, where the group is walking between higher trees on a narrower path. Thus, the next excerpt documents another solution the cameraperson finds on her way:

(6) [meta2_19.13 = moy2_21.03 formes]

```
((the group is walking along a narrow path, in line one behind the other)
1  JEA    c'est l'jardin des formes là?
          that's the garden of forms here?
   cam    >>walks backwards-->
2  LUC    c'est le jardin des [formes
          that's the garden of [forms
3  YAN                        [(        )
```

```
4  LUC    mais mal- maltgré* toùt on retrou%ve# beaucoup de ↑vie,
              but th- though we find a lot of life,
   yan                    ↑looks at and leans over on his R----↑points->
   luc                    *looks at Yan--------------->
   jea                                      %turns back, stops and pivots->
   fig                                      #fig.1a/b
```

Figures 6.1a and 6.1b   Metacamera and camera views at the same instant.

```
5  LUC    beaucoup* de::•
              a lot of::
                 --->*stops-->
   cam →                •raises the camera->
6         •(0.2)•
   cam →  •stops•walks forward, holding the camera-->>
7  YAN    et pourta+nt.#
              though.
                     ->+
   fig                #fig. 2a/b
```

Figures 6.2a and 6.2b   Metacamera and camera views at the same instant.

```
8  LUC    y *ent a hein des des p'ti[ts (.) %des p'tits* insectes*
              there are aren't there lots of of li[ttle (.) of little insects
9  YAN                               [(    )
   luc    ->*walks back towrds Yan-------------------*leans forward*
   jea                                  -->%walks back-->
   yan       ->↑
```

```
10         (1.2)
11 YAN     [pis mê:me la [for::me,            [de (tou:te beauté)
           [and even the [form,              [so (beautiful)
12 LUC     [e-           [>des petites# guèpes< [des toutes petites guèpes
           [e-           [>little wasps<        [very little wasps
   fig                                 #fig. 3a/b
```

Figures 6.3a and 6.3b   Metacamera and camera views at the same instant.

Jean is walking ahead, followed by the rest of the group. He asks for con-firmation from Luc (line 1) about the section of the garden they are walking in (the garden is organized in different thematic and formal sections, and this one is called "*jardin des formes*," garden of forms) and gets a positive response (2). In overlap, Yan notices something (3), and even though Luc continues by com-menting on the fact that the garden of forms does not exclude being a garden of life (4), the attention of the participants turns to what Yan is doing. Yan has spotted something on his right, looks at it, leans over, and then points at it (4); Luc immediately looks at him, and Jean begins to turn back (Figure 6.1b), stop-ping and pivoting back to look at what he is noticing (see Figure 6.2b).

Such sudden noticings along the way are a common phenomenon in visits and are particularly challenging for video recording. The camera is con-fronted with a contingency that is not projectable as such and that changes the trajectory of the ongoing action, setting up new relevances and new focuses, all in a new interactional space.

Participants realign their actions to this new event too: Luc leaves his turn unfinished (5) and stops walking, addressing the new relevancies raised by Yan's noticing. At this point, the cameraperson modifies her ongoing trajec-tory (5) too: even before stopping, she begins to raise the camera (Figure 6.2a), using the steadycam mount as a tripod allows her to hold the camera higher than her arms and above her head. Once she has raised the camera, she stops her walk backward and inverts its direction, beginning to walk forward (9) (see Figure 6.3a).

At that point, the participants are looking back, not yet walking back. Yan, having secured the attention of the group, utters a short enigmatic turn (7). Luc promptly adjusts to the new action by offering a comment on the insects

Yan spotted and by walking back to him (8). Jean walks back too. The camera follows them, continuing to walk forward (Figure 6.3a). In this way, the camera captures the new interactional space, constituted by the participants' regrouping of their bodies around Yan and their sharing of his noticing the form of the insect (11), promptly named by Luc (12).

The relevancies of changing foci and bodily reorientations are visible not only in the work of the cameraperson but also in the way in which this work is recorded by the metacamera filming it. The next excerpt shows evidence of these multiple orientations. The group has stopped at the margins of the footpath and has just observed a plant—"*les joubarbes*"—lying on the floor. We join the action as Luc is still looking at them, but Yan introduces another focus of attention, the fruits on the tree above that plant:

(7)   [Moy2_6.20 = meta2_4.29 fruits foncés]

```
1   LUC     .h par con*tre les
            .h by contrast the
                    *points down-->
2   YAN     les ↑les [fruits↑
            the  the [fruits
                 ↑points up--↑
3   LUC              [les jou]barbes sont con*ten*tes*
                     [the hou]seleeks are happy
                        ------------>*,,,,*looks at YAN*
4           *c- c'est c'est •joli hein?
            i- it's it's nice isn't it?
            *looks up behind him and pivots back---->
    cam              •zoom in-->
5   YAN     ah oué.# (.) >°c'très beau°<
            oh yep. (.) >°it's beautiful°<
    fig            #fig. 1
```

Figure 7.1   Metacamera view.

```
6 LUC     alors *>plus plus< ils •ont les feuilles- les •fleurs (0.4) claires,
          so >the more the more< they have light sheets- flowers
              ->*points up------>
    cam           --->•
    cam   >>stopped on the R-------------------------•moves to the L---->
7         >et plus les fruits# sont foncés<. celui-là devait avoir des fleu-
          >and the more the fruits are bright<. the one there should have flo-
    fig            #fig. 2
```

Figure 7.2   Metacamera view.

```
8            des:, .hh des fleurs pratiquement blanches .h et# quand* les fle-
             ART    .hh almost white flowers                .h and when the flo-
                                                           -->*gesticulates-->
   fig                                                       #fig.3
```

Figures 7.3 and 7.4   Metacamera views.

```
9            quand les ffleurs sont• rouges, les: les fruits sont blancs.
             When the flowers are red, the: the fruits are white.
   cam                               -->•
   meta  >>posit on Lfmoves towards R----------->
10           (.) donc# voyez c'- [c'est c'*est
             (.) so you see it- [it's it's
                                           -->*reorients tow group->
   fig               #fig.4
11 YAN                         [ah::,f         c'est l'in[verse
                               [oh::           that's the op[posite
   meta                         ->f
```

When Yan points at the fruit on the tree (line 2), Luc promptly realigns with this new focus, looking at him and uttering a positive assessment (4), responded to with an upgrade by Yan (5). At this point, a shared focus of attention is established.

The cameraperson responds to this initiation of a new sequence and new focus by zooming in (4). The cameraperson has stopped on the right side of footpath (Figure 7.1) and responds first with a technical close-up (4). Nevertheless, secondly, she modifies her position as Luc begins to describe the relation between the colour of the sheets and the colour of the fruits (6), pointing up. The camera stops zooming in, and the cameraperson begins to move from the right side of the path to the left side, adjusting her perspective to the new focus (6) (Figure 7.2).

Interestingly, this movement generates a practical problem for the metacamera documenting the camerawork: if the metacamera remains where it stands, on the left side of the path, the cameraperson ends up obscuring the group it is filming (Figure 7.3). To preserve the documentation not only of the camera movements but also of the recorded group, the metacamera switches position, moving to the right (Figure 7.4). This enables the camera operator to document the entire interactional space of the camerawork, which comprises the camera and its focus, the group.

This movement of the metacamera also shows a general phenomenon addressed by the camerawork: the attempt to keep together the participants *and* the objects they are orienting to. This attempt also shows that the camera and its focus constitute an entire recognizable configuration, "belonging together." This gestaltic feature is also shown by the orientation towards the camera filming and what it is filmed, displayed by other persons walking in the park who avoid crossing the line between the camera and the participants.

These analyses show the variety of micro practices through which the cameraperson projects and adjusts to new foci of attention of the participants: zooming in, walking closer to the participants, raising and holding the camera in a higher position. In these cases, there is an inversion of the mobile relation between the recorder and the recorded: the camera does not walk ahead of the group (backward) anymore but follows the group (forward). This entails a different temporal coordination: anticipating backward is not the same as anticipating forward. These analyses also point towards the relevant aspects of constituting a focus as it is practically defined by the camerawork: the camera orients to a gestaltic configuration constituted by the participants and what they are looking at, in a way that is similar to how the metacamera orients to the gestalt created by the shooting camera and the filmed participants.

8.   WALKING AT SEQUENCE COMPLETION

In the previous sections, I have demonstrated how the camerawork orients and treats the constitution of a new interactional space with a new disposition of the participants and the emergence of a new shared focus of attention. In this section, I deal with the dissolution of this common focus and the closing of the sequence. In guided visits, sequence closings are implemented in walking forward (Broth & Mondada, 2013; Mondada, 2012c; vom Lehn, 2013) and responded to by the camera walking backward again.

The next excerpt shows how all of the participants orient to this movement, including the cameraperson:

(8)   [meta2_8.53 = moy2_10.30]

```
1   LUC    .h mais c'est sympa, parce que: .hh voyez dans^un
           .h but it's nice, because: .hh you see in a
2          un en- un endroit .h où on pourrait dire eh ben:: voilà
           in a pl- a place .h where you could say well:: there it is
3          c'est un jardin FORmel justement, où les plantes sont
           it's precisely a formal garden, where the plants are
4          taillées, où c'est .h c'est euh c'est
           trimmed, where it's .h it's ehm it's
5   JEA    tai[llées?
           tri[mmed?
6   LUC       [rigoureux, non, c'est pas rigoureux,
              [rigorous, no, it's not rigorous,
7          .hh y a de la vie, y a d'la vie partout,
           .hh there is life, there's life everywhere,
8          †(.) .h[hh et* vous allez** voir* sur• les +sur les% .h les^
           (.) .h[hh and you will see on the on the .h the
                  *................*walks frwd->>
                                  **points frwd----->>
    yan    †comes out from the bush---->>
    eli                                              +walks frwd--->>
    jea                                                    %walks frwd->>
    cam                                      •walks backwards--->>
9   YAN        [(    )
10  LUC    les^érémurus par exemple là- les lys, .hh vous allez voir
           the eremurus for example the- the lily, .hh you will see
```

After advocating that the formal garden is in fact full of life (lines 1–7), Luc announces the next objects that will be seen ("*vous allez voir*," 8), projecting the next steps of the visit and pointing forward. While uttering the verb in the future tense, he also begins to walk forward. The other participants promptly align with this closing and begin to walk too: Yan comes out of the bush where he was inspecting something, and Elise and Jean walk forward on the footpath.

The camera operator begins to step back as soon as Luc has initiated his walking. It focuses on him as the guide, responding to him as the other participants do too. Contrary to what happens in sequence openings, where the camera tends to wait for all the participants to stop, here the camera responds faster and orients to the walking of the leading participant (see also excerpt 2).

Thus, the camera tends to *anticipate* closings, as in the following excerpt:

(9)   [meta1_12.10=moy1_13.46]

```
1   LUC    oui, oui parce qu'il y a les étamines qui sortent alors là elles
           yes, yes because there is stamen coming out so it
2          sont peut-êt- mais *y en a peut-ê•tre **+qui sont déjà en en •
           is mayb-       but there are maybe some that are already at at
                              *................*leans down->
    eli                                        +leans down->
    cam                                  •1 step frwd--------------•
```

```
 3  ELI    là
            there
 4  LUC    stade voilà, au stade plus ↑avancé, et du coup et
            at the stage yes, at a more advanced stage, and so and
    yan                            ↑leans down--->>
 5         c'est très joli eh
            it's very nice eh
 6         (.)
 7  LUC    voi↕+*là↕+*
            there it is
            ->↕+*stand up↕+*
 8  ELI    comment ça s'appelle?
            what is that called?
 9  LUC    c'est de la briza media en: •latin, c'est le l'amourette,
            it's briza media in latin, it's snakewood,
    cam                               •walks slowly backwrds----->
10  JEA    l'amourette?
            snakewood?
11  LUC    l'amourette
            snakewood
12  ELI    ouais
            yeah
13  LUC    c'est joli hein?
            it's nice isn't it?
14  ELI    c'est mignon
            it's cute
15  JEA    entre briza ↕media et l'amourette::,•
            between briza media and snakewood::,
    elya                  ↕walk back to the footpath->>
    cam                        ---->•moves faster to path
                                    and backwards-->>
```

We join the action as Luc is showing "*les étamines*" (line 1) and the participants are leaning over the ground (2, 4) to observe them. The camera adjusts to the new focus by making a step forward towards the group (2) (cf. supra). The sequence is achieved by a closing assessment (5) and the sequence-closing particle "*voilà*" (7), both uttered by Luc. Immediately after the particle, all the participants stand up together (7). But before the sequence is definitively closed, Elise asks a question about the name of the plant (8), and Luc responds (9). In guided visits, sequence closing is a sequential position at which participants often ask questions: questions both orient to the ongoing closings and delay them.

The cameraperson orients to this sequential feature: during Luc's answer, she begins to slowly walk backward. This *slow* movement lasts during all of the final closing comments on the name (15) and closing assessments (13–14). As two participants initiate walking on the footpath, the cameraperson *accelerates* the pace of her movement down the path. So the camera movements, speed, and pace are finely adjusted to the sequential features of the closing sequence.

Another similar adjustment is observable when the closing sequence is not only delayed but momentarily suspended by a question or a noticing occurring in the preclosing phase. The next excerpt shows how the camera adjusts to this sequential contingency.

(10)   [Moy2_6.55 = meta2_5.07]

```
1  JEA    mais comment tu fais pour tailler là haut?
           but how are you managing to trim up there?
2  LUC    be: je j'y arrive plus maintenant. c'est fini hé hé
           well I I'm not able to do that anymore now. it's gone eh eh
3         j'monte plus *HI% HHE HE
           I don't climb anymore HI HHE HE
                         *walks frwd->
   jea                   %walks frwd->
4  YAN    (   [•    )
5  LUC        [•ben j'faisais comme les cueilleurs de noix% de% coco
              [well I was doing as the coconut pickers do
   jea                                       -->%stops%
   cam →       •walks back->
6         hein HE °à l'ancie[nne°
           right HE °as in the [old days°
7  YAN                        [mais c'est *marrant* parce qu'on dirait
                              [but it's funny because one would say
   luc                              -->*stops--*pivots back-->
8         qu'ils ont été pelés* par un animal
           that they have been peeled by an animal
                           -->*
9  LUC    ah *ouais?
           oh yeah?
              *looks at YAN--->
10 YAN    à cou à •long• [cou, (.) on dirait ↑tune girafe
           with a neck with a long [nexk (.) it looks like a giraffe
                                    ↑walks frwd->
   cam →        ->•stops and does a lateral step•
11 LUC                   [c'est moi l'animal he he* eh ha ha ha ih
                         [it's me the animal he he eh ha ha ha ih
                                 -->*walks frwd---->>
12 ELI    +c'est lui l'animal [à long •cou
           that's him the animal [with a long neck
          +walks frwd---->>
   cam →                        •walks back->>
13 JEA                         [c'est toi Luc %d'accord
                               [that's you Luc alright
                                       %walks frwd--->>
```

We join the action as Luc has just explained how a tree needs special trimming of its high branches. Jean asks a question (line 1), and Luc answers (2–3), laughing about his current tree-climbing incapacity. On the completion of the adjacency pair, both begin to walk forward (3). The camera operator immediately begins to walk back too (5).

Luc adds some information about the way he used to climb the tree (5–6), and Jean stops, turning to him (5). At that point Yan, who was already saying something before that was not addressed by the others, does a noticing, which is a joke about both the tree and Luc (7–8). Luc orients to this noticing by stopping his walk and even pivoting back towards Yan (7), responding with a change-of-state token (9). This prompts Yan to elaborate on his joking remark (10). At that moment, the camera stops and begins to move laterally, refocusing on this post-closing extension of the sequence and on Yan.

As soon as Yan has produced the pun of the joke (*"on dirait une giraffe,"* 10), he walks again. Luc finally understands the joke and aligns with it (11), walking forward too, followed by Elise and Jean, who also recognize that Luc is the object of Yan's joke (12–13). The camera operator also walks to follow their walking.

This episode shows how sequence closing can be negotiated by the participants and how expansions can be given various degrees of importance; participants can treat them either as being just an extension of the ongoing closing sequence or as suspending the closing. In the guided visit, the suspension of the walk embodies the latter interpretation. The camera is sensitive to the very same sequential features. By anticipating the closing, the camera can organize a continuous slow progression towards closings; when an expansion of the sequence is under way, the camera interprets it—on the basis of her interpretation of the participants' conduct—in a manner that is immediately implemented either in her continuing walking or in her stopping and focusing again on the participants.

9.   CONCLUSIONS

Although there is an increasing literature about video materials, giving methodological advice about how to produce them, there is a surprising absence of studies of the detailed embodied practices of researchers actually producing their video data in situ and in vivo. This chapter begins to fill this important gap.

The chapter has focused on a perspicuous setting—the guided visit as the *paragon* of a mobile activity—in which the mobile work of the cameraperson is particularly observable in its step-by-step organization. On this basis, I have offered a systematic analysis of some key sequential moments of the guided visit: the opening and closing of sequences and the introduction of a new focus of attention. I demonstrated how the participants achieve them and how the cameraperson adjusts to them, providing an online situated protoanalysis of what happens and incorporating it into the embodied camera movements in the here and now.

Hence, the chapter has studied the methodic production of a set of micro practices and described their distribution in specific sequential environments—sketching a "grammar" of video recording with a mobile camera:

- anticipating/following participants' walk;
- projecting/responding to the sequence organization of participant's talk;
- walking again, stepping aside, walking slowly/faster;
- walking backward/forward;
- stopping;

- focusing: using the zoom-in/-out (as technically mediated movements) versus approaching/distancing (as embodied movements);
- raising the camera above the head (creating a vertical perspective) versus keeping it at level of the torso (creating an horizontal perspective);
- inspecting the environment before moving on; finding open spaces versus encountering obstacles for filming;
- positioning the metacamera in order to document the camera and its focus;
- filming the participation framework/changing participation frameworks;
- filming joint attention on a close/distant object;
- identifying and covering the adequate interactional space;
- and so on.

These embodied movements of the cameraperson are produced by orienting to, interpreting, *protoanalysing* the sequential features of the video-recorded action. The cameraperson orients to the embodied movements of the participants, to the structure of their activity, and to the sequential organization of their talk and action. The analyses provided here show that the cameraperson strongly orients to embodied actions of the filmed participants, such as their incipient walking or stepping. By so doing, she takes into consideration not only their bodies but, more fundamentally, the sequential organization of their action.

This sequential organization is *visible* but also *audible* for the cameraperson (who, in the case studied, was close enough to the group to be able to listen to it; moreover, the group's conversation is also audible in the microphones of the metacamera, which is even more distant from the group). This raises interesting questions about the relevant details to which an *observer* orients. Does the observer privilege some specific sequential features over others for the practical purposes of her situated perspective? Systematic study not only on this corpus but on other data sets reveals that the feature first oriented to is the specific sequential organization of the activity that is being recorded. The cameraperson orients primarily to sequence organization—rather than to the formatting of turn-constructional units or turn-taking organization. She orients to the way in which the activity is structured in sequences, episodes, and typical actions, involving characteristic arrangements of bodies in interaction. More particularly, she orients to sequence openings and closings as the most relevant sequential features for the work of filming the activity in its naturally occurring emergence.

Moreover, the cameraperson acts as an *overhearer* and an *overviewer* of the filmed scene: it would be interesting to investigate whether the features relevant for a scientific observer are also relevant for other categories of bystanders. In this case, the study of the camera orientations would also contribute to an understanding of how strangers adjust, for various practical purposes, to the collective behaviour of a group and more generally to its *publicly intelligible character.*

The study of camerawork as a form of embodied protoanalysis casts light not only on the praxeological grammar of recording video for analytic purposes but also on the specific features of the video-recorded activity. In this respect, the analyses developed here contribute to the understanding of sequence openings and sequence completions and their embodied organization (Mondada, in press b), as well as of sequences in which joint attention is progressively established (Goodwin, 2000; Heath & Luff, 2000; Hindmarsh & Heath, 2000; Mondada, 2012c). It also contributes to the grammar of walking as a social activity (cf. Broth & Mondada, 2013; Depperman, Schmitt, & Mondada, 2010; Relieu, 1999; Ryave & Schenkein, 1974), showing the methodic organization of walking, stepping, stopping, stepping back, pivoting, changing trajectory, and so on. It also highlights the finely tuned coordination of these practices with the grammar of turns-at-talk, characterized by projections, completions, suspensions, expansions, and the like, recognizing the literal power of "stepwise" organization. Time is crucial for both types of organization, and the perspicuous setting studied here reveals some important differences in the temporality and sequentiality of *following* versus *anticipating*, as well as the complex temporalities of *adjusting.*

Furthermore, the study of the practical problems solved online within the work of video-recording a mobile group also reveals specific issues related to participation—be it in terms of participation framework, vehicular unit, interactional space, or mobile formation. The camera orients to the "group" both as a whole and as a differentiated ensemble led by a guide and constituted by various categories. At times, it makes relevant what the guide is initiating and, at other times, what the entire group is achieving, thereby highlighting different aspectual features of the trajectory of this plastic vehicular unit (Goffman, 1971). In this light, a group stopping at some place is an emergent process taking some time, which might be variously treated by the cameraperson, having to decide whether she favours the projected/incipient stopping trajectory as it emerges or waits until all of the participants have stopped, as well as whether she takes into account possible divergent or delayed individual trajectories. Thus, a group stopping might take the form of different contextual configurations (Goodwin, 2000) defined by the participants' gaze, gesture, body orientation, and walk as they are shaped within the ongoing situated action (of showing, explaining, admiring, assessing, etc.). This in turn shapes the conceptualization of embodied participation: participants' bodies are not only positioned within the space but also dynamically assembled in various F-formations (Kendon, 1990), producing a dynamic interactional space that is also constrained by the objects and places they are looking at. This interactional space and its multimodal features is precisely what the camera attempts to continuously document in situ and in vivo.

In this sense, the detailed study of the researcher's camerawork as a practical, situated, embodied ongoing accomplishment constantly adjusting to the recorded action not only reveals the methodic organizational principles of video practices but also casts some light on broader and fundamental features of social interaction—such as the organization of sequence and participation.

APPENDIX: TRANSCRIPT CONVENTIONS

Talk has been transcribed according to conventions developed by Gail Jefferson (see Jefferson, 2004).

An indicative translation is provided line per line, in italics.

Multimodal details have been transcribed according to the following conventions (see Mondada, 2007):

* *	Each participant's actions are delimited by the use of the same symbol.
*--->	Action described continues across subsequent lines.
*--->>	Action described continues until and after excerpt's end.
---->*	Action described continues until the same symbol is reached.
>>--	Action described begins before the excerpt's beginning.
. . . .	Action's preparation
,,,,,	Action's retraction
luc	Participant doing the action is identified in small characters when he/she is not the current speaker or when the gesture is done during a pause.
fig	screen shot
#	Indicates the exact moment at which the screen shot has been recorded.

REFERENCES

Birkner, K., & Stukenbrock, A. (2010). Multimodale Ressourcen für Stadtführungen. In M. Costa & B. Müller-Jacquier (Eds.), *Deutschland als fremde Kultur: Vermittlungsverfahren in Touristenführungen* (pp. 214–243). München: Judicium.

Broth, M., Haddington, P., & McIlvenny, P. (Eds.). (in press). Mobile formations in social interaction [special issue]. *Space and Culture*.

Broth, M., & Lundström, F. (2013). A walk on the pier. Establishing relevant places in mobile instruction. In P. Haddington, L. Mondada, & M. Nevile (Eds.), *Interaction and Mobility* (pp. 91–122). Berlin: Mouton de Gruyter.

Broth, M., & Mondada, L. (2013). Walking away. The embodied achievement of activity closings in mobile interactions. *Journal of Pragmatics, 47*, 41–58.

Büscher, M. (2005). Social life under the microscope? *Sociological Research Online*, 10(1) www.socresonline.org.uk/10/1/buscher.html

Büscher, M., Urry, J., & Witchger, K. (Eds.). (2010), *Mobile Methods*. London: Routledge.

Deppermann, A., Schmitt R., & Mondada, L. (2010). Agenda and emergence: Contingent and planned activities in a meeting. *Journal of Pragmatics*, 42(6), 1700–1718.

De Stefani, E. (2010). Reference as an interactively and multimodally accomplished practice: Organizing spatial reorientation in guided tours. In M. Pettorino, A. Giannini, I. Chiari, & F. Dovetto (Eds.), *Spoken Communication* (pp. 137–170). Newcastle upon Tyne: Cambridge Scholars Publishing.

De Stefani, E. (Ed.). (2007). Regarder la langue. Les données vidéo dans la recherche linguistique [special issue]. *Bulletin VALS-ASLA, 85.*

Erickson, F. (1982). Audiovisual records as a primary data source. *Sociological Methods and Research, 11,* 213–232.

Garfinkel, H., & Wieder, D.L. (1992). Two incommensurable, asymmetrically alternate technologies of social analysis. In G. Watson & R.M. Seiler (Eds.), *Text in Context: Contributions to Ethnomethodology* (pp. 175–206). Thousand Oaks, CA: Sage.

Goffman, E. (1971). *Relations in Public: Microstudies of the Public Order.* Harmondsworth, UK: Penguin.

Goldman, R., Pea, R., Barron, B.J., & Derry, S. (Eds.). (2007). *Video Research in the Learning Sciences.* Mahwah, NJ: Erlbaum.

Goodwin, C. (1993). Recording interaction in natural settings. *Pragmatics, 3*(2), 181–209.

Goodwin, C. (1994). Professional vision. *American Anthropologist, 96*(3), 606–633.

Goodwin, C. (2000). Action and embodiment within situated human interaction. *Journal of Pragmatics, 32,* 1489–1522.

Goodwin, C. & Goodwin, M.H. (2004). Participation. In A. Duranti (Ed.), *A Companion to Linguistic Anthropology* (pp. 222–244). Oxford: Blackwell.

Haddington, P., Mondada, L., & Nevile, M. (Eds.). (2013). *Interaction and Mobility. Language and the Body in Motion.* Berlin: De Gruyter.

Heath, C. (1986). *Body Movement and Speech in Medical Interaction.* Cambridge: Cambridge University Press.

Heath, C., & Hindmarsh, J. (2002). Analyzing interaction: Video, ethnography and situated conduct. In T. May (Ed.), *Qualitative Research in Practice* (pp. 99–121). London: Sage.

Heath, C., Hindmarsh, J., & Luff, P. (2010). *Video in Qualitative Research.* London: Sage.

Heath, C., & Luff, P. (2000). *Technology in Action.* Cambridge: Cambridge University Press.

Hindmarsh, J., & Heath, C. (2000). Embodied reference: A study of deixis in workplace interaction. *Journal of Pragmatics, 32,* 1855–1878.

Hindmarsh, J., Heath, C., vom Lehn, D., & Cleverly, J. (2005). Creating assemblies in public environments: Social interaction, interactive exhibits and CSCW. *Computer Supported Cooperative Work, 14,* 1–41.

Jefferson, G. (2004). Glossary of transcript symbols with an introduction. In G. H. Lerner (Ed.), *Conversation Analysis: Studies from the first generation* (pp. 13–31). Amsterdam: Benjamins.

Kendon, A. (1990). *Conducting Interaction: Patterns of Behaviour in Focussed Interaction.* Cambridge: Cambridge University Press.

Knoblauch, H., Baer, A., Laurier, E., Petschke, S., & Schnettler, B. (Eds.). (2008). *Visual Methods. Forum: Qualitative Social Research, 9*(3). www.qualitative-research.net/index.php/fqs/issue/view/11/showToc

Knoblauch, H., Schnettler, B., Raab, J., & H.-G. Soeffner (Eds.). (2006). *Video Analysis: Methodology and Methods. Qualitative Audiovisual Data Analysis in Sociology.* Frankfurt: Lang.

Laurier, E., & Philo, C. (2006). Natural problems of naturalistic video data. In H. Knoblauch, J. Raab, H.-G. Soeffner, & B. Schnettler (Eds.), *Video-Analysis Methodology and Methods, Qualitative Audiovisual Data Analysis in Sociology* (pp. 183–192). Bern: Lang.

Lomax, H., & Casey, N. (1998). Recording social life: Reflexivity and video methodology. *Sociological Research Online, 3*(2).

Luff, P., & Heath, C. (2012). Some "technical challenges" of video analysis: Social actions, objects, material realities and the problems of perspective. *Qualitative Review, 12,* 255–279.

Lynch, M. (1993). *Scientific Practice and Ordinary Action.* Cambridge: Cambridge University Press.

Macbeth, D. (1999). Glances, trances and their relevance for a visual sociology. In P. Jalbert (Ed.), *Media Studies: Ethnomethodological Approaches* (pp. 135–170). Lanham, MD: University Press of America.

McIlvenny, P., Broth, M., & Haddington, P. (Eds.). (2009). Communicating place, space and mobility [special issue]. *Journal of Pragmatics, 41*(10).

Mondada, L. (2006). Video recording as the reflexive preservation and configuration of phenomenal features for analysis. In H. Knoblauch, J. Raab, H.-G. Soeffner, & B. Schnettler (Eds.), *Video Analysis: Methodology and Methods. Qualitative Audiovisual Data Analysis in Sociology* (pp. 51–68). Bern: Lang.

Mondada, L. (2007). Multimodal resources for turn-taking: Pointing and the emergence of possible next speakers. *Discourse Studies, 9,* 194–225.

Mondada, L. (2009). Emergent focused interactions in public places: A systematic analysis of the multimodal achievement of a common interactional space. *Journal of Pragmatics. 41,* 1977–1997.

Mondada, L. (2012a). The conversation analytic approach to data collection. In J. Sidnell & T. Stivers (Eds.), *Handbook of Conversation Analysis* (pp. 32–56). Chichester, UK: Blackwell-Wiley.

Mondada, L. (2012b). The establishment of a common focus of attention: Issues for participants, camera(wo)men and analysts. In J. Hindmarsh, P. Luff, & D. vom Lehn (Eds.). *Work, Interaction and Technology: A Festschrift for Christian Heath* (pp. 43–56). London: King's College.

Mondada, L. (2012c). Garden lessons: Embodied action and joint attention in extended sequences. In H. Nasu & F. C. Waksler (Eds.), *Interaction and Everyday Life: Phenomenological and Ethnomethodological Essays in Honor of George Psathas* (pp. 293–311). Lanham, MD: Lexington Books.

Mondada, L. (in press a). Video as a tool in sociology and anthropology. In C. Müller, A. Cienki, E. Fricke, & D. McNeill (Eds.). *Body—Language—Communication* (pp. 978–988). Berlin: de Gruyter (HSK 38.1).

Mondada, L. (in press b). Multimodal completions. In A. Deppermann & S. Günthner (Eds.), *Temporality in Interaction.* Amsterdam: Benjamins.

Relieu, M. (1999). Parler en marchant: Pour une écologie dynamique des échanges de paroles. *Langage & société, 89,* 37–67.

Ruby, J. (2000). *Picturing Culture: Explorations on Film & Anthropology.* Chicago: University of Chicago Press.

Ryave, A. L., & Schenkein, J. N. (1974). Notes on the art of walking. In R. Turner (Ed.), *Ethnomethodology* (pp. 265–274). Harmondsworth, UK: Penguin.

vom Lehn, D. (2013). Withdrawing from exhibits: The interactional organisation of museum visits. In P. Haddington, L. Mondada, & M. Nevile (Eds.), *Interaction and Mobility*. Berlin: de Gruyter.

Zouinar, M., Relieu, M., Salembier, P., & Calvet, G. (2004). Observation et capture de données sur l'interaction multimodale en mobilité. *Mobilité & Ubiquité '04*, 1–3 June 2004, Nice, ACM.

2 Pans, Tilts, and Zooms

Conventional Camera Gestures in TV Production

Mathias Broth (Linköping University)

1. INTRODUCTION

This chapter considers video as action within interactive sequences involving talk and camera movement in TV production. Based on video-recorded live production of a series of French studio interviews, it focuses on how camera operators move their cameras in conventional ways to achieve locally relevant actions. The focus here is thus rather on the handling of the camera as reconstructable through the shot it produces than on the filmed reality as represented in its shot.

Live TV production is an activity whose overarching aim is the production and simultaneous broadcast of video sequences and sound of live events. It is a form of collaborative work carried out within a production crew whose members are ordinarily dispersed in at least two different locations, a control room and a shooting site, classically a television studio. This study is based on the work of a French TV crew. In their control room (Figure 1) are positioned, among others, the Director, who selects and constantly switches among the camera operators' different shots, the Production Assistant (PA), who keeps track of time and the order of planned events, as well as technical, sound, and lighting engineers. In the studio (Figure 2), the Floor Manager embodies a link with the control room, giving cues and instructions to the studio audience and the studio host, and camera operators provide shots of the studio debate to be broadcast. Four out of five operators (operators 1–4 in Figure 2), using cameras on stands, occupy particular positions and shooting angles in relation to each other and the participants in the TV debate, whereas a fifth operator (operator 5), using a portable camera, moves more freely in search of good shots. The five operators' shots are displayed in a bank of screens in the control room (cameras 1–5 are visible from left to right in the bottom row of screens in Figure 1). Through close collaboration, the members of the crew ongoingly participate in the production and broadcast of an emergent sequence of shots and carefully controlled audio uptake.

Communicative resources are asymmetrically distributed among camera operators and the participants in the control room. Whereas the control

Figure 1 The control room.

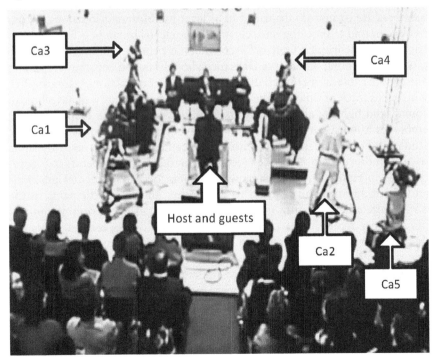

Figure 2 The studio.

room can talk to operators over an audio interface, operators can't normally talk back (as they hardly ever use the microphones of their headsets). Further, although neither side can actually see each other, operators can display their activity through the continuous shot they make with their cameras. So the main resources used are (1) talk by control room participants and (2) camera movement by operators.

The particular video practices to be studied here are part of a larger set of conventional "visual signals" (Millerson, 1999: 111) that is arguably constitutive of any television camera operator's professional competence (cf. C. Goodwin, 1994): tilting the camera repeatedly up and down to mean yes, panning it repeatedly left and right to mean no, and zooming repeatedly in and out to highlight one's own shot.[1] An example of one of these practices can be found in the following excerpt, where a camera operator in the studio (Ca3, Bertrand), following a question from the Director in the control room (line 1) repeatedly tilts his camera to produce an affirmative response (line 2, camera movement in grey overlay). (See the Appendix at the end of this chapter for transcription conventions.)

(1)   RR031120 [22.24:10–22.24:13]

```
01 Dir:    donc Bertrand, tu m'entends+::?
           ok so Bertrand, do you hea::r me?
02 Ca3:                          +tilt down&UP&DOWN&UP&down+
03                                  (0.7) bon, (.) tu vas+ avoir
                                    alright   you will have
```

Although repeated pans, tilts, and zooms are basically associated with no, yes, and highlighting, their meaning as a situated action—what a particular camera movement "does" or "achieves" and what practical problem it actually addresses—can be assumed to be reflexively related to just where a movement is produced in an emergent sequential (cf. e.g. Drew & Heritage, 1992) and praxeological context (Chapter 3 in this volume by Mondada; cf. Linell, 2011: 14). Just how camera operators produce and time repeated pans, tilts, and zooms in relation to ongoing talk and other local contingencies is the topic of this chapter. These practices will be considered in two distinct activities: *off-air*, preparing for the next live-editing session, and *on-air*, as the team is currently involved in producing sequences of shots that are broadcast live. The analysis will yield a description of how repeated pans, tilts, and zooms may be relevantly produced by operators to achieve a number of crucial actions for the live-editing work.

2. LIVE TV PRODUCTION AS A SOCIALLY ORGANIZED ACTIVITY

How television is produced and consumed is a recurrent research topic in fields such as semiotics, sociology, and media studies. However, with the notable exception of the recent interdisciplinary field of "Production

Studies" (Mayer, Banks, & Caldwell, 2009), the interest in television production does not generally base its analyses on observations of production processes but rather on its product, i.e. the broadcast program. Even within Production Studies, there is still a lack of attention to the fine and emergent details of the work of TV production. As a result, only very few empirical studies actually consider televisual production processes as they happen in real time.

Drawing on previous EMCA work on the sequential organization of actions and activities (Sacks, 1992; Schegloff, 1968; Heritage, 1984a), "centres of coordination" (Suchman, 1993), video mediated interaction (Heath & Luff, 1993), the accountability of camera shots (Macbeth, 1999; Mondada, 2003), and of film editing (Jayyusi, 1988), I have already explored (Broth, 2004) some of the basic interactive mechanisms involved in the live-editing of TV debates. A fundamental editing sequence was found to be (1) multiple proposals of "broadcastable" shots produced by camera operators holding their cameras steady, and (2) acceptance of one of these at a time by the Director, effectuating the switch from a current shot to a next one. The communication between camera operators and control room personnel also involved mediated sequences built using talk and camera movement. There, precise timing was identified as central for achieving sequence coherence and situated meanings of actions.

This early study also hinted at the fact that structures inherent in the broadcast (i.e. the "on-stage") activities play a crucial role in the workings of the live television production process. Production crews exploit these structures as a "contextual resource" (Broth, 2008), providing a background against which members of the crew make sense of the highly indexical (Garfinkel & Sacks, 1970) and technologically mediated actions of other members. This is not only the case for talk-based activities such as TV interviews and TV debates (see also Mondada, 2009) but applies more generally (see Engström, Juhlin, Perry, & Broth, 2010, on the live production of sports replays). In subsequent works (Broth, 2006, 2008, 2009), I have developed analyses of how interactional practices in the TV debate—e.g. in terms of projectable questions and answers, address terms, and the current topic—are crucially relevant for the crew to be able to show particular studio participants as they take turns in the ongoing TV debate.

3.   TWO BASIC CONCERNS IN TV PRODUCTION

There is a widely established prescriptive "grammar" of TV production (see e.g. Millerson, 1999). A brief description of two basic concerns in the production and sequencing of shots is in order because these concerns are consequential for when, how, and often also why camera operators produce conventional camera movements. A first one is the ongoing and incessant achievement of the *invisibility* or transparency of the production work in most TV productions. This effort involves the content of shots, as operators systematically avoid making shots of production-related objects, including equipment and personnel (camera operators should always avoid "shooting their colleagues"). This orientation also involves the ongoing framing activity, which is manifest in camera operators' careful use of camera movement when the team is on-air and a general avoidance of putting unstable or jerky shots on-air (Broth, 2004).

A second concern relates to the production of spatial intelligibility for the viewer in and through the ways in which the edited sequence of shots is assembled. For example, to visually create the understanding that two interlocutors are indeed facing each other, shots of studio participants are standardly produced from complementary angles. This is achieved by following the so-called 180° rule—well known within the television professions—which stipulates that the two camera operators involved should be on the same side (the same 180°) of an imagined line cutting through the current interlocutors. In contrast, if operators are on different sides of this line, their shots will show the two interlocutors looking in the same direction. Editing these back to back would visually create the erroneous understanding that they are positioned side by side rather than opposite each other (cf. Jayyusi, 1988).[2] Having direct visual access to all participants in the studio (participants to the ongoing debate as well as the other operators), camera operators are normally in a better position than the control room to understand which operators should shoot which studio participants so as to honour this rule; and conventional camera movement allows them to communicate their understanding to the control room.

4. ACTION SEQUENCES IN CAMERA-AND-TALK-IN-INTERACTION

Sequence organization, i.e. "the organization of courses of action" (Schegloff, 2007: 2) is both a fundamental topic and a methodological resource in EMCA forms of interaction analysis. Ever since the "discovery" of the sequence in the early 1960s (Sacks, 1992, I: 3–11), work in this broad discipline has continued to explore how action sequences are organized for the interactional achievement of actions and activities, mainly in and through talk. The present chapter contributes to this body of work by considering how also *camera practices* may be used to build interactional sequences (see also Chapter 3 by Mondada, this volume).

In reflexively responding to some prior, ongoing, or anticipated event, camerawork is "accountable" (Garfinkel, 1967: 33): both what is shown in a shot and the way in which it is ongoingly framed amount to a public display of how events in the world are relevantly understood by a camera operator (Macbeth, 1999; Mondada, 2003; Introduction by Broth, Laurier, & Mondada, this volume; see also Broth & Lundström, 2013). Operators exploit the accountability of the shot in their interactive sense-making with the distant control room personnel, who perceive operator shots as they appear in the row of monitors in front of them. In moving one's camera, operators can thus show the control room what they are orienting towards and currently working to achieve (Broth, 2004).

Camera movement is generally responsive either to talk in the control room as mediated through the internal radio circuit or to an event within the broadcast studio interaction (cf. Broth, 2008, 2009). In the former case, camera movement is standardly a second pair part in a so-called adjacency pair, i.e. a pair of actions where the first makes the second expectable and missing if not produced (Schegloff, 1968: 1083). In the studied setting, control room talk and camera responses most frequently take the form of "directive–compliance" sequences (cf. Craven & Potter, 2010; Chapter 3 by Mondada, this volume), produced each time the Director performs the basic task of directing operators to produce particular shots. In the latter case, operators move their cameras to adjust to new studio contingencies, i.e. on their own initiative. However, because such initiatives may or may not be noticed by the control room personnel, who are not necessarily oriented to that particular operator's monitor when the movement is produced, there is an inherent problem of control room attention of camera operator initiatives. This characteristic of the setting impacts on how members of the crew format and time talk and camera actions (Broth, 2004, 2008).

5. CONVENTIONAL CAMERA GESTURES (CCGs)

A distinction can be made between, on the one hand, camera movement (directed or not) towards making usable shots for the live-editing and, on the other, camera movement having a conventional meaning potential that transcends the local situation in which it is used (cf. e.g. Linell, 2011). Conventional camera gestures (CCGs) include repeated pans for no and repeated tilts for yes (in analogy with head movement in many cultures). Just like the very similarly restricted word set of the aphasic man studied by C. Goodwin (whose only words were "yes," "no," and "and"), these two resources "presuppose links to other talk" (2003a: 91), within which they get their situated meanings as action. A third CCG is repeated zooms in and out for indexing or highlighting, not unlike pointing in face-to-face interaction, similarly a practice that relies on surrounding talk for its intelligibility (C. Goodwin, 2003b). Different CCGs differ in the ways in which they depend on the shot's *content*. For pans and tilts, the intelligibility is crucially based on the perceivability of the camera as moving laterally or vertically, which only presupposes some kind of visual structure in the shot to allow for such reconstructive understanding. In contrast, because repeated zooms typically refer to something visually available in the shot or to the shot itself, the content of the shot is central to its understanding.

As we will see, reflexively, CCGs make it possible for the control room to engage with operators by launching other sequence types than directive ones in the particular "language game" (Wittgenstein, 1953) and workplace of TV production, e.g. *asking* yes/no-questions and *producing informings* that demand a response. It also allows operators to actually *comment* on control room talk, confirming or disconfirming particular spoken turns.

CCGs are recognizable and accountably set off as distinct from other camera activity by (1) their initiation immediately following some prior—studio or within-crew—action (to which it reacts or responds), (2) their limited repertoire (horizontal pans, vertical tilts, and zooms), (3) their repeated character (e.g. minimally, left-right, up-down, and in-out). Although conventional, their meanings are, just like other language resources, *potential* rather than actual, in the sense that the meaning of a movement always has to be locally achieved. To produce the locally relevant meaning of a CCG, the context(s) of its use must be taken into account (cf. e.g. Garfinkel & Sacks, 1970: 339; Drew & Heritage, 1992: 18; Linell, 2011: 14).

6.   A NOTE ON DATA AND METHODOLOGY

The study is based on five video-recorded production sessions of the French live TV interview programme *Rideau Rouge* (broadcast from Paris on *TV5 International* between 2002 and 2005), taking place in 2003 and 2004. Each session lasted for about 1 hour 35 minutes, and the total corpus used involves almost 8 hours of TV production work. The activity was filmed in the control room and is therefore documented from a control room perspective rather than, for example, a camera operator perspective. Three different cameras were used: one for a wide-angle view of the PA, the Director, and his assistant in front of the screens (from left to right in Figure 1); one for a closer view of the screens only; and one for a very close view of a monitor in the control room relaying a wide-angle view of the studio, including the five camera operators (Figure 2). The broadcast programme was also recorded on a VHS recorder.

The recordings were carefully searched for instances of CCGs. Twenty-five sequences where at least one CCG was produced were identified. Ten sequences were found during a total of 6 hours of on-air production work and 15 sequences during the 1.5 hours that the team was off-air. All CCGs were then studied in their local sequential and praxeological environment to identify when and how they were produced, whether they were recognized as actions by the participants in the control room, and in that case, what action they were demonstrably doing, as evidenced in the control room's subsequent uptake (cf. Sacks, 1992, II: 251–253).

7.   CONVENTIONAL CAMERA GESTURES
IN INTERACTIVE SEQUENCES OFF-AIR

When the team is not live-editing (before the show or during the broadcast of a prerecorded video clip), CCGs are relatively frequent. They are used to produce different sequentially relevant actions.

7.1.   Answering Questions

CCGs can achieve positive or negative answers to questions from the control room. Questions to operators typically require a yes/no response, and operators can respond with either repeated tilting or panning movement. One example is excerpt (2), where Léonard is camera operator 2.

(2)   RR040122 [22.43:04–22.43:10]

```
01 PA:   Léonard il est un peu battu mais bon¿
         Léonard he is a bit beaten but well¿
02       (0.5)
03 Dir:  ouai[s mais:: euh (0.4) tu lui as expl]iqué# Léonard hein?
          yeah but:: eh (0.4) did you explain it to him, Léonard?
04 PA:       [il est assis maintenant le : : --]
              is he seated now         the:: --
   fig                                           #fig.2.1
```

Figure 2.1

```
05       (0.2)+(0.5) ++(0.5)
06 Ca2:       +unstab++tilt down&UP&DOWN&-->
07 Dir:  #ouais okay (0.2)+(0.1) c'est bien!
          yeah okay (0.3)        it's good!
08 Ca2:  &UP&down       -->+
   fig   #2.2
```

Figure 2.2

After a period of live broadcast, the PA notices that one of the camera operators, Léonard (Ca2), is a bit "beaten" (line 1). By this she means that he has had a hard time finding good shots from his position behind the host in the studio. At this point, the Director, leaning closer to his microphone and looking at Ca2's monitor (Figure 2.1), puts a question directly to Ca2, checking whether he has explained the reasons for his difficulties to the host or not (which the Director had earlier asked him to do) (3). After a short pause, this question gets its projected and conditionally relevant (Schegloff, 1968) response as Ca2 takes control of his camera and shortly thereafter tilts it rather vigorously up and down to produce an affirmative answer to the question (6; tilt visible as blur in Figure 2.2). That the Director sees this movement as sequentially relevant and understands it as embodying an affirmative answer is manifest to Ca2 (and to the researcher) through his production of an audible "sequence closing third" (Schegloff, 2007: 118), whereby he accountably acknowledges Ca2's answer ("*ouais, okay*," "yeah okay," 7). It can be noted that the Director's action is initiated already after 0.5 seconds of tilting, which, in terms of camera movement, amounts to only a part of the entire repeated tilting ("down&UP&DOWN. . ." and as the camera is still tilting downward). This is then what it takes for the Director to understand the mediated camera movement as doing the relevant responsive action in this sequence.

A sequentially relevant and recognizable answer can also be produced by zooming in and out, as in excerpt 3 below. Following the request of a journalist present in the control room to show a particular member of the studio audience (Pierre Lagrange, the same person who is now talking in the prerecorded clip currently broadcast), the PA relays this request to the camera operators (line 1).

(3)   RR040122 [22.58:45–22.58:49]

```
01 PA:     >alors< (.) Pierre Lagran:ge? hein,
           okay then (.) Pierre Lagrange? PRT
02 Dir:    (.) no::n [euh(ais)]
           (.) no::   eh(eah)
03 PA:            [il est- ]+%il% il fau#&[drait-]+=
                   he is     we  we need-
04 Ca3:                     +ZOOM OUT          -->+
    dir
                                     &prep. pointing-->
05 Jou:                              [il est]=
                                      he is
    fig                              #fig.3.1
```

Figure 3.1

```
06 Jou:    [ d+ans la salle&]&+        [c']est bi+en [(lui)].
              in the room              that is him alright.
07 PA:     [il+faudrait qu'&]&+ t'#aie[s-]        [voilà]:.+
              we need            you to           that's it.
   dir                  -->& &points Ca3-->
08 Ca3:    +ZOOM IN      -->+            +ZOOM OUT -->+
   fig                       #fig.3.2
```

Figure 3.2

```
09         (0.2)+(0.1)
10 Ca3:        +ZOOM IN-->
11 Dir:    ou&ais d'a++ccord merci Bertrand.
              yeah ok     thanks Bertrand.
   dir     ->&
12 Ca3:        -->++close up Pierre Lagrange-->>>
```

The PA produces her request for shots of a particular guest by uttering, after a connective particle (*"alors"*), the name of this person (Pierre Lagrange) loudly and with upward intonation. Just after this interrogative turn, no fewer than three of the five operators (Ca3, Ca4, and Ca5) begin to work towards producing a shot of this person in the audience. Here, I will focus only on Ca3, who, in fact, already has a shot of the person as the PA produces her question. Although the Director expresses doubt, presumably about the possibility of such a shot (line 2), the PA begins to specify what they would need to be able to get one (3), and the journalist asserts that Lagrange is in the room (5–6). Ca3 zooms out quickly from his current close-up shot of Pierre Lagrange (4, Figure 3.1). In this sequential position, the quick zooming out can be seen to make the camera's monitor in the control room salient: after only a very short while, and as Ca3 is still zooming out, the Director begins to point towards it (4). After a very brief wide-angle shot, Ca3 then zooms back in again (8). In a strikingly coordinated collective movement, the zooming in and the Director's pointing gesture reach their end points (i.e. their *apex*) at the very same moment (7–8, Figure 3.2). Seeing this happen, both the journalist and the PA manifestly understand these two forms of indexical reference—note how the way their two turns are formatted (*"c'est bien lui,"* "that is him alright" [6]; *"voilà,"* "that's it" [7]) displays their responsive character—as highlighting the relevant person in the audience. To close the sequence, the Director then acknowledges and also thanks Ca3 (11).

The last two excerpts demonstrate that camera movement can be used to constitute sequentially relevant actions in the mediated and asymmetrical interaction within the TV production crew. They also show how camera movement is integrated in action sequences through a mutual sensitivity to the relative timing of actions that are produced as part of a coherent interactional sequence. However, the particular resource used differs in the two excerpts: in excerpt 2, there is a tilt, and in excerpt 3, there is a zoom. An assertive tilt is a relevant response to a yes/no question (2), whereas the operator's zooming out and in in 3 can be considered an artfully designed response to a request to show someone who is in fact already visible in his shot, thereby highlighting it.

7.2. Acknowledging Informings

A second kind of action that camera operators are able to produce by repeated tilts and zooms is *acknowledging* an informing that is verbally addressed to them directly. What is at stake here is to make manifest, using the camera as the only communicative resource, that a message has been received while not producing a new shot (in contrast to any directive–response sequence, where the operator produces the asked-for new shot and by this same movement also shows recognition of the directive). In the following excerpt, a repeated tilting movement is produced to acknowledge reception of control room talk.

(4)   RR040122 [23.34:18–23.34:43]

```
01 Ca5:    -->>middle shot host-->
02 Dir:    ah oui c'est bien, Patrick.#
           oh yes that's good, Patrick.
   fig                                #fig.4.1
03         (11.7)+         (2.1)        ++      (7.4)
04 Ca5:       -->+tilt & pan down-right-up++shot behind screen-->
```

Figures 4.1–4.2

```
05 Dir:    #ouais je te prendrai pour sor+ti:r, Patrick. (0.3)& #
           yeah I'll use you     for going live Patrick.
06 Ca5:                              ->+tilt down&UP&DOWN&UP&DOWN-->>
   dir                                                 &turns away>>
   fig     #fig.4.2                                       #fig.4.3
```

Figure 4.3

During a break in the broadcast, Ca5 finds a shot of the host (Figure 4.1) that the Director notices, assessing it positively (1–2). In the corpus *Rideau Rouge*, such positive assessment is a recurrent Director's method for "securing" good shots for upcoming cuts in live-editing (Broth, 2004). Ca5 then holds this shot for almost 12 seconds, before suddenly redirecting his camera so that it produces a shot of one of the other operators sitting behind the reverse side of the big screen used for projecting images in the studio, clearly not suitable to broadcast (3–4, Figure 4.2). We can only speculate as to why Ca5 does this; maybe he needs a bit of rest (Ca5 operates a portable camera). After a while, the Director (re-)informs Ca5 (notice the "*ouais*," "yeah," beginning of line 5) that he will use him for the transition between the currently broadcast video clip and the upcoming live studio broadcast (5). Even before the end of the Director's turn, and interestingly also before his name is mentioned, Ca5 begins tilting his camera repeatedly down and up (6). As the camera is still tilting, the Director turns away from Ca5's monitor (6, Figure 4.3), indicating (to us as observers, although not to Ca5) that he has indeed received this camera-mediated acknowledgement.[3]

Our next excerpt (5) does not show any display of acknowledgement. It is nevertheless useful to show that an acknowledgement by an operator may be pursued if not produced at its relevant sequential position next to a piece of information. Following a question by the Director, the PA states who will be the first guest to be interviewed after the break; Ca2 (Léonard), the camera operator to be used for showing this guest, does not move his camera.

(5)   RR040122 [22.44:10–22.44:23]

```
01 Ca2:    +close up shot of studio guest-->>
02 Dir:    hein- il parle avec qui, principe euh:::
           hey- he talks to whom, in principle eh:::
03 PA:     alors on SORT, sur <BIgnaMI:>, normalement.
           okey we go on air with Bignami normally.
04         (0.7)
05 PA:     >LéoNArd euh<.
06         (0.7)
```

```
07 PA:      c'est:: euh:: c'est pas lui:, hein:, euh::
            that's:: eh:: that's not him right eh::
08 PA:      ah SI¿ c'est lui, Bignami, (°xx photo°).=
            oh yes that's him Bignami (°xx photo°).
09 PA:      =>pardon mais il a- il a< pas de lunettes¿
            excuse me but he does- he doesn't wear glasses¿
10 PA:      (.) °ah si:°.
            (.) °oh yes:°.
11 Dir:     (1.7) ah ben les photos:,
            (1.7) well you know how photos are,
```

During this entire sequence, Ca2 produces a close-up shot of one of the guests in the studio (line 1). With less than a minute of going live again, the Director turns to the PA to enquire about who will be interviewed next (2). This is consequential for what cameras to use for going on-air. The PA answers that normally it should be the participant called Bignami (3). At this point, Ca2 has the possibility to confirm this understanding. There are two ways to do this: (1) panning to produce a close-up shot of some other participant who will then be understood to be claimed to be Bignami by the operator (Broth, 2009); (2) in case the operator already has a shot of the relevant participant, as here, producing a repeated tilting or zooming movement that will then be understood as both acknowledging the stated understanding and as claiming that it is really Bignami who is visible in the operator's shot (cf. Broth, forthcoming). In this case, Ca2 does neither, and his shot remains steady, which creates a situation where the control room can't be sure whether he has heard the preceding talk or not. That the PA expects some kind of immediate response from Ca2 in this sequential position is visible as she produces Ca2's name after only 0.7 second of stable shooting (4–5) and thereby prompts him to respond. After yet another 0.7 second, she goes on to explain that the person currently visible in Ca2's shot is not Bignami (6–7). She gets past yet another moment in which a camera response would have been relevant (end of 7), but the camera still does not move. It is only now that the PA realises, after looking at a photo of Bignami (not shown in transcript), that, indeed, Ca2 is currently shooting Bignami (8).

Although Ca2 does not move his camera at all in this excerpt, the lack of camera movement is taken as embodying the operator's accountable action, and the expected response is pursued by the PA when it is not forthcoming (cf. Davidson, 1984; Stivers & Rossano, 2010). As a result, the absence of confirming camera movement becomes sequentially relevant and eventually leads the PA to reconsider her first assumption regarding who is visible in Ca2's shot.

7.3. Confirming or Disconfirming a Control Room Statement

In addition to merely producing a public display of actually hearing a piece of information, camera operators may also resort to CCGs for *confirming* or *disconfirming* a statement made in the control room, whereby they can confirm or reject some hearable display of understanding. Contrary to the control room personnel, operators are in a position to directly observe the studio ecology. This asymmetry of access can be highly consequential for understanding what shot to produce. Not surprisingly, operators' confirming or disconfirming camera actions are therefore generally related to spatial, interactional, or epistemic aspects of the studio ecology.

The next excerpt (6) shows how first one, then two operators confirm the same understanding. The Director and the PA are discussing which camera operator, Ca3 (Bertrand) or Ca4 (Pierre-Alain), should be used for the host (Claude) when they go live.

(6)   RR030311 [23.27:51–23.28:02]

```
01 Dir:    et: euh: il me faut+ <Claude, su+r euh+:> su+r qui: là:.
           and eh: I need      <Claude on eh:>    on who (there).
02 Ca3:                        +small pan rt+      +sml pn lt+
03         (0.1)+(0.2)
04 Ca3:          +zoom in Pierre-Alain-->
05 Dir:    ah ouais,
           oh yeah,
06 PA:     (.) ben c'est Bertr[and:¿ ]
           (.) well it's Bertrand:¿
07 Dir:                       [Pierre]-Alain¿
08         (0.1)+(0.2)+(0.1)
09 Ca3:    -->+       +small zoom out-->
10 PA:     Bert+and- (0.1)+     (0.7)        ++ (0.3)
11 Ca3:    -->+           +tilt up&#DWN&UP&dwn++pan right/zoom out-->
   fig                         #fig.6.1
```

Figure 6.1

```
12 PA:     tu est sû:r?
           are you su:re?
13 Dir:    (0.6) il l'a+[(dit ouais)].
           (0.6) he (said so yes)
14 PA:                 +[  >oui oui ]oui+:<.
                          >yeah yeah yeah:<.
15 Ca3:                -->+           +tilt DOWN(&UP&DOWN etc.)-->
16 Dir:    (0.2)+(0.1) c'est Pierre-Alain, hein:, (euh)=
           (0.2) (0.1) it's Pierre-Alain, right:, (eh)
17 Ca4:         +tilt DOWN&UP&DOWN&UP&DOWN&UP&DOWN&UP-->
18 PA:     =oui c'est Pierre-Alain, c'est #Pierre-Alain. (0.1)+(0.1)+
           yeah it's Pierre-Alain,  it's  Pierre-Alain. (0.1) (0.1)
19 Ca3:                                                       -->+
20 Ca4:                                                              -->+
   fig                              #fig.6.2
```

Figure 6.2

A minute before going live, the control room is checking which camera operators should shoot which guests. Prior to the Director's turn-at-talk in line 1, the team has established that Ca1 should cover the next guest. The remaining question, addressed in the Director's turn, is who should cover the host (Claude). Although his turn is initiated as an assertion, it soon becomes a question (end of line 1). Almost immediately, Ca3—who has already shown some signs of incipient "contributorship" by beginning to move his camera during the Director's turn (2)—initiates a big zooming in on one of the camera operators in the studio (4). Even as this zoom has hardly begun, the Director, looking at the monitor, displays a new understanding in a turn that involves "*ah,*" a "change-of-state" token (Heritage, 1984b), and Ca4's first name ("Pierre-Alain," 5 and 7). Shortly afterwards, Ca3 confirms this understanding by a clear but brief down-up-down tilt (11, Figure 6.1). Apparently not taking any of this into account, the PA simultaneously asserts in an almost self-evident way that it is Bertrand (Ca3) who should cover Claude (6). Hearing the Director state that it should be Pierre-Alain (7), she questions this understanding (12). However, he begins to account for it by explicitly referring to the activity of one of the operators ("he [said so yes]"), presumably Ca3 (13). Before the Director gets very far into this turn, the PA, who also looks at the monitors, now manifests a change in understanding to one that is congruent with the Director's ("*oui oui oui*") (14). At this point in the emerging sequence, Ca3 begins to repeatedly tilt his camera again, and Ca4 soon also joins in (15–16, Figure 6.2). This dual tilting activity stretches over the last verbal adjacency pair, which is constituted by a try-marked assertion by the Director (16) and a rather intensely produced confirmation by the PA (18). In this way, the camera operators manage to confirm this understanding as it is being interactively established as a fact in the control room. The operators' repeated tilting does not stop until the PA actually finishes her turn (19–20).

An understanding in the control room can also be confirmed through a repeated panning movement. This is the case for negatively formatted displays of understanding, as in the next example, where the PA formulates her understanding of where a studio participant is looking.

(7)   RR030918 [23.04:08–23.04:14]

```
01 PA:      et ensuite euh (.) (connaît) hein (.)
            and then eh (.) (know) right (.)
02 PA:      pour euh:: (.) (pour) Léonard.
            for eh:: (.) (for) Léonard.
03          (1.1)
04 PA:      (            ne +regarde Claude).
            (            doesn't look at Claude).
05 Ca2:                    +pan RIGHT&LEFT&-->
06          (0.5)
07 PA:          °non°. (0.7)+
08 Ca2:     &RIGHT#&LFT&RGHT->+
   fig            #fig.7.1
```

Figure 7.1

Here, the PA states which guest Ca2 (Léonard) should cover next (lines 1–2). In fact, Ca2 already provides a shot of this participant and does not move his camera at the end of the PA's turn. Although the sound quality of the recording makes it quite hard to hear just what is said in this excerpt, it is possible to understand that what the PA produces a second later is a negatively formatted formulation of what must be the case in the studio: most likely, that the guest shot by Ca2 is not looking at the host (Claude) (4), which would explain why his head is not turned in the expected way in Ca2's shot. This topic seems to be expected by Ca2: even before she finishes her turn, Ca2 begins to confirm this understanding through repeated pans (5, Figure 7.1). As in the previous case, this movement is produced over and past its subsequent own sequential uptake in the form of a brief utterance (7–8), whereby the PA verbally formulates what she understands Ca2 to be doing (i.e. saying no).

In this excerpt, Ca2 confirms the PA's negatively formatted turn through repeated pans. This suggests that the "polarity" logic of many ordinary languages (cf. Enfield, Stivers, & Levinson, 2010)—whereby, for example, a negative utterance is agreed with through the production of a no rather than a yes type of action—can also hold for talk-and-camera interaction. Further, in terms of how this asymmetrical kind of interaction is sequentially organized, the analysis suggests that the panning can be taken as achieving different actions at different moments over the course of its production in sequential time (Rawls, 2005): as it is begun, it confirms the PA's displayed understanding, and its continuation over and beyond its uptake can be taken as confirming the correct understanding of its interactional import, thereby closing the sequence.

8. CONVENTIONAL CAMERA GESTURES IN AN ON-AIR CONTEXT

In an on-air context, CCGs are far less frequent. This is understandable considering the risk that camera movement may inadvertently go on-air when a shot is chosen and broadcast as part of the live-edited sequence of shots.

8.1. A "Flaw" in the Broadcast

In the entire corpus, there is only one case of a CCG broadcast by mistake.[4] It is presented here in the next excerpt (8), wherein the studio interview is transcribed in grey characters, providing temporal landmarks for the transcription of the crew's activity. Miguel-Angel Moratinos (MM) is talking in the studio, and the control room personnel are struggling to determine which camera to use for the corresponding close-up of the host.

(8)   RR030610 [22.59:27–22.59:33]

```
01 MM:    =on {a dit  il  FAUT  avoir     la fe}uille de route.
           it was said that we must have  the Road Map.
02 TecA:       {(he[in c'est ÇA qui est faux). ]}
                yeah   that's  what's  wrong.
03 PA:         {   [là il le regarde (.) voilà.]}
                there he looks at him  that's it.
04 MM:    (.) il FAUT: la publi*{cation >d'un feuille de route< .H=,}
               we need a Road Map to be published              .H
    dir                         1*3
05 PA:                          {et c'est mieux sur la quatre, hein¿}
                                 and it's better on four,       right¿
06 MM:    =.HH il FAUT: +un nouveau=
           .HH we need   a new
07 Ca3:                      +tilt down&up&down&up&do=--->
```

Figure 8.1

```
08 MM:      =#*premier mi+{nistre palestinien,}
                Prime Minister of the Palestinians
09 Ca3:     =*wn&up  -->+
    dir     3*1 ((clearly hearable))
10 Dir:                    {(faut pas        )}
                            shouldn't
    fig     #fig.8.1
```

The control room has just understood why the team is unable to produce complementary shooting angles of the guest and the host and is thus
seemingly unable to honour the 180° rule: the interviewed guest is currently not looking at the host (lines 2–3). This situation generates shots by
Ca3 and Ca4 wherein both participants are looking in the same direction
(Figure 8.1). Prior to this excerpt, the control room had dismissed Ca4 and
called forth Ca3, only to realize that this did not solve their problem. In
fact, Ca3 shoots the host from an even worse angle than Ca4. This is what
the PA alludes to, as she says, *"c'est mieux sur la quatre"* ("it's better on
four") (5). Just as she initiates her turn, the Director switches to Ca3 (4)
and thus puts this second best camera on-air. As it happens, Ca3, who
for some reason does not notice that his shot is now on-air, confirms this
understanding through a repeated camera tilt (7 and 9, Figure 8.1). Even
though it is produced with fairly small movements, it is very noticeable as
it enters the live broadcast, and the Director switches quickly away from
Ca3 back to the shot of the current interviewee. The Director also issues
what sounds like the beginning of a negative rule formulation (*"faut pas,"*
"you shouldn't,") (10), which indexes this event as a mistake.

In the face of the risk of such flaws, because the team is on-air, CCGs are
generally avoided and, when actually produced, done using relatively small
movements. Among the cases of CCGs in an on-air context that we do get,
the majority can be associated with highly problematic situations for the
crew that seem to make taking the risk necessary. Many such situations are
related to the crucial problem of which camera operator should provide
footage of which participant in the studio (as in excerpt 8). A second
reason for the relative lack of CCGs in an on-air context is that this lack
is reflexively produced because operator responses are hardly ever made
relevant in a "conditional" way by the control room personnel.

On-air, the "praxelogical context" (Chapter 3 by Mondada, this volume)
becomes more complex than off-air. Camera operators attend not only to
the control room personnel over the audio interface but also to the ongoing studio interview. Providing relevant, intelligible, editable, and broadcastable footage of the latter is in fact their main concern. On-air, camera
operators are thus simultaneously oriented to two and partly distinct participation frameworks (cf. e.g. M. H. Goodwin, 1996: 439). As we will
see, both can be drawn upon by camera operators to minimize the risk of
finding one's CCG actually hitting the air.

I will now indicate a number of sequentially relevant actions that may be produced through CCGs in an on-air context.

8.2.   Agreeing in a Safe Way (as Primary Recipient)

Only one case in the corpus involves an assessment primarily directed to an operator. This is produced when the Director invites Ca3 (Bertrand) to agree with him regarding a previous decision regarding a camera angle. The guest currently talking is Jean-Pierre Bibring (JPB).

(9)   RR040122 [22.49:21–22.49:29]

```
01 JPB:   =et qu' cette planète {était   très    sembla}ble.
          and that this planet   was     very    similar.
02 Dir:                          {c'est bien Bertrand.}
                                 it's good Bertrand.
03 JPB:   .h:::*(.) on essaie de le savoir¿
          .h::: (.) we try to get to know¿
   dir        2*3
04 JPB:   (0.3) et ensuite on essaier{a* d' se dire pourquoi y a eu}=
          (0.3) and then we will try to ask why there have been
   dir                              3*2
05 Dir:                             {c*'est bien:,   c'est bien:.  }
                                    it's goo:d,    it's goo:d.
06 JPB:   ={+des parc- des- des évolutions tellement différents.  .h:}+:
           ART parc- ART- ART evolutions so very    different    .h::
07 PA:    {+°(mhm:°)=
08 Dir:           =(et) ton angle, il est finalement très utile euh.}+
                  (and) your angle, it is finally very useful eh.
09 Ca3:   +slow pan left                                         -->+
10 JPB:   +un{e GRAN:}de pa+r+tie d'ce qu'on recherche aujour+d'hui,=
          a big part of what we are studying today,
11 PA:       {°ouais°.}
             °yeah°.
12 Ca3:   +pan left&zoom ->+#+tilt up&down&up&down      -->+
   fig                     #fig.9.1
```

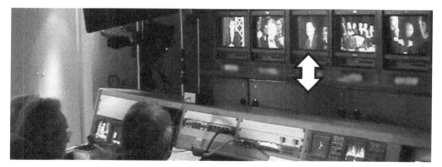

Figure 9.1

Shortly after positively assessing Ca3's shot (that shows two of the listening guests), the Director puts it on-air (lines 2–3). As he cuts away from this shot (3), the Director repeats that it's good (5), evaluating either the shot again or maybe the current situation. Soon afterwards, he adds a more general assessment of the usefulness of Ca3's shooting angle (8). This assessment is directly addressed to Ca3 ("*ton angle,*" "your angle") and therefore rather strongly projects an agreeing response (Sacks, 1987) by this participant. And shortly afterwards, just following the PA's verbal agreement (11), Ca3 agrees by gently tilting his camera (12, Figure 9.1).

In excerpt 9, the CCG is produced in an environment that would seem to be analysed by Ca3 as very safe with regard to the risk of going on-air. First, Ca3 is directly spoken to by the Director, who is in control of the switches. Because the Director addresses him directly, inviting an agreeing answer from him, it is highly unlikely that he will put that camera on-air at this moment. Second, Ca3 has just been on-air and is still panning left as the tilting is begun. Therefore, Ca3 does not produce any stable and broadcastable shot just prior to the tilting. Third, the interviewee is currently shot by Ca2 and the host by Ca1, which makes Ca3's shot a relatively less needed one, to be used mainly for providing listening shots of the nonspeaking guests in the studio. And fourth, when Ca3 starts tilting his camera, the interviewee is well into a new turn at talk (lines 10 and 12), which projects him as the current speaker—maintaining the current situation—for a while longer. Nevertheless, we notice that the tilt is done in a much more restricted manner compared to the tilts that were previously observed in an off-air context.

8.3.   Acknowledging Information

On occasion, the control room may inform operators of some problematic aspect of the production. In the next excerpt (10), as the current interviewee (Polly Estabrook, PE) produces a long turn, Ca5 (Patrick) is made aware that his lens hood is falling down, so that it is visible in his shot.

(10)   RR040122 [22.37:38–22.37:53]

```
01 PE:    mon métier- (.)  c'est (.)  la communication
          my profession    that is   communication
02 PE:    .h: e{t   (.)   euh- qui  est  (.)   }
          .h: and   (.)   eh-  that is    (.)
03 Dir:        {fais gaffe Patrick à ton volet¿}
               watch out Patrick for your hood¿
04 PE:    spécial, pou:r euh .h: p- pou:r (.) ce que nous,=
          special, for   eh  .h: f- for       what we,
05 PE:    =on appe{lle      .h-      (.)     l'appro}ch:e,
            call             .h-              flying in,
06 Dir:           {ton volet est dans le champ Patrick.}
                  your hood is in the shot Patrick.
07 PE:    et: (.) des centres sur la planète.
          and: (.) centres on the planet.
08 PE:    .h{ : :  et : :    alors  je  suis:  toujours,   }=
          .h : :   and::     so     I   am     still,
09 PA:    {Patrick+ton volet tombe sur++(ton eh ton °vas-y°.)}
          Patrick your hood falls into (your euh your °go ahead°.)
10 Ca5:           +tilt upward    -->++tilt dwn&UP&dwn&UP&DWN&-->
11 PE:    =avec les gens qui+ travaillent,
          with  people  who work,
12 Ca5:   #&UP&down&UP    -->+
   fig    #fig.10.1
```

Figure 10.1

Seeing that the lens hood is falling down, the Director warns Ca5 about this (line 3). The most straightforward way to respond to such a warning would arguably be for Ca5 to try to deal with the problem by adjusting it so that it would no longer be visible. Because no indication of any such attempt is perceivable in his shot, after a while, the Director repeats his warning (6). A few seconds are allowed to pass before the PA repeats it once more, in a more explicit way (9). This time, Ca5 finally begins to move his camera just after his name is produced, and he soon produces a repeated tilting movement (10, Figure 10.1). Although the control room does not produce any verbal response related to this sequence, the fact that they stop pursuing a camera response following this excerpt implies that they have indeed received the camera movement. The camera movement is taken as an acknowledgement of the warning, good enough as a response in the absence of Ca5's actually fixing the problem with his hood.

8.4.   (Dis-)agreeing with Control Room Statements (as Overhearer)

Outside the cases where camera operators are directly addressed, operators may also use CCGs as overhearing members of the crew. By producing a CCG, an operator may take sides in an issue discussed in the control room.

In many on-air cases, camera operators are involved in *disagreeing* with something that is said in the control room. However, when these actions follow a turn in the control room that is already indicating disagreement with a previous statement, on a locally sequential level the CCGs are in fact analysable as *agreeing* with this disagreement. One example of disagreeing is shown in the next excerpt (the talk of the current interviewee, who is on video link and in the middle of a long turn, is not shown for reasons of space). The Director announces an upcoming cut to Ca2 (Léonard).

(11)   RR031120 [22.53:07–22.53:22]

```
01 Dir:    je vais passer (0.7) Léona::rd,=
           I will put (0.7) Léona::rd on air,
02 Dir:    je vais la passer elle, parce qu'on va la voir,
           I will put her on air, because we will see her,
03 Dir:    c'est Pio,
           that's Pio,
04         (1.0)
05 PA:     ÇA ça c'est pas Pio: hein¿
           That (that) is not Pio: right¿
06 Dir:    (0.3)+la+ deux: là:?
           (0.3) (camera) two (there)?
07 Ca2:        +slight panning jerk+
08 ??:     (.)+(mhm¿)
09 Ca2:        +pan RIGHT&-->
10 PA:     (0.2) NON: #ça c'est- non- ça c'est+pas Pio:.=
           (0.2) NO:  that is-  no- that is not Pio:.
11 Ca2:    &LEFT&RIGHT&LEFT&RIGHT&left       -->+
   fig                  #fig.11.1
```

Figure 11.1

```
12 Dir:    =>°bon alors°< c'est qui.
           >°well ok°< who is it.
13 PA:     (0.6) Léonard faut que tu prennes Pio+:, hein:,
           (0.6) Léonard you have to shoot Pio:, right,
14 Ca2:                                        +pan right-->
15 PA:     en sortie: hein, (0.7)+(0.4)
           when we go live, right (1.1)
16 Ca2:                       -->+
17 PA:     >voilà<. ça c'est Pio:.
           there you go. That's Pio:.
18 Dir:    (.) d'accord.
           (.) okay.
```

At the beginning of the excerpt, the Director announces that he will cut to Léonard (Ca2), in whose shot Madame Pio is visible in a close-up (lines 1–3). After a second of pause, the PA disagrees with an assumption in the Director's turn, namely that it is Pio who is in Léonard's shot (5).

Displaying surprise, the Director asks her to confirm this challenge of his assumption by referring to the camera in question, Ca2 (6). However, it is not the PA who answers first: before her, Ca2 initiates what turns out to be a repeated panning (9, Figure 11.1). This produces a negative polarity action that aligns with the PA's earlier challenge in line 5. Initiated right after the Director's turn in line 6, it is also understandable as a first confirming response to the Director's request for confirmation. Soon after the beginning of the repeated panning, the PA confirms her previous challenge in a second negative turn (10), and her talk and the camera pan simultaneously produce negative assertive actions pertaining to the issue of the identity of the person shown. That the person visible in Ca2's shot is not Pio is subsequently implicitly accepted by the Director (12), and the PA then asks Ca2 to produce a shot of Pio in the studio, asserts that the new person that Ca2 shows is indeed Pio, and also gets the Director's acceptance of this claim (13–18).

The preceding excerpt (11) shows how camera operators can get involved in some current issue in the control room, using a CCG to support one conclusion rather than another. By their precise placement with regard to an unfolding course of verbally organized control room actions, CCGs can acquire highly specific meanings (contrary to their basic yes or no values). In the above excerpt, for example, this meaning involved disagreeing with a previous assumption about the identity of a particular guest in the studio.

The next excerpt (12) shows how pans, tilts, and zooms can all be combined as an operator (Ca3), not addressed to begin with, initiates and gets involved in a sequence, intensely arguing for which operator should be chosen for making shots of the host in the studio. As the excerpt begins, Louis-Marie Houdebine (LMH) is talking in the studio; in the control room, the Director and the PA urgently direct Ca4 to produce a close-up shot of the host (Claude).

(12)   RR030918 [22.56:59–22.57:13]

```
01 LMH:    (0.4) le-1{e- >le problème s'est< répandu.}
           (0.4) the- the- >the problem has< spread.
02 Dir:             { PIERRE - ALAI[N  TU  (SERRES)]}
                      PIERRE — ALAIN  YOU ZOOM IN
03 PA:              {              [PIERRE-ALAIN    ]}
04 LMH:    {(0.2)+D:Ès que+ ça} a commen+CÉ:¿
           (0.2) as soon as it has started.¿
05 Ca4:          +smll pan+              +pan left-->
06 Dir:    {[SUR  +CLAU::DE+ ]}
           ON CLAU::DE
07 PA:     {[SUR  +CLAU::DE+.]}
08 LMH:    (0.9) cette euh:-+cette euh+ mo:rt,
           (0.9) this eh:-   this eh dea:th,
09 Ca4:                 -->+            +zoom in-->
10 Ca3:                              +pan right, moves-->
11 LMH:    de des++#va:ches, euh: britannIques¿ (0.5) les chercheurs¿
           of of british eh: cows¿              (0.5) the researchers¿
12 Ca4:        ->++#stable shot of host-->>
   fig          #fig.12.1
```

Figure 12.1

```
13 LMH:     +(°euh°) #se so{nt+< É l e v é s : > ,   }
              (°eh°)  have stood up
14 Ca3:    ->+zoom in#&out -->+
15 Dir:                 {°no+n c'est Bert[rand°.
                         °no it's Bertrand
16 PA:                  {                [Bertrand}.
   fig              #fig.12.2
```

Figure 12.2

```
17 LMH:    (0.1+0.3) en disant, (.) <ARrêtez>¿
             (0.4)     saying,    (.) <stop it>¿
18 Ca3:        +pan left&right&left&right&left&right&-->
19 LMH:    vous allez+ con+ta{miner:.     }
             you are going to contaminate
20 Ca3:    &left  -->+    +zoom in&-->
21 PA:                    {c'est Bert}=
                           it's Bert=
22 LMH:    {(0.3) +} TOUS les+troupeaux:,
             (0.3)    ALL the heards
23 Ca3:    &out -->+       +tilt dwn&up&-->
24 PA:     ={rand:,+}
             =rand:,
25 LMH:    (0.4) n'ont pas++été atten- entendus très+=
             (0.4) weren't wait- weren't listened to very
26 Ca3:    &down&up&down->++zoom in&out&in        -->+
27 LMH:    =vi{te, (0.3) >et quand quel}que jour
             quickly (0.3) >and when some day
28 PA:        {il ne regarde pas Claude}.
                he doesn't look at Claude.
```

The control room is in a difficult situation because it is currently hesitating regarding what shot to use for the host. Having identified a potential problem of shooting angles with the operator chosen at first (Bertrand, Ca3, who shows the host from the same angle as the current interviewee), they urge Pierre-Alain (Ca4) to make a close-up shot of Claude (lines 2–7). Ca4 follows the instruction and soon stabilizes a close-up of the host (9 and 11) that also shows him from the same angle and even more from the side than Ca3's shot (Figure 12.1). Seeing this shot—and possibly also Ca3's repositioning his camera, ending in a quick zoom in and out (10 and 14, Figure 12.2)—the control room realizes that, after all, Ca3 should be used (*"non c'est Bertrand,"* "no it's Bertrand") (15–16). Following this display of control room understanding, Ca3 pans back and forth (18–21). By virtue of its placement, this pan may be somewhat ambiguous, as either agreeing with the *"non"* or disagreeing with the indication of the name of the relevant operator (Bertrand). There is evidence that the PA does not consider the issue fully resolved because she again produces an indication of the right operator (20 and 23) for Ca3 to confirm. As she produces this turn, Ca3 zooms rapidly in and out on the host (21 and 24), thereby highlighting himself. And in the sequential slot that appears after the PA's turn, he provides a series of tilting movements (24) to which he also adds another quick zoom in and out (26), thereby clearly confirming the PA's display of understanding. Based on this confirmation that Bertrand is the right operator, the PA then also concludes that the current guest is not looking at the host (28).

The preceding excerpt (12) shows how a camera operator can use repeated pans and tilts to reflexively adapt to changing polarities in the emergent control room talk, arguing for a particular understanding—in this case, that he himself (also highlighted by repeated zoomings) should be used for the host.

8.5. Making Refusing Accountable

A particular kind of action that can become relevant in an on-air context is to *refuse* a directive from the control room. Such refusals are rare and may be publicly displayed by a CCG. This happens in the next excerpt (13), where Ca2 (Léonard) refuses to follow the PA's directive to make a shot of the guest Nicolas Duntze (ND), who has just been given the floor by the host.

(13)   RR030918 [23.24:31–23.24:37]

```
01 Hos:    monsieur Duntze,
           mister Duntze,
02 Ca1:    >>pan right-->
03 Ca2:    >>pan right-->
04 ND:     j[e++peux pas:  ]°euh°--
           I   can't:      °eh°--
05 Hos:    [e++st-ce que::]
              can::
06 Ca2:    -->++close up guest-->
```

```
07 ND:      {j e  peux  pas : : :}++laisser di{re   }ça+:{  : : : : :     }
             I     can't:::           let this be said
08 PA:     {Duntze[Duntze]Léonard}.              {NO++N}
09 Dir:          [Duntze]                              {Léonar+d Duntze}
10 Ca1:                     -->++zoom in Duntze  -->+#
11 Ca2:                                  -->++pan lft&rgt&lft+
    fig                                           #fig.13.1
```

Figure 13.1

```
12 ND:    à ce monsieur,=
          by this mister,
13 ND:    =parce que c{'est--  .h:::::::   on a la preu:ve} là,
          because   it's--    .h:::::      we here have the proof,
14 PA:                {c'est Maria+.=
                       it's Maria.
15 Dir:                          =ouais Maria bouge plus}+
                                  yeah Maria move no more
16 Ca2:                          +pan left&RIGHT&LFT&RT -->+
```

When the host addresses a new guest, as in line 1, the crew immediately work to produce a close-up shot for this participant so as to be able to broadcast the shot as soon as possible (Broth, 2009). In this particular case, both Ca1 and Ca2 have already begun to pan (2–3). Because Ca2 is the first to produce a stable shot of a studio participant (6), the control room (mistakenly) assumes that Ca2 thinks that he is producing a shot of the upcoming interviewee, Nicolas Duntze. However, the control room recognizes that the person visible in Ca2's stabilized shot is *not* Duntze and therefore directs him to make, instead, a shot of Duntze (8–9). In response, Ca2 at first does nothing. And as Ca1 (Maria) simultaneously zooms in on Duntze (10, Figure 13.1), the PA now sees that they were wrong: it is Ca1 who is the good operator (8 and 14). The PA's display of change of understanding ("NON," 8) is hardly begun before Ca2 initiates a small but repeated panning movement, by which he carefully makes his refusing the directive accountable in an unambiguous way (11, Figure 13.1). Apparently not perceiving this beginning response by Ca2 to the PA's previous directive, the Director repeats it once more (this happens slightly after the PA's first sign of understanding and as Ca2 has just begun panning) (9). Ca2 again refuses this directive, through a second and more pronounced series of pans back and forth (16). By making it possible for Ca2 to openly refuse the directive,

the CCG allows Ca2 to initiate repair of the Director's and the PA's erroneous understanding of which camera to use for the new interviewee.

8.6.   Arguing for One's Own Shot

In addition to producing stable shots, whereby operators are generally taken
to *propose* their shots for inclusion in the broadcast (Broth, 2004), operators may also *argue* for the particular usability of their own shot in a more
active way by means of CCGs. This is a very rare phenomenon (only one
instance found), which is understandable considering the risk, as noted, of
getting such moving shots on-air and the Director's need to have several
stable shots to chose from at all times.

Just prior to the following excerpt (14), the control room has discussed
which operator (Ca3 or Ca4) should cover the host (Claude), who has just
started interviewing a new guest (Jacques Myard). They have come to the
conclusion that it should be Ca4 and directed him to produce a close-up of
the host. As the guest is speaking (line 1), on-air in a close-up shot that is
slightly more zoomed in than the shot of the host, the control room instructs
Ca4 (Pierre-Alain) to zoom in a bit more on the host (2).

(14)   RR031120 [23.19:01–23.19:11]

```
01 JM:    c'est c{lair, .h: et je trouve que} mons{ieur  +  } #Perle,=
          it's clear,  .h: and I think that  monsieur        Perle,
02 Dir:        {s:erre un peu Pierre-Alain}      {°°ouais+°°}
               zoom in a bit Pierre-Alain         °°yeah°°
03 Ca3:                                               +pan right&-->
   fig                                                #fig.14.1
```

Figure 14.1

```
04 JM:    =+a vérita{blement+ du       }talent++{pour nier l'évi+*den}ce.
          really       has     a       talent for denying what's evident.
05 Ca4:   +slow zoom in -->+
06 Ca3:   &left&right&lft&RIGHT&LEFT&RIGHT-->++#big zoom out->#+
   Sw:                                             2*1
07 Dir:        {ben c'e+st bien:là}.
               well it's good there.
08 PA:                                     {Perle sur la u+*ne,}
                                            Perle  on     one,
   fig                                      #fig.14.2      #fig.14.3
```

Figures 14.2–14.4

```
09 JM:    +.h:: ++parce que franchement+:, (.) il+faut quand+même pas¿=
          .h::    because frankly speaking (.) you can't after all¿
10 Ca3:   +z.i&o++zoom in          -->+#          +zoom out->+#
   fig                             #fig.14.4                #fig.14.5
11 JM:    =p+ousser le+ bou+chon tr+op loin.
          push the cork too deep. (into the bottle)
12 Ca3:   +zoom in->+#    +zm out +#
   fig                #fig.14.6    #fig.14.7
```

Figures 14.5–14.7

```
13 JM:    (.) .h{:* et} je le dis[:],        [   très    directe*ment].
          .h: and   I say: it,                   very directly.
14 Hos:                             [e]n généra[l il dit les ch*oses]=
                                    in general he says things
   Sw:           1*2                                        2*3
15 Dir:          {a*h: }
```

Just after Ca4 is asked to zoom in (2), we can see, in the monitor just to the left of Ca4's monitor, Ca3 producing repeated pans (3, Figure 14.1). However, the control room does not attend to these movements, instead following and responding to Ca4's production of the slightly more zoomed-in close-up shot just asked for (7). But Ca3 continues his project of getting the control room's attention: stopping panning, he now zooms out very rapidly, which transforms his shot from a close-up of the host to a wide-angle shot in which both the host and the currently speaking interviewee are visible (6, Figures 14.2 and 14.3). At the same time, the PA, who attends to something completely different, notices that the person just mentioned by the interviewee (end of 1) is available in Ca1's shot, and the Director also switches to Ca1 (6 and 8). There is thus still no sign of the control room's attention to Ca3, who nevertheless continues to produce a series of zooms in and out (10 and 12, Figures 14.4–14.7). It is only when the Director switches from Ca1 to Ca2 that he manifests seeing Ca3's shot and its usability for the editing with a brief *"ah"* (15) that displays a new knowledge state (cf. Heritage, 1984b). After this, Ca3 holds his shot stable, and a brief while later, without any further warning, the Director also cuts to Ca3's shot (14).

Not being a primary addressee by the control room, Ca3 clearly has trouble getting its attention. The ways in which Ca3 uses his camera nevertheless orients to the *possibility* of being seen. The careful repeated panning that he first produces to object to Ca4 being chosen for the host is not very salient among the monitors in front of the Director and the PA. Because it is subsequently clear that the control room takes no notice but continues working with Ca4, Ca3 uses more dramatic (upgraded) movements in the form of zooms in and out. This activity continues until he receives a reaction from the Director, after which he completely stabilizes his shot, making it available for the live-editing.

The shot that Ca3 is able to produce (after not being chosen for the close-up of the host), which he promotes through his repeated zooms, is a shot in which both the host and the speaking guest are visible. The independent production and promotion of this shot display the operator's awareness of the crew's collective tasks and orientations (cf. Chapter 3 by Mondada, this volume) because it nicely solves a rather urgent problem of the crew: that of making the spatial and orientational relations between the different participants in the studio intelligible for the viewers during those frequent moments when the current interviewee does not look at the host. Having the two participants in a single shot, all this becomes very clear, and viewers can understand that the interviewee is looking at somebody else (i.e. one of the other guests, visible and showable at any time in Ca1's shot [Figure 14.1]).

In promoting his medium shot by zooming in and out, Ca3 must, however, not at the same time destroy it by zooming in and out too much. Zooming in heavily on only the host would arguably be taken to refer to the host (cf. excerpt 3) or himself (excerpt 12), not to the shot itself; zooming out too much would soon become a shot of the entire group of people in the studio. By zooming in and out in a way that both—and only—the host and the back of the speaking guest remain visible in the shot (Figures 14.3–14.7), Ca3 preserves the relevant features of his shot for the current practical live-editing purposes.

8. CONCLUSIONS

This study has demonstrated how camera operators in a French-speaking TV production crew engage in interactive sequences with the control room, using camera practices that are conventionally associated, in their professional culture, with particular kinds of meanings. The ways in which such conventional camera gestures (CCGs) are produced, their frequency, and the range of actions found differ depending on whether or not the team is currently live-editing. Whereas camera movements were salient (using big movements) and fairly common as the team was still off-air, on-air CCGs were much less frequent and more subtly produced. These observations all indicate a general orientation towards avoiding CCGs during live broadcast.

The kinds of actions that CCGs are used to accomplish differs off-air and on-air. Acknowledgements of information were found in both contexts. But whereas answers to questions were frequently produced by means of CCGs off-air, on-air answers were virtually missing. This lack is reflexively produced because the control room generally does not pose questions to operators when the team is on-air. Further, whereas overhearing operators may confirm control room understandings off-air, there was only one such case on-air (and where the confirming camera tilt was mistakenly broadcast). There is thus a significant reduction from the control room of actions making a CCG a relevant next action, and from operators of its use as a communicative resource. This reduction is arguably the outcome of a shared and constant orientation by the members of the crew to the risk of putting nonbroadcastable shots on-air by mistake.

On-air, CCGs were almost exclusively produced in problematic situations and by operators who can be relatively sure of not being put on-air instantly. Here, problems relate not only to the distant control room's understanding of the studio ecology (which operator to use for which studio participant and who a particular participant is), but also to the quality of an operator's shot (a visible lens hood) and the achievement of a proper intelligibility of the studio space in the edited sequence of shots (the interviewee not looking at the host). By using repeated pans to *dis*confirm an assertion or to explicitly refuse a directive, or by repeatedly zooming to highlight their own shot, operators indicate problematic control room understandings and thereby initiate repair of them. Once having entered a repair sequence, operators may use pans, tilts, and zooms to participate in the interactive resolution of the problem.

How sequences of talk-and-camera interaction are emergently constituted reflects the communicative resources used. Because talk is exclusively
audible and camera movement is visual, actions to an emergent sequence
can coexist and "bleed into" each other. Specifically, in this context, we saw
a number of examples where responsive talk is begun soon after the beginning of a CCG, after which the two actions were produced simultaneously.
For some cases, we argued that the CCG could then seamlessly turn into a
next action as it outlasted and thereby responded to a turn-at-talk, confirming its display of understanding.

This chapter has focused on what actions CCGs may accomplish in
sequences of talk-and-camera interaction. In so doing, it shows how these
camera practices enable operators to actively participate in the crew's collaborative work, and in other ways than just to propose or to project proposals
of specific shots as the next shot in the live-edited sequence of shots (Broth,
2004). Fundamentally, CCGs allow operators to contribute their knowledge
and understanding of the studio to the distant control room, where a proper
understanding of relevant studio aspects is the very basis for appropriate
live-editing decisions.

APPENDIX: TRANSCRIPTION CONVENTIONS

Talk has been transcribed following the Gail Jefferson conventions (see e.g.
Drew & Heritage, 1992). An indicative translation is provided line per line,
in italics.

In addition, the following conventions are used:

+ +	Delimit descriptions of actions other than talk.
& &	When needed for clarity, other symbols may be used,
+ +	When the action is a camera movement, grey overlay is used.
--->	Action described continues below.
--->+	Until the same symbol is reached
+--->>	Action described continues until and after the end of the excerpt.
Dir	Participant doing a gesture is identified by lower-case characters.
Fig	Figure, frame grab.
#	Indicates the exact moment at which the frame grab was extracted.
up	Lower case indicates relatively slight camera movement.
UP	Upper case indicates relatively salient camera movement.
n*n	Director's editing switch from camera (n) to camera (n).
talk	Studio talk in grey characters.
{ }	Simultaneity between talk in studio and control room

NOTES

1. These signals are mentioned in television handbooks, e.g. by Millerson: "Where there is no intercom circuit, or you cannot speak to the director (e.g. when on-air), you may use visual signals such as: '*Yes*' (tilt up and down); '*No*' (pan left and right); '*I've a problem*' (pan/tilt round in circles); '*I've focus problems*' (rapidly rock focus); '*I need to speak on the private wire*' (quick in- and out-zooms)" (1999: 111–112). However, the basic meanings of at least some of these signals may be subject to variation. In the French television crew studied here, quick in- and out-zooms are clearly used for highlighting.
2. An orientation to the 180° rule normally already underpins the way in which the participants in the studio interview and camera operators are spatially distributed relative to each other prior to the broadcast (see further Broth, 2009).
3. Additionally, as Ca5 responds to the director's new turn before he has been explicitly identified as a recipient (5–6), the transcript also suggests that the director's first assessment (line 2) created some enduring pressure on Ca5 to produce his previous and positively assessed shot as they later go live.
4. See Broth (2009) for an extensive analysis of this case.

REFERENCES

Broth, M. (2004). The production of a live TV-interview through mediated interaction. In C. van Dijkum, J. Blasius, H. Kleijer, & B. van Hilten (Eds.), *Proceedings of the Sixth International Conference on Logic and Methodology* August 17–20). Amsterdam: SISWO.

Broth, M. (2006). La pertinence des formes d'adresse pour la construction interactive d'une interview télévisée. In I. Taavitsainen, J. Härmä, & J. Korhonen (Eds.), *Dialogic Language Use, Mémoires de la Société néophilologique de Helsinki*, Vol. LXVI (pp. 275–294). Helsinki: Helsinki Modern Language Society.

Broth, M. (2008). The studio interaction as a contextual resource for TV-production. *Journal of Pragmatics*, 40, 904–926.

Broth, M. (2009). Seeing through screens, hearing through speakers. Managing distant studio space in TV-control room interaction. *Journal of Pragmatics*, 41, 1998–2016.

Broth, M. (forthcoming). Naming faces, facing names. How a TV-crew collaboratively memorizes who is who in the studio. In E. de Stefani (Ed.), *Names in Everyday Usage*. Berlin: De Gruyter.

Broth, M., & Lundström, F. (2013). A walk on the pier. Establishing relevant places in a guided, introductory walk. In P. Haddington, L. Mondada, & M. Nevile (Eds.), *Interaction and Mobility: Language and the Body in Motion* (pp. 91–122). Berlin: de Gruyter.

Craven, A., & Potter, J. (2010). Directives: Entitlement and contingency in action. *Discourse Studies*, 12(4), 419–442.

Davidson, J.A. (1984). Subsequent versions of invitations, offers, requests, and proposals dealing with potential or actual rejection. In J. M. Atkinson & J. Heritage (Eds.). *Structures of Social Action: Studies in Conversation Analysis* (pp. 102–128). Cambridge: Cambridge University Press.

Drew, P., & Heritage, J. (Eds.). (1992). *Talk at Work: Interaction in Institutional Settings*. Cambridge: Cambridge University Press.

Enfield, N.J., Stivers, T., & Levinson, S.C. (Eds.). (2010). Question–response sequences in conversation across ten languages [special issue]. *Journal of Pragmatics, 42*(10), 2615–2860.

Engström, A., Juhlin, O., Perry, M., & Broth, M. (2010). "Temporal hybridity: Mixing live video footage with instant replay in real time." In *Proceedings of ACM CHI 2010* (Atlanta, Georgia). New York: ACM.

Garfinkel, H. (1967). *Studies in Ethnomethodology.* Englewood Cliffs, NJ: Prentice-Hall.

Garfinkel, H., & Sacks, H. (1970). On formal structures of practical action. In J. C. McKinney & E. A. Tiryakian (Eds.), *Theoretical Sociology: Perspectives and Developments* (pp. 338–366). New York: Appleton-Century-Crofts.

Goodwin, C. (1994). Professional vision. *American Anthropologist, 96*, 606–633.

Goodwin, C. (2003a). Conversational frameworks for the accomplishment of meaning in aphasia. In Goodwin C. (Ed.), *Conversation and Brain Damage* (pp. 90–116). Oxford: Oxford University Press.

Goodwin, C. (2003b). Pointing as situated practice. In S. Kita (Ed.), *Pointing: Where Language, Culture, and Cognition Meet* (pp. 217–242). Mahwah, NJ: Erlbaum.

Goodwin, M. H. (1996). Informings and announcements in their environment: Prosody within a multi-activity work setting. In E. Couper-Kuhlen & M. Selting (Eds.), *Prosody in Conversation: Interactional Studies* (pp. 436–461). Cambridge: Cambridge University Press.

Heath, C., & Luff, P. (1993). Disembodied conduct: Interactional asymmetries in video-mediated communication. In G. Button (Ed.), *Technology in Working Order. Studies of Work, Interaction, and Technology* (pp. 35–54). London: Routledge.

Heritage, J. (1984a). *Garfinkel and Ethnomethodology.* Cambridge: Polity Press.

Heritage, J. (1984b). A change of state token and aspects of its sequential placement. In J. M. Atkinson & J. Heritage (Eds.), *Structures of Social Action: Studies in Conversation Analysis* (pp. 299–345). Cambridge: Cambridge University Press.

Jayyusi, L. (1988). Towards a socio-logic of the film text. *Semiotica, 68*, 271–296.

Linell, P. (2011). *Samtalskulturer. Kommunikativa verksamhetstyper i samhället.* Linköping: Linköpings University.

Macbeth, D. (1999). Glances, trances, and their relevance for a visual sociology. In P.L. Jalbert (Ed.), *Media Studies: Ethnomethodological Approaches* (pp. 135–170). Lanham, MD: University Press of America.

Mayer, V., Banks, M.J., & Caldwell, J.T. (2009). *Production Studies. Cultural Studies of Media Industries.* New York: Routledge.

Millerson, G. (1999). *Television Production.* Oxford: Focal Press.

Mondada, L. (2003). Working with video: How surgeons produce video records of their actions. *Visual Studies, 18*(1), 58–73.

Mondada, L. (2009). Video recording practices and the reflexive constitution of the interactional order: Some systematic uses of the split-screen technique, *Human Studies, 32*(1), 67–99.

Rawls, A. (2005). Garfinkel's conception of time. *Time & Society, 14*(2/3), 163–190.

Sacks, H. (1987). On the preferences for agreement and contiguity in sequences in conversation. In G. Button & J.R.E. Lee (Eds.), *Talk and Social Organisation* (pp. 54–69). Clevedon, UK: Multilingual Matters.

Sacks, H. (1992). *Lectures on Conversation* (2 vols.). G. Jefferson (Ed.) & E. A. Schegloff (Intro.). Oxford: Basil Blackwell.

Schegloff, E.A. (1968). Sequencing in conversational openings. *American Anthropologist, 70*, 1075–1095.

Schegloff, E. A. (2007). *Sequence Organization in Interaction: A Primer in Conversation Analysis*, vol. 1. Cambridge: Cambridge University Press.

Suchman, L. (1993). Technologies of accountability: Of lizards and airplanes. In G. Button (Ed.), *Technology in Working Order: Studies of Work, Interaction and Technology* (pp. 113–126). London: Routledge.

Stivers, T., & Rossano, F. (2010). Mobilizing response. *Research on Language & Social Interaction*, 43(1), 3–31.

Wittgenstein, L. (1953). *Philosophical Investigations* (2nd ed.). G. E. M. Anscombe & R. Rhees (Eds.). G. E. M. Anscombe (Trans.). Oxford: Blackwell.

3 The Surgeon as a Camera Director

Manoeuvring Video in the Operating Theatre

Lorenza Mondada (University of Basel)

1. INTRODUCTION

Medicine is a professional area in which the use of video cameras is playing an increasingly crucial role within a diversity of practices, like visual examinations, video-assisted operations, collaborative surgical operations at a distance (telemedicine), and training. One of the most significant of these is endoscopy, which is a technique that allows the exploration and operation of the anatomy of the patient in a minimally invasive way. A camera is inserted into the body by means of trocars, and it is then manipulated inside the body by means of various instruments inserted in the trocars. By using videoscopic techniques, medical expects enhance their scopic access to the body in its anatomical details.

Professional vision, visibility, and the achievement and negotiation of what is visible through in situ reading activities are pervasive features of medical contexts (see Hartswood, Procter, Rouncefield, & Slack, 2002 on mammographies; Nishizaka, 2011 on ultrasound examinations; Rystedt, Ivarsson, Asplund, Johnsson, & Bath, 2011 on radiography). The visibility of the operating theatre is a crucial condition for surgery too: it does not preexist the surgical procedure but has to be achieved through it (Koschmann, LeBaron, Goodwin, & Feltovich, 2011; Mondada, 2003; see also Hirschauer, 1991, and Aanestad, 2003 for an STS perspective). Visible phenomena are actively and collectively achieved by medical teams, realized moment by moment through various situated practices, among which the positioning and manoeuvring of the video camera are central.

Camerawork in the operating theatre is implemented in a variety of practical actions: exploring the anatomy, searching for landmarks, visualizing the operative field, cleaning the optics, choosing the adequate angle, changing lenses, zooming in and out, and so on. These actions are often topicalized in the context of teaching: questions are asked about the chosen angle, comments are offered retrospectively about the importance of a clean optics, comments are made online while trying to visualize details, and the quality of the light, colour, and contrast is constantly assessed.

In this chapter, I offer a systematic description of some micro practices through which the video camera is mobilized, manoeuvred, and instructed within the team in the operating theatre, achieving the visibility of the patient's anatomy both for operating and for demonstrating the operation. Building upon and completing a series of previous analyses (Mondada, 2003, 2007a, 2007b, 2011a), I focus on the way in which the team collectively and interactively produce the relevant camera views, either when the chief surgeon directs the endoscopic camera while operating and demonstrating the operation for an audience of advanced trainees or when an exterior camera on the operative field is adjusted to the surgical action and demonstration by the technical staff, producing a view for the audience. In this context of multiactivity (Mondada, 2007a, 2011a, in press), the team is involved in at least two concurrent courses of action: the operation and its demonstration for the trainees. Both rely on the visibility of the shared focus of attention achieved by the video cameras. Instructions to the camera(s) display a division of labour within the operating room: often, surgeons do not control the endoscopic camera themselves but rely on assistants; moreover, at some points of the demonstration, they might request an external view that shows what is happening outside the patient's body, which is controlled by technicians in a control room. So camera manipulations reveal the collaborative and collective dimension of surgical activity.

This chapter will focus both on the situated practices through which the visibility of the anatomy is achieved by manipulating video cameras and on the sequential organization of how these manipulations are collectively achieved by the team. Through a systematic analysis of instructions concerning the camera, of responses to these instructions, and of actions made possible by them, the chapter will demonstrate how camerawork is embedded in routine activities and is sequentially organized.

More broadly, the chapter contributes to ongoing reflections on sequential organization and on action formation and sequences in complex settings and in embodied activities. It demonstrates the role of multimodal resources and of the local ecology for the organization of sequences constituted by paired actions such as instructions, directives, requests, and the actions complying with them (see also Mondada, 2011b). It also shows how these paired actions are organized as sequences even when they are not always verbally realized and when talk is not always the primary vector either for initiating action or for responding to it.

Moreover, the analysis of collections (Schegloff, 1996), demonstrates that these practices are methodically organized and that it is possible to develop a systematic sequential approach integrating both talk, gestures, gestures performed with tools, instrument manipulations, as well as features of the local spatial and material ecology. In this sense, the chapter also contributes to the development of a multimodal conversation analysis interested in the organization of sequentiality as it is reliant on embodied material and spatial features exploited as resources for the organization of social action—integrating the role of the camera into the core of sequential organization.

2. THE SURGEON AS A FILM DIRECTOR

This chapter offers a systematic analysis of video practices in a distinctive workplace setting: an operating room in which a surgical team operates on a patient and comments on the operation for an audience. This multiactivity setting, although particular, is recurrent in medicine (cf. Chapter 5 by Lindwall, Johansson, Rystedt, Ivarsson, & Reit, this volume): the surgeon operates on a patient using an endoscopic camera and at the same time uses these images to explain what he is doing for an audience of trainees and experts located in an auditorium and connected live via a videoconferencing or closed-circuit television (CCTV) system.

The video image is essential to these activities. Laparoscopic surgery (also called "keyhole surgery") is a minimally invasive technique that consists of placing the instruments and an optic system within the patient's body through small incisions and by means of trocars in which the instruments are inserted. The camera is generally handled by an assistant; the surgeon operates while looking at a TV monitor where the endoscopic image is made available. This image (Figure 1) can be transmitted to other participants: online advice from remote experts is made possible by the accessibility of the surgical theatre through videoconferencing; remote learning is also made possible thanks to the transmission of the image to trainees (Mondada, 2003). Another image is also produced by a traditional camera mounted on the light above the operating theatre, making visible the movements of the surgeons' hands and the surface of the patient's body (Figure 2). This camera is mobilized only for teaching purposes; the chief surgeon can request the control room to transmit it to the amphitheatre alone or in an inset image together with the endoscopic view (Figure 3).

Thus, video is the major link between the various participants and the key technological tool for accomplishing multiple activities.

Video shooting is constitutive of the action the participants perform: not only do they orient towards the camera and reflexively organize their conduct in relation to it, but also it is the camera that makes their work possible—a surgical gesture needing a particular camera angle to be performed (Mondada, 2003).

The video images presented in this chapter have been recorded with the same videoconferencing device that transmits and produces them, thereby integrating and to some extent naturalizing the recording itself. Moreover, videos of surgical operations are routinely recorded by surgeons for archiving and training purposes: therefore, the production of video data is done by the participants themselves for their practical purposes. As a researcher, I have made substantial use of their videos, although I have also produced my own recordings in the operating room, capturing a more global view (Figure 4).

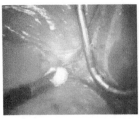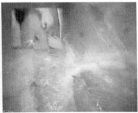

Figures 1–3   Views produced by the surgical team. Figure 1: endoscopic (internal) view; Figure 2: external view; Figure 3: endoscopic view with external inset view (picture in picture).

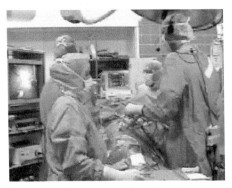

Figure 4   The view produced by the researcher.

In this chapter, I am interested in how visibility is achieved within the mundane video work of surgeons; I will examine how camerawork is collectively achieved in the operating room by focusing on the instructions given by the surgeon in two video environments: directives concerning the movements of the endoscopic camera held by an assistant (line 3), and requests and checks concerning image editing, alternating or superposing the endoscopic image with an external image, which is manipulated by the control room (4). Moreover, I will also examine the way in which these camera actions are responded to not only by the person complying with the directive but also by the overall audience. This is observable in sequences of instructions closed by assessments and compliments (5).

3.   DIRECTING THE ENDOSCOPIC VIEW: INSTRUCTED CAMERA

The endoscopic camera is generally manipulated by the assistant under the supervision of the surgeon, who instructs her. This is a key aspect for the achievement of the activities carried out—both operating and demonstrating. In the operation, the camera is indispensible for making the next surgical step, guided by seeing and looking—such as cutting, dissecting, coagulating, clipping, cleaning, and the like. In demonstrations, the camera is crucial for making visible anatomical landmarks and relevant peculiarities, shapes, forms, and colours characterizing the anatomy. In order for these aspects to be seen by the audience, they are not only focused upon by the camera assistant, they are also pointed at by the surgeon in different ways. So the relevant and efficient manoeuvring of the camera is essential for the activity at hand and for the production of the *visibility* of the operating field.

The endoscopic camera operator constantly adjusts in a tacit way to the surgical action they make possible, both following and anticipating the actions of the chief surgeon. However, in some circumstances—for instance, when the surgeon initiates a new step in the procedure, changes the surgical plane, or spots a new problem—the position and zoom of the camera are treated by him in specific instructions: when this happens, he initiates a sequence constituted by a directive followed by a complying action by the camera assistant.

Directives have been studied in a rich literature and in studies of social interaction (Davidson, 1984; Goodwin, 1990; Lindström, 2005; Heinemann, 2006; Curl & Drew, 2008). However, they remain scarcely studied as far as embodied action in context is concerned (but see Mondada, 2011a, 2011b, in press; Goodwin, 2006; Cekaite, 2010; Goodwin & Cekaite, 2012). Directives and related actions complying with them constitute a sequence, where the first action sets up the "conditional relevance" for the second. The fact that the latter is conditionally relevant ensures that if a second is produced, it is seen as being "responsive" to a first; if it is not produced, it is seen as "noticeably, officially, consequentially, absent" (Schegloff, 2007: 20).

In our data, directives take the form of instructions given by the surgical team. They initiate a pair, constituted by an "instruction" followed by an "instructed action." As shown by Garfinkel (2002: Ch. 6; Amerine & Bilmes, 1988), rather than unilaterally determining instructed action, instructions acquire their sense in that they are followed in instructed actions. More particularly, instructions are always incomplete, and "following" them supposes a competent interpretation that retrospectively and reflexively configures their meaning (Mondada, 2011a, 2011b).

In this section, I examine the contingencies and systematicity characterizing the instructed camera, manipulated by the assistant responding to the directives issued by the surgeon.[1]

3.1.   Instructing/Instructed Camera: A Paired Action

During the operation, as well as within anatomical demonstrations, the endoscopic camera is instructed by the chief surgeon addressing his assistant. His action is implemented as a directive taking the form of a paired action, constituted by the directive or instruction (first pair part), followed by the directed or instructed action (second pair part).

Here are some occurrences. (See the Appendix to this chapter for transcription conventions.)

(1)   [1106k1d2-11.31]

```
1   SUR     %zoom arrière.
            zoom back
            %fig.1
2           (0.2) + (0.3)   + %
    cam           +zoom back+
    fig                       %fig.2
```

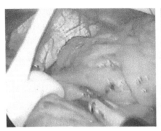

Figures 1.1–1.2

(2)   [2702k1d1-8.17]

```
1   SUR     %au: milieu s'il vous pla+ĭt,
            in the middle please
    cam                             +recenters-->
    fig     %fig.1
2           (3.+3)%
    cam      ->+   %
    fig          %fig.2
```

(3)   [2702k1d1-27.16]

```
1   SUR     %°okay. get close°
    fig     %fig. 1
2           +(0.9)
    cam     +zoom in-->
3   SUR     °okay°.+%
                 ->+
    fig           %fig.2
```

(4)   [2702_k1d1- 43.24]

```
1   SUR     center +here,  that little   + vein
    cam            +goes below and centres+
```

(5)   [2702_k1d2-50.23]

```
1  SUR    get close to the spleen now
2         + (0.8) +
   cam    +zoom in+
```

In all cases, an instruction is produced, followed by a movement of the camera operated by a (silent) assistant. The instructions are implemented in directives, which can take different forms: they are generally brief, essentially formulated by a verb of action, often in the imperative form, but also in the present progressive ("get close," lines 3, 5; "we are going now do:wn," 2; "*zoom arrière*," 1; "center here," 4) and/or by a spatial indication ("close," 3, 5; "*au: milieu*," 2; "*arrière*," 1; "here," 4), which is most frequently expressed by a deictic expression. Less frequently, a more precise landmark is formulated ("that little vein," 4; "to the spleen," 5). Often, the instruction is produced by code-switching into French, the language of the operating team (Mondada, 2007b).

These paired actions raise several questions. The main analytical issue here concerns how the assistant is able to move the instructed camera in a way that successfully complies with the directive, given that the latter is produced in a very indexical way. This adequate response of the camera assistant is precisely what practically achieves the visual arrangement for the ongoing surgery.

3.2.   Responding to Instructions: Indexicality of Instructions and Accountability of Their Praxeological Context

Instructions are underspecified and indexical. As already noted, the camera operator does not merely respond to what is said in the instruction but does much more than that. How does he know what exact camera movement and view are requested at which precise moment? How is the response to the instructions organized in a relevant way?

To grant the directive, the assistant mobilizes other embodied and material resources, interprets the praxeological context and the ecology of the ongoing action, and displays her professional vision (Goodwin, 1994). In the following analysis, I look at these paired actions in more detail.

Instructions are not formulated in a vacuum: they are produced in relevant contexts of action, which reflexively give the instructions their intelligible and even their evident character. Here, I focus on two recurrent praxeological environments that reflexively make instructions to the camera accountable.

3.2.1.   *Camera Directed by Showing Instructions and Pointing Gesture*

In the first type of environment, verbal instructions, often containing a deictic term, co-occur with "pointing gestures" made by the surgeon with the hook: he suspends the dissection and literally points towards the relevant space to cover with the endoscopic camera.

(6)   (= 2) [2702k1d1-8.17]

```
1  SUR     au*: mili*eu s'il vous pla+%ît,*
            in the middle please
               *hook back and forth*       *positions hook-->
   cam                                   +recenters-->
   fig                                   %fig.1
2          (3.+%3)
   cam     ->+
   fig     %fig.2
```

Figures 6.1–6.2

In this extract, which reproduces extract 2 with a detailed multimodal transcription, the surgeon stops using the hook to dissect and moves it back and forth, indicating the place that is supposed to be visualized in the middle of the screen. This zone was originally visible on the left side of the picture (Figure 6.1); after the instruction, it ends up being in the centre (Figure 6.2). In this case, operating constraints merge with more aesthetic criteria, relative to the presentation of the operating field for an audience.

In the next extract, the instruction is uttered in French, code-switching in the middle of an ongoing explanation, and it contains a deictic term ("*à gauche*").

(7)   [2702k1d1-35.59]

```
1  SUR     after that we know *that montre à gauche (.)
                                show on the left
            >>hook gest above last clip*shows on the left->
2          *on +the RIGHT si:de,+ we have no problem,
            *hook covers a yellow surface various times->
   cam          +moves to the left+moves below following hook->
3          and the dissection* will be very+ very easy, .h
               -->*hook goes down-->>
   cam                               -->+cam goes down-->>
```

The instruction "*montre à gauche*" co-occurs with the hook showing something at the left of the screen; at that point, the camera begins to move to the left too (line 2). The next camera movements literally follow the hook. Interestingly, the use of French for the instruction and English for the comment refer to two different spaces that are oriented in opposite ways. The former ("*à gauche*") refers to what is visible on the screen, whereas the latter ("on the RIGHT si:de") refers to the body of the patient. This shows that the relevant space of action for the camera operator is not the body itself but the visible field—both being seen within two different praxeological perspectives.

In the next extract, the relation between the camerawork and the work of showing to the audience—in order to make them to see the relevant aspects of the operating theatre—is particularly clear.

(8) [1106k1d1-50.24]

```
1   SUR     you see* here, (.) eh:: eh eh zoom arrière jean,
                                              zoom back
            >>.....*points w hook-->>
2           + (0.5) +
    cam     +zoom out+
```

The operating surgeon first addresses an instruction to the audience ("you see"), accompanied with a pointing with the hook; then he produces a directive addressed to the assistant. Here, the directive achieves the instructed vision of both the audience about what has to be seen and the camera operator about what has to be relevantly shown.

3.2.2. Camera Orienting to the Ongoing Trajectory of Dissection

There is a second type of environment for directives. In it, no pointings are addressed to the audience or to the camera operator; instead, the operating surgeon is fully engaged in the surgical procedure. The sequential organization of the surgical action projects the next step to come and reflexively instructs the camera operator. The next two extracts document this coordination between the surgeon's hook and the assistant's camera.

(9) (=1) [2702k1d1-27.16]

```
1   SUR     °okay. get close°
            >>dissecting-->>
2           +(0.9)+
    cam     +zoom in--->
3   SUR     °okay°.+
            --->+
```

The operating surgeon is working with the hook at a particular point visible on the screen; his action constitutes the focus of his indexical instruction ("get close," line 1). Indeed, the camera assistant immediately operates a zoom in focusing on that particular place. The camera movement and its completion is further directed by the terminal "°okay°" in third position (3).[2]

In a similar way, in the following case, the instruction is formulated first with a deictic ("here," 2); the camera moves as soon as the verb is uttered and as this spatial description is completed with a demonstrative ("that little vein," 2).

(10)   (= 5) [2702_k1d1- 43.24]

```
1              *        (1.5)                 *      (0.5)      *
   sur      *approaches a bleeding spot w hook*cauterizes it*
2  SUR      center +here, that little+ vein
   cam             +goes below and centres+
3          *(2)
   sur      *continues cauterization-->>
```

The operating surgeon is cauterizing a bleeding spot, which is made visible by blood spilling out and by the surgical action that treats it. The camera assistant grants the instruction even *before* the demonstrative description is completed. So here we have an *early response* by the camera assistant, who orients to the projections made possible by the operating actions of the surgeon and anticipates them in his response.

Interestingly, this early response is also observable in some cases in which the verbal spatial description of the surgeon is particularly explicit.

(11)   [2702k1d1-28.18]

```
1  SUR      *okay. .hh +°show me this+ ligament°
            *moves the scissors toward the ligamt+dissects-->>
   cam             +moves in dir of the scissors->>
```

The surgeon moves his scissors towards the ligament before naming it. The camera operator orients immediately to his action, following the movement of the scissors before the verbal instructions. Moreover, the surgeon begins to dissect immediately—an action that relies on the relevant visualization of the operative field—before the name of the anatomical landmark has been uttered. So, although the instruction is particularly explicit, the instructed action is achieved *before* it. In this context, the explicit character of the description seems to orient to the fact that the surgeon is not just operating but also demonstrating the operation; it is addressed more to the audience of trainees than to the assistant.

In sum, these *early movements* show that, although instructions are always indexical, their indexicality is often not a problem because they are accountably formulated within a *praxeological context* that reflexively achieves their intelligibility. This context is configured by trajectories of the surgical action that highlight and project the relevant landmarks for the next surgical step. In these early camera movements, the assistant controlling the camera and the surgeon directing it display their common orientation to the ongoing surgical action. The assistant exhibits, through these anticipating moves, her skilled participation in the operation (see Sanchez Svensson, Heath, & Luff, 2007, on a team's anticipation of the next move while passing instruments).

The camera response can be produced relatively early or late depending on the way in which this praxeological context evolves dynamically within the temporal and sequential unfolding of the surgery. Responses tend to be fast in the course of a projectable trajectory of action (see also Mondada, 2011a); they tend to be delayed when a new surgical step is initiated or when the movement of the hook initiates a new trajectory—that is, in cases in which the incipient praxeological context is not yet intelligible enough to permit a recognition of the relevant operating space to be focused on by the camera.

After some early occurrences like these just analysed, in the next two extracts I give instances of late ones. The camera response occurs quite late after the instruction, being granted only once the position referred to has been clearly indicated by the placement of the hook.

(12)   [2702k1d1-6.04]

```
1   SUR     on+ va là+ he*in
            we go there okay
            >>moves hook-*turns the hook---->
    cam        +moves slightly+
2           (1.2)
3           on se rapproche enco*+re,+
            we go closer again
                          ---->*positions hook for dissection->>
    cam                       +zoom+
```

When the surgeon says "*on va là*" (line 1), the camera moves slightly, responding to the directive but without clearly moving to a specific target. A pause follows (2), in which the surgeon rotates the hook without orienting or using it in a precise direction. The second directive (3) is completed as the hook is finally positioned for the dissection: at that precise moment, the camera operator immediately zooms in a relevant way. We can clearly see here that although the movement of the camera displays an immediate response to the verbal directive, it actually grants it only once the emergent spatial configuration indicated by the hook has been made recognizable.

Difficulties in recognizing this configuration can delay the camera response, as in the following excerpt.

(13)   [2701 k1d1-13.55]

```
1   SUR     %oké* on va se rapprocher enco*re%
            okay we get closer again
                 *hook advances-->
    fig     %fig.1                          %fig.2
2           (0.2! %0.8* 1.5)
    pea          !peanut enters the field, advances, until it's positioned->
    sur             ->*hook is positioned-->
    fig             %fig.3
3           so we begin no%w!*
                         -->*hook under the adrenal vein back and forth->>
    pea              --->!
    fig              %fig.4
```

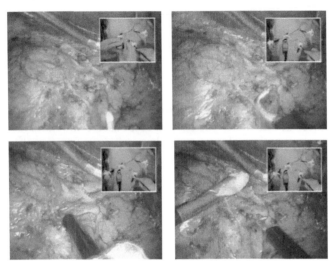

Figures 13.1–4

```
4           (1+.5)
    cam          +zooms in quickly->
5   SUR     to pass% under+ the (1.0) the adrenal vein
    cam              ->+
    fig          %fig.5
```

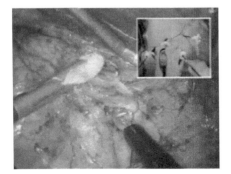

Figure 13.5

At line 1, the surgeon's instruction is *not* followed by a camera movement. At that point, the context is still evolving: a new spatial configuration is defined first by the movement of the hook, which was almost out of the screen at the beginning of the "°oké°" (1), and then by the peanut (a special grasper having a piece of mesh gauze rolled and fixed on its tip), an instrument manoeuvred by another assistant, which becomes visible in Figure 13.3. Both the hook and the peanut enter the visual field of the camera and position themselves progressively in the middle (Figure 13.4). This positioning is completed when the surgeon announces the new step in the procedure (3) and shows the adrenal vein with his hook positioned just under it (at the end of "now," 3; see Figure 13.4). At that point, the camera assistant responds to the instruction and does a fast zoom-in, towards the adrenal vein (Figure 13.5), just before the surgeon describes his action and space of action (5). Again, what seems to be crucial for the assistant to be able to grant the directive is the recognizable emergence of a visual field graspable in terms of the surgical action that the camera will make possible.

In sum, the analysis of the instructed action of the camera assistant cannot rely only on the description of the paired action directive/compliance but has also to include the progressive establishment of a relevant praxeological context that makes the instruction intelligible and accountable. The temporality of the instructed action depends on the emergent character of this context. This temporality is further characterized by early versus late responses, displaying the possibility of anticipating versus following the requested action. These responses, then, do not only exhibit the competent action of the assistant but also adjust to the different trajectories of either a continuous (thus projectable) or a new course of action.

3.3.   Repairing Camera Movements

The indexicality of instructions is addressed in various ways by the participants, who orient to the accountable ecology of action and to the temporal emergence of a recognizable spatial configuration both in the production of and in the response to directives. In some cases, however, the underspecification of instructions occasions either no responses or responses that are treated as displaying an inadequate grasping of the previous action—generating repairs of the camera assistant's action.

Often instructions are self-repaired in repeated directives. These repetitions orient to the observable absence of a response (displaying the normatively expected occurrence of a second paired action) or to a not yet satisfactory response (displaying a trouble in grasping the requested action). Repetitions can be multiple and adjust to the temporality of the ongoing action (cf. Mondada, 2011b). Here are some occurrences.

(14)   [2702k1d1-20.25]

```
1   SUR     get close.
2           (1.3)
3   SUR     get clos+e,
    cam            +zoom->>
```

(15)   [1106k2d2-4.29]

```
1   SUR     ouais, zoom, ici,
            yeah   zoom  here
2           (0.5)
3   SUR     >zoom %zoom, zo+om, zoom, °zoom°<
    cam                 +zoom in-->
    fig        %fig.1
4           (1.%0) + (4.0)
    cam         ->+
    fig        %fig.2
```

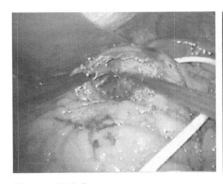 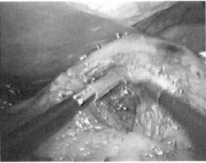

Figures 15.1–2

(16)   [1106-k2d2-0.59]

```
1   SUR     <à droite image, droite image,> >droi+te, droi+te,<
            to the right image, right image, right,    right
    cam                                        +moves R-+
```

(17)   [1106k2d1-32.40]

```
1   SUR     ΔSO,Δ *(0.3) now we try to (.) have a better exposure,*
                  *with pliers tries to control the fat----------*
    cam     Δmoves slightlyΔ
2           >zoom avant. zoom avant. zoom avant.< (.) Δ°zoom avant.°Δ
            zoom forward. zoom forward. zoom forward.  °zoom forward.°
    cam                                               Δzooms-------Δ
3           *(5.0)
    sur     *arranges fat-->>
```

In excerpts 14 and 15, repetitions orient to the absence of response and offer again a slot for a responsive action. Furthermore, excerpts 16 and 17 show that the directive can be repeatedly uttered, accompanying the movement and eventually directing it step by step and repairing and even correcting its inadequate trajectory. In the latter case, directive and progressive guidance merge as the emergent action continues.

The directive can be repeated once (excerpt 14) or several times (excerpts 15–17). The temporal dimension of these repetitions is crucial because directives can guide the action until it is correctly granted. "In this way, both parties are reciprocally and continually calibrating their actions so as to respond to each other and to the developing situation" (cf. Lindwall & Ekström, 2012: 36). They adjust to the temporality of the action, for instance by accelerating the delivery of the directive (excerpts 16–17), both in its prosody and its form (in extract 16, the directive is produced in a form that is shorter and shorter). Generally, the repetition stops as soon as the instructed camera *begins* to move since this clearly projects the new view. The initiation of the camera movement is relevant, whereas its completion is not addressed (contrary to what happens for other instructed actions in the surgical room; see Mondada, 2011a).

Accelerations of the directive achieve a sense of urgency and an intensification of the command. This can also be achieved through repetitions followed by modifications of the initial directive.

(18)   [2702k1d1-30.50]

```
1    SUR    *you can see the vein now, (1.7) °I think° (1.6) possi*bly
            *passes on the possible vein w aspirater-------------*asp back->
2           (0.9)
3    SUR    .h back,
4           (0.5)
5    SUR    back,
6           (.)
7    SUR    we might have* to get this here*
                        -->*asp at the limits of vis. field shows something*
8           (0.7)
9    SUR    recule
            go back
10          +(1.5)+
     cam    +zoom back and mov tow right+
```

In this extract, the operating surgeon aspirates blood and other liquids from the anatomical field and then instructs the camera assistant to move back (line 3). In the absence of a response (4), the instruction is repeated (5), and the surgeon adds a description of the target of the next action (7), which is formulated with a deictic term and indicated by the position of the aspirator, at the limits of the visual field of the camera. The response being still absent (8), the surgeon utters the directive again (9), by code-switching from English to French: finally, the camera moves to the target (10).

In some cases, repair can occasion a treatment of possible troubles of shared understanding as well as of interpretation of the indexicality of instructions in the form not only of repetitions but also of negative particles ("*non*," "no"), followed by a more explicit instruction, directly repairing the first camera response.

(19)   [2702_k1d1_1.00.10]

```
1   SUR     allez vas-y là-bas,
            go    go over there
2           (0.3) + (1.0)  + (2.0)
    cam           +zooms up+
3   SUR     non, la caméra en bas, douce+ment doucement+ doucement,
            no   the camera below slowly    slowly     slowly
    cam                            +moves right/below+
```

When the camera assistant responds (line 2) to the initial directive (1), the zoom highlighting an anatomical region in the upper part of the visual field is repaired by a "*non*" (3), followed by a new formulation of the directive, more explicit about the location and progressively accompanying its dynamic movement (3).

Repairs can concern not only the direction of the camera, as in the previous excerpt, but also the amplitude and temporality of its movements (typically in the case of zooming), as in the following one.

(20)   [2702-k1d2-42.43]

```
1           (2)%
    sur     >>does a knot-->
    fig        %fig.1
2   SUR     recule-toi un peu,
            go back a bit
3           +(1.%5)                                    + (0.5)+%
    fig        %fig.2                                       %fig.3
    cam     +zoom back at the limits of the trocar+zoom in again+
4   SUR     pas trop. hh
            not too much. hh
```

  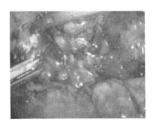

Figures 20.1–3

As he is doing a knot (Figure 20.1), the surgeon asks the camera to move back to give more space for this action (line 2). The camera operator grants the directive by zooming back (3) but does it a bit too much, almost exiting the internal visual field (Figure 20.2). Interestingly, before being repaired by the surgeon (4), this movement is self-repaired by the camera operator himself (end of line 3, Figure 20.3).

Repairs and negative directives can be integrated within another course of action. Whereas in the previous excerpts, the surgeon's talk was entirely devoted to directing the camera, in other cases instructions are inserted within his online commentary, as in the following case.

(21)   [2702k1d1-35.07]

```
1   SUR     and +we are here *on the diaphra*gm=
                            *points w hook*
    cam         +zoom slightly back-->
2   EXP     =yeap+
    cam         ->+
3   SUR     e*t:, (.) montrez là, (0.4)+ after that,* we go: (.) and
            and   (.) show there
                *hook in the air moves forth a bit on the left*stays-->
    cam                                 +re-centres around the hook-->
4           we have dissected (0.4) °montre-moi +mieux. non, (.)
                                     °show me better.     no
    cam                               -->+moves and zoom in->
5           plus* là-bas,° the (0.6) SU+perior artery,*
            more there,°
            -->*grasps the artery-------------------*clips->>
    cam                           --->+
```

The surgeon is describing his position and pointing with the hook (line 1): the camera assistant anticipates and then accompanies his gesture (1–2). The next step (3) is achieved by a directive in French (3) and by the hook moving, followed by the camera. The comment continues in English, with a verb of action projecting its argument; but instead of the argument, a new directive is uttered again in French (4), granted by a camera movement that is immediately repaired by the initiator "*non*" (4), followed by a new spatial description, co-occurring with the movement of the hook grasping the artery before clipping it. In this case, the comment in English alternates with directives in French (Mondada, 2007b), which follow the hook actions and at the same time make the next action possible (grasping and clipping the artery).

Finally, in some—rare—cases, a radical form of repair can be observed: unlike most of the repairs, that are other-initiated by the surgeon and self-achieved by the camera assistant, in this case the surgeon can other-correct the video movement by directly taking the control of the endoscopic camera (see Keevallik, 2010; Parry, 2004 about corrections controlling the body of the dancer in dance lessons or of the patient in physiotherapy). This is what happens in the following excerpt.

(22)   [1106-d2k2-2.01]

```
1   SUR    montre un petit peu là pierre-alain, là-bas au fond% à droite,
            show a bit there pierre-alain, there at the bottom to the right
    fig                                                           %fig. 1
2          (0.6)
3   SUR    (j'y *vais;j'ai* vu)% °non°?
            (I go;I've seen)      °no°?
    sur         *abandons his trocar and grasps the camera, directing it->
    fig                        %fig.2
4   SUR    °comme ça comme ça,% oui comme ça.°* là j'ai vraiment la %vision.
            °like that like that, yes like that° there I really got a view.
                                         -->*takes his plier again->
    fig                         %fig.3                               %fig.4
```

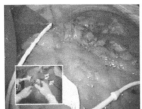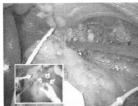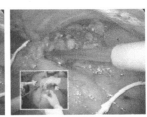

Figures 22.1–3

```
5          (0.6)
6   SUR    et zoom avant,
            and zoom in
7          (0.3) +(1.7)
    cam              +zoom-->
8   SUR    ok+é, (0.2) comme ça c'est bon.%
            okay, (0.2) so it's fine.
    fig                                 %fig.5
```

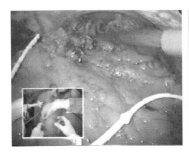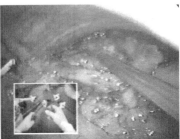

Figures 22.4–5

This extract begins with a directive addressed to the camera assistant, Pierre-Alain: a first deictic description ("*un petit peu là,*" line 1) is followed by a modified and more elaborated one ("*là-bas au fond à droite,*" 1).

Pierre-Alain does not reorient the camera (2) and instead produces a repair (3): during this turn, the surgeon abandons his own instrument and grasps the camera from the assistant's hands (Figure 22.2). He reorients the camera in a demonstrative way (Figure 22.3), by formulating and assessing what a good view is (4). Then he leaves the camera to the assistant, while controlling his instrument again (Figure 22.4). The next directive (6) is granted by the assistant, who immediately zooms in (7) (Figure 22.5).

Although in the vast majority of the cases, a preference for self-repair (Schegloff, Jefferson, & Sacks, 1977) is visible both in the fact that the surgeon waits for the assistant's response and that he initiates the repair only if this is not adequately accomplished. In this rather exceptional case, the surgeon achieves the repair himself by taking the control of the camera and correcting the view. This case is even more interesting because the action of the surgeon is recorded and displayed by the external camera in an inset exterior view on the instruments and the hands holding them, which makes visible for the audience this change of control of the endoscopic video in its embodied details.

In sum, in this section, I have focused on the endoscopic camera producing an interior view as directed by the surgeon and operated by the assistant. The production of the relevant internal view requires a comprehension not only of the instruction but also of the ongoing activity. Professional vision (Goodwin, 1994) is both the condition for a good video image and the condition for the next step of the procedure. Because of the indexicality of instructions as an essential feature, instructed action relies in crucial ways on the praxeological ecology and the comprehension of its emergent relevancies and projections. When this context of action is not intelligible enough, the action of the instructed camera can be delayed, absent, or wrong: repairs and corrections reinitiate the instruction, just repeating it or elaborating it, in concomitance with the surgical action going on and by orienting to a precise expected outcome of the action. In this sense, camerawork reveals the complex relevancies and projectable actions constituting the surgical procedure as a shared collective but also as a hierarchical accomplishment.

4.   ONLINE EDITING FOR THE DEMONSTRATION: REQUESTING AND CHECKING THE EXTERNAL VIEW

While demonstrating the operation, the surgeon will orient to the relevance of showing the operating theatre to the audience: the surface of the patient's body, the disposition of the trocars, and the manipulations of the instruments by the hands of the team. In this section, I focus on the surgeon requesting the control room to switch the monitors of the audience on the external view. The manipulation of the external camera is recipient oriented:

it is manoeuvred and used for the benefit of the audience of trainees for demonstrative purposes.

Whereas the internal view is directed by the surgeon for the practical purposes of the ongoing operation, the external view is manoeuvred by orienting to the practical purposes of the demonstration. The former is moved by the assistant; the latter is controlled by the technical staff.

Like the internal view, the external view can be made available at different stages by the control room without being requested by the surgeon. This is typically the case when the endoscopic camera is taken out of the body and cleaned. The technicians in the control room can also decide to offer a combination of internal and external views, editing one or the other as an inset image (picture in picture). In this way, although they are not part of the medical personnel, they also display a professional vision of the surgical events going on (Mondada, 2003).

In this section, I focus on sequential environments in which the surgeon orients to the relevance of the external view and requests it from the technical staff. Interestingly, there are several differences in the manipulation of the external versus the internal camera: (1a) the surgeon addresses the technical staff with *requests* and not with *directives,* thus showing a different form of entitlement (Curl & Drew, 2008) in asking for something to be done; (2) these requests are often uttered because the requested action has already been anticipated by the staff; they are often converted in checking questions concerning the availability of the external image. This shows a different form of control by the surgeon on the internal (endoscopic) versus external image: the former is directly relevant for the surgical procedure, and the surgeon has full epistemic, authoritative, and praxeological control of it, whereas the latter is relevant for the explanation of the procedure and treated by the surgeon as not entirely depending on him.

In the following analyses, I focus on the way in which the surgeon requests the external view, on the way in which this is made available by the technical staff following or anticipating the request, as well as on the subsequent use of the image by the surgeon within the dissection. Once the availability of the external view is established, the action not only takes place in the field of vision of the camera but also is organized in such a way that it exploits the visibility of the space that is displayed and recorded on video. Exploiting the visual field created by the external view, the surgeon displays, exhibits, and spatializes his embodied demonstration *for the camera* and therefore for its recipients, the trainees (see also Mondada, 2007a about the constitution of a *space for action*).

Two environments will be studied here, in which the external view is particularly relevant. The first concerns the beginning of the procedure, when the surgeon requires the external camera for demonstrating the position and insertion of the trocars—including the position of the endoscopic camera. The second concerns the request of the external view to show a particular instrument or a specific gesture during the procedure.

4.1.   Showing the Position of the Trocars at the Beginning of the Operation

At the beginning of the operation, the external view is recurrently requested to show the organization of the operating theatre: the position of the team members, the insertion of the trocars, the choice of where to position the camera, and which optics to use. In this sense, the external view makes visible for the audience the very conditions at which the operation can be not only carried on but, more fundamentally, can be seen endoscopically.

Interestingly, this is a sequential environment that makes the use of the external view projectable; indeed, the staff often anticipate the switch from the internal to the external view even *before* the request of the surgeon. Moreover, the surgeon's primary monitor in the operating room does not display these switches; the video perspective transmitted to the trainees is displayed on another monitor, which is checked by his team but at which he does not constantly look himself.

Here is a first extract, taken from the very beginning of an operation.

(23)   [1106_k1d1-7.15 (V)]

```
1   SUR     so eh::m, (.) I- I would like to have an external view,
    scr     >>external view already in place-->>
2           (1.0)
3   ?       °°(elle est là) monsieur daccard.°° ((in DAC's headphones))
            °°(it's there) mister daccard°°
4           (1.1)
5   SUR     *ehm (0.7) *and% (0.8) i s:tay (0.7) between (0.4) the legs,
            *..........*puts two parallel hands on both sides of the body->
    fig                %fig.1
```

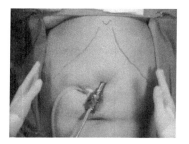

Figure 23.1

```
6           (0.4) i'm standing between the legs,* (1.7) ant*oine wittig,
                                            -->*     *points Lindex->
7           (0.2)% is on the (0.3) right side of the patien*t (0.4) the sc?
                                                       -->*,,,,,,,,,,,,,,,,
    fig            %fig.2
8           nurse, is *on (0.3) the* two scrub nurse is on the% left si*de
                      *...........*points Rindex--------------------*,,,
    fig                                                      %fig.3
```

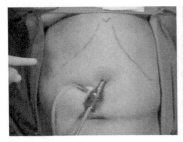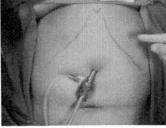

Figures 23.2–3

```
9            of the patie*nt. (1.8)* he%re you see% a subcostal area,* (0.3)
             ->*.........*parallel hands along the ribs----*,,,->
   fig                    %fig.4          %fig.5
```

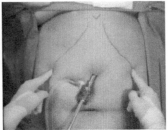

Figures 23.4–5

```
10           and *the xyphoid% appendice. (*2.1)* here, (.) is the ombelicus.
             ->*points Rindex------------*,,..*points----------------->
   fig                %fig.6
11           (3*.1) because of *eh (0.3) close angle, (1.*1) i put eh %(0.4)
                            *hands form a triangle on appdx*RH tw optics->
   fig                                                %fig.7
12           my optical system (0.4) a 1- (0.3) a litt' bit (0.7) eh (0.7) em
13           more down as usually, (2*.2) euh (.) so *the first trocar %is a
                        --->*                *palm vert open----->
   fig                                            fig.8%
```

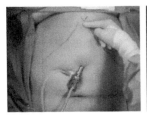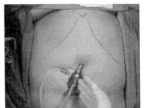

Figures 23.6–8

```
14        ten milli*meter trocar, (0.8) and euh (.) in *order to*: (1.0)
          ->*                                        *palm vert open*
15        to introdu:ce (0.4) *the optical *system, and *we use (0.3)
                              *points------*          *points-->
16        a thir*ty degree optical system.
          -->*
```

Just before the extract, the surgeon has explained the procedure on the basis of some slides. Now he turns to the operative field. He requests the external view (line 1). A member of the staff responds via the audio connection with the surgeon, confirming that the external view is in place (3). Even if this view is already available, the surgeon's request projects a specific configuration of the action to come, which is not the operation but the demonstration. The latter is not just done but is *performed for the camera*.

From line 5 on, the demonstration is verbally and gesturally formatted in a recipient-designed way for the audience watching the image. The surgeon describes his position relative to the patient: despite the fact that the external camera does not capture the entire operating room and that the body of the surgeon is not visible, the surgeon produces a self-description by doing a gesture with his two parallel hands (Figure 23.1), which allows reconstructing the position of his entire body. In a similar way, he points respectively from the left (Figure 23.2) and from the right (Figure 23.3) of the image, to indicate where the assistant and the nurse are positioned. In this way, he reproduces for the limited space of the camera view the structure of the bigger space of the operating room.

Next, the surgeon describes a series of landmarks: again, his spatial description co-occurs with gestures that are exhibited for the camera, in an embodied explanation formatted for being visible for it. The hands are not just pointing to landmarks; they are displayed in a way that does not obscure the view and that exhibits the gesture for the vertical perspective of the camera.

This initial demonstration also topicalizes various choices concerning the endoscopic camera (11–13): the point at which it is inserted and its orientation within the body are related to the position of other trocars and to the patient's anatomy; the kind of optic chosen is also formulated (15–16).

The next extract shows another beginning, done by a different surgeon, in quite similar ways. The excerpt begins as the video transmitted to the audience switches from another operating room to the one in which the surgeon is operating. The first view offered by the technical staff is the external one.

(24)   [2702k1d2-45.42]

```
1   SUR    now, i have inserted my three trocars,
           >>external view-->
2          can we show the outside for a few seconds,
3   ?      °vous avez la vue externe [alain°
           do you have the external view? Alain
4   SUR                             [hein?
                                    [what?
```

```
5   ?        °(      )°
6   SUR      i can't s- >okay okay.<
7            (0.4)
8   SUR      so*: three% tens,* (.) and%:* we will do: we'll try a three
             *touches vert H*points to 3 troc*
    fig                %fig.1            %fig.2
```

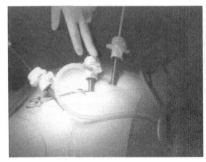 

Figures 24.1–2

```
9            trocard technique, if it doesn't work then we will put
10           a *forth one,% and .h* (.) for retraction, I did an open
             *points----------*
    fig                %fig.3
11           tech*nique, I %use a eh:* .h (0.4) tsk towel clip eh *(0.4)
             *points-------------*                                *points->
    fig                %fig.4
```

 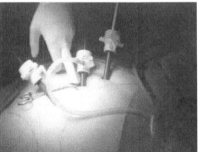

Figures 24.3–4

```
12           for the extra mi*limi*ters so i don't* get any leaks (0.6) eh:
             -->*    *points---------*
13           I will put the camera here, a thirty degree angle scope (0.4)
14           into this *first tro%card, and * now* | I'm
             *points--------------*,,,,*palm altern btw 2 troc->
    scr                                -->|ext.view+inset int.v.->
    fig                    %fig.5
15           working with two handed technique,*
                                      --->*
```

Figure 24.5

As in the previous extract, the external image is requested by the surgeon (line 2), although it is already visible for the trainees. A member of the staff confirms, in a message received by the surgeon in his headphones, the availability of the external view (3). After a repair initiation (4) and a new confirmation (5), finally ratified after a suspended negative utterance (6), the surgeon begins the demonstration (8). Thus, the latter does not begin before the external view is definitively established.

Then, like his colleague in the previous extract, the surgeon begins to gesticulate for the camera, pointing at the first trocar (Figure 24.1), at the three trocars he has already inserted (Figure 24.2), as well as at the position of a possible fourth one (Figure 24.3). Each instrument is both named and pointed at; the choice of the camera's position and optics is also presented (13–14; Figure 24.5).

In sum, in these two excerpts, the surgeon secures the availability of the external camera *before* actually beginning his demonstration. He requests the exterior view at the beginning of the procedure, although the staff has already anticipated it—both orienting to the relevance of that view at that particular moment. As the staff confirms its availability, he begins his explanation. The demonstration is an embodied action, in which talk and gesture are synchronized in a finely tuned way; moreover, gestures are done *for the camera,* literally recipient oriented, turned—via the video—towards the audience. Gestures are made for the camera also in the sense that they take into consideration its zenithal view, avoid covering the visual field, and are displayed in a way that maximizes their visibility for the camera.

4.2.   Showing the Instruments

A similar use of the external camera is observable during the operation: the surgeon exploits it for presenting the new instruments he uses. This is the case in the next two extracts.

(25)   [1106-k1d2-14.51]

```
1   SUR      now, *    (0.7) tsk   * (0.4) i open the lesser omentum
                 *approaches sciss*takes it out of the visual field-->>
2            (3.9)
3   SUR      c'est pas comme ça hein, c'est::, (1.2) ciseaux à l'extérieur
             it's not like that isn't it, it's:: (1.2) scissors outside
4            (0.7)

5   SUR      okay.    |
    scr      >>intenal|external view-->>
6            (2.1)
7   SUR      grasping forceps,
8            (0.3)
9   SUR  →   would you like °to-° okay. you have the external view?
10           (0.3)
11  SUR      so we change now and we put *the grasping forceps* (0.7)* here,
                                         *shows gf------------*introd it*
```

(26)   [1106-k2d1-52.50]

```
1   SUR      so, you know the device, underreticula|tor?
    scr      >>internal view--------------------- |external view-->>
    com      ((no instrument is visible on the internal image))
2            *(0.8)
    ver      *holds the instrument across the visual field-->
3   ASS  →   °ext[ernal view°

4   SUR          [i think it (.) it-
5   ASS  →   °external view°
6   EXP      lu[c?
7   SUR  →     [external view, *(.) you know this device?%
                             -->*shows the end point of the device-->
    fig                                          %fig.1
8   EXP      do you always use this device?
```

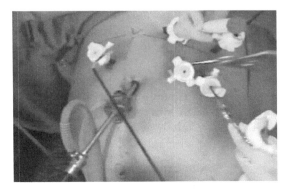

Figure 26.1

These two extracts show the interactional work devoted to the establishment of the external view. As was the case in extracts 23 and 24, the
technical staff *anticipates* its relevance in excerpt 25 on the basis of a problem encountered by the surgeon, addressed in French by referring to the

withdrawal of the scissors (line 3); in excerpt 26 on the basis of the reference to an instrument that is not visible on the internal view (1). The surgeon requests the view: interestingly, in excerpt 25, this request is sketched ("would like °to-°," 9) but promptly suspended, probably when the surgeon notices that the external view is available and transforms the request in a checking question ("you have the external view?," 9). In excerpt 26, as the surgeon has initiated his demonstration of the under-reticulator (1), the assistant orients to the relevance of the external view and requests it (3, 5), followed by the surgeon (7). In both cases, the surgeon delays the beginning of the next turn until the external view has been secured.

Once the external view is established, the way in which the surgeon displays the instrument is again turned towards the camera: in both cases (27 and 28), the instrument is positioned in such a way that it crosses the visual field of the external camera; in both cases, the light colour of the skin is used as a visual background that makes the instruments' shape particularly visible—in a way that the use of the instrument within the body, as visible on the endoscopic camera, does not make possible (see Mondada, 2007a, for other examples of exhibited displays of tools on the body).

In sum, this section has shown that the external camera is managed in a very different way than the internal one: its relevance is mostly anticipated by the competent manoeuvring of the technical staff; it is requested by the surgeon or by his assistant, displaying its relevance at some point of the procedure, where a switch from the operation to the demonstration is to be made; instructions concerning the external view are formatted as requests using modal verbs (as in "I would like," "would you like," "can we") and thus display less entitlement on the part of the surgeon—contrasting with the high entitlement of the directives used for the endoscopic camera. More generally, this makes accountable the difference between the operation, under the responsibility of the surgeon, and the demonstration, which is a collective production involving not just the medical team.

5. RECIPIENT'S IMAGE RECEPTION: ASSESSMENTS AND COMPLIMENTS

The relevance, as well as the recipient-oriented character of the way in which the camera is manoeuvred and chosen, is displayed by the active reception of the views that are being produced. This reception is observable in the assessments and compliments produced by third parties outside the operating room. Often, there are experts commenting on the operation for the trainees (cf. Chapter 5 by Lindwall, Johansson, Rystedt, Ivarsson, & Reit, this volume). Assessments are frequent; they are produced in specific sequential positions, which exhibit an orientation and responsiveness towards the camerawork: this is namely the case of assessments produced as closing third turns at the end of a sequence constituted by the paired action directive/request plus response of the assistant/control room.

However, it is important to note that many other types of assessment are produced as well: assessments can refer and respond to dissecting actions that achieve the visibility of the operating theatre; to demonstrations, anatomy explanations, and other comments addressed to the trainees (often prefaced by "you see"; cf. Mondada, 2003); to checks initiated by the surgeon (such as "do you have a good view?"); to negative assessments of the surgeon about the image quality (to which a positive assessment in opposed), and so on.

In the next section, I focus on the first type of assessment, directly responsive to the camerawork. I show that assessments can close both types of sequences previously analysed here: directives concerning the internal view and requests concerning the external view.

5.1. Assessments Addressing the Endoscopic Camerawork

Assessments closing the sequence of paired actions that is constituted by the instruction and granted by the action of the instructed camera display the way in which the movement of the endoscopic camera is explicitly addressed by the audience—most often, the experts. Here are some occurrences of the phenomenon, showing its recurrent and methodic form.

(27) [2702-k1d1-43.46]

```
1   SUR        go up,
2              (2.0)
3   SUR        go up,
4              (2+.7)+
    cam        +up+
5   EXP  →     it's beautiful,
6   SUR        we [gonna join our superior (1.0) middle opening,
7   EXP  →        [beautiful picture
```

(28) [2702-k1d2-47.00]

```
1   SUR        get- get closer now the camera,
2              (0.8)
3   SUR        +center here
    cam        +zoom in--->
4   EXP  →     it's+ a very nice picture (.) very nice.
    cam           ->+
```

(29) [2702-k1d2-50.46]

```
1   SUR        okay, (0.6) NOW, (0.5) rotate +your thirty degree (0.3) a bit+
    cam                                     +rotates----------------------+
2              +THIS way,
    cam        +zoom in-->
3              (0.8)
```

```
4   SUR      oka+y
    cam       ->+
5            (1.8)
6   SUR      and *((clears throat)) (1.3) we will just lift (0.2)
                 *approaches w scalpel--->>
7            come clo+se+
    cam                +zoom in+
8   EXP  →   it's a very nice [picture
```

(30)   [2702-k1d1-56.51

```
1   SUR      get back, back so I can see this instrument +coming,+
    cam                                                 +zoom out+
2            (4.5)
3   SUR      ok*ay.     come       *close
                 *introduces scissors*moves in w scissors->
4            (0.5)
5   SUR      come clos+e
    cam               +zoom in---->
6            (0.4)
7   SUR      °oké°. (.) you SEE,+ it's holding the sple*en
                                 --->*cuts adhesions->>
    cam                 --->+
8            (7.1)
9   EXP  →   we have a very nice picture Michel
```

In all of these excerpts, the expert, a surgeon colleague, produces an assessment that follows a camera movement responding to an instruction. These assessments explicitly deal with an *assessable* that is an image (the word "picture" is used in all the cases). They orient to the aesthetics ("beautiful," "nice") of a view that is coproduced by the action of the surgeon (who is dissecting) and the assistant (holding the camera). This aesthetics is functional not only to the surgical work (a clear image allows for the precision and safety of the surgical procedure) but also to the training activity (a clear image allows the trainees to see the relevant details of the operation). "Seeing" is here clearly the product of a complex array of professional practices that produce the "visibility" of the anatomy.

The fact that the picture is a situated achievement of the team and of the camerawork is also observable in assessments positively evaluating the chosen optics.

(31)   [1106-k2d1-33.52]

```
1   SUR      tu peux m'montrer?
             can you show me?
2            +(0.7)
    cam      +moves--->
3   ASS      °(hein)°?+
             °(what)°?
                     -->+
```

```
4              (0.4)
5    SUR      t'peux m'mon:trer? (.) *°o:ké°.
              can you show me? (.) °okay°.
                              *positions the hook--->
6              (1.4)
7    SUR      SO, (0.3) here is my landmark,
8              (0.9)
9    SUR      sorry there is eh h (1.0) *some blood, (0.6) coming from the:,
                              --->*dissects--->>
10             (0.7) .hh the liver
11             (9.3)
12   EXP →    I think in such case, the use of a thirty degree angle
13             optics is VERY very useful.
14             (3.2)
```

(32)   [1106-k1d1-44.45]

```
1    SUR      oké. you SEE he+:re,+
     cam                    +zoom in+zoom out-->
2              (3.3) + (0.2)
     cam          ->+zoom in-->
3    SUR      you see: (0.9) °°mich+elle°° (1.7) the:, upper part of
     cam                       -->+
4              the spl*een, (1.*5)        *the left (1.5) pillar,* (1.1)* and
                     *points w hook*,,..*points----------------*,,,,.*points->
5              the phreno- (0.2) gastric, ligament he*re. (0.8) very
                                                  --->*
6              short. (1.0) .hh and I create a window (0.3) HEre
7              *(5.7)
              *begins dissection-->
8    EXP      and the thirty degree angle optic helps you (0.5) very well here
9    SUR      tha- (0.2) that's correct
```

In the first except (31), the surgeon asks the assistant to show him (lines 1, 5) the relevant anatomic space. After a repair (3–5), the camera view is ratified by an "°o:kay°." Consequently, the surgeon can position his hook for the next step of the operation (the dissection begins a few seconds after, line 9) and point out, for the audience, the landmark that will guide it (7). After a noticing concerning a small haemorrhage, the expert offers an assessment praising the camera angle (30°) (12–13). In this case, the specific kind of optics is identified as making that step of the operation possible.

In the second excerpt (32), which prefaces the beginning of the dissection, the surgeon is directing the assistant (Michelle) who is holding the camera during an anatomical description (lines 1–6) that prefaces the beginning of the dissection (7). The expert produces an assessment of the optics as making the action of the surgeon—and the vision obtained— possible.

These assessments of the endoscopic view show that the participants orient to the quality of the image, treating it as relevant for the successful achievement of the operation. In this sense, the camerawork is not a sub-ordinate or invisible activity but becomes a central feature of the operation itself.

5.2. Assessments Responding to Online Editing (Requests for External View)

The majority of image assessments concern the endoscopic view; the external view is much less frequently commented upon. This shows that, contrary to the former, the latter is not considered a central dimension of the surgical operation.

Nevertheless, some topicalizations of the external view are observable, which interestingly refer to the editing work of the surgeon and to the skilled combination of internal and external views. I give two occurrences of the phenomenon.

In the first, the surgeon engages in online editing work by requesting both the endoscopic and the external images.

(33) [1106-k1d1-57.50 REQ IV]

```
1   SUR   oké, (0.2) and NOw, I ask to Michelle, *(1.0)  to put (0.9)
          >>external view-------->
                                          *holds M's hand-->
2         the: trocar in the direc*tion of the SPLeen.
                              -->*slowly moves and orients M's hand--->
3         (1.2)
4   SUR   okay,*
           ->*
5         (1.2)
6   SUR   *becau:se, (0.8) while I introduce *my prosthesis, (0.7) euh:m
          *takes the band-------------------*approaches it to trocar-->
7         (0.4) I eliminate immediately, (0.7) the pneumoperitoneum. (0.8)
8         okay, (.) *so. (0.8) look, perhaps also (.) u- (0.4) the- the
                  -->*introduces it only a little bit-->
9         (0.3)**BOTH** external view (0.3) a- | okay/% (0.3) fine,
               **points**
    scr                                         |ext.view+insert int.view
    fig                                              %fig.1
```

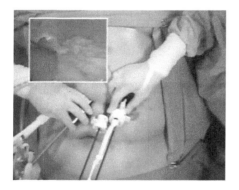

Figure 33.1

```
10        *(2.4)
    sur   *introduces the band--->
11  EXP   tu les as aux ordres hein les techniciens là hein? .h HH
          you totally control the technicians do you? right? .h HH
```

As the external view is transmitted, the surgeon first demonstrates the positioning of the trocar holding the camera by distinctively directing the assistant's hand (lines 1–2). What is made relevant here is the embodied manoeuvring of the video, made visible thanks to the external camera. But this is not enough: the orientation of the endoscopic camera is functional for making visible the introduction of the prosthesis by the surgeon, which is announced next (6) and which is made visible by the internal view. The surgeon instructs the audience to look at both views (8–9) for appreciating the step demonstrated here.

The temporality of this instruction is adjusted to the finely tuned coordination between the introduction of the nasogastric band in the trocar and the request for an inset internal view within the external image. The surgeon delays the introduction of the band (8), as well as his turn at talk ("look, perhaps also (.) u- (0.4) the- the (0.3) BOTH external view (0.3) a-," 8–9), until the inset image appears on screen (ratified with an assessment: "okay, (0.3) fine," 9). Only at that point—at which the visibility of its action is secured—does he finally introduce the prosthesis (10). This complex coordination of surgical gesture, the assistant's manoeuvring of the endoscopic camera, and the control room's editing of the internal and external views is addressed as the assessable of the compliment addressed by the expert (11): the compliment topicalizes the distant editing skilfully achieved by the surgeon. It is done in French, a linguistic choice that restricts the participation framework in which the evaluation is done.

Another occurrence of assessment referring to the video editing is observable in the following extract, in which the surgeon, before using a gastrostenometer, shows it to the audience.

(34)   [1106-k1d2-5.51]

```
1   SUR     okay NOW:, (.) we will talk about the gastro-stenometer,
2           (0.5)
3   SUR     is it possible to have an external view? (0.7) euh: (0.4) of
4           the gastrostenometer?  (0.2) euh
5           (1.8)
6   SUR     okay,
7           (0.9)
8   SUR     ne|xt-, ooh là: quell% beau mixage à la régie| ooh lalala:, .hh
                      what a nice editing in the control room
    scr     |ext.view on the gastrostenometer----------|internal view-->
    fig                        %fig.1
```

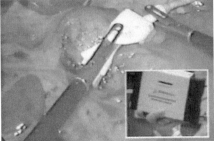

Figures 34.1–2

```
9            (1.5)
10 SUR       |o:kay:. so: (.) is it possible,  °oh no the inclusion is
   scr       |int.view + insert ext.view-->
11           perfect.° %look, (0.2) at the red light,
   fig                 %fig.2
```

First, the surgeon announces the next topic of his explanation (line 1). But before actually talking about it, he requests the external view (3) from the control room. What is produced by the technicians is assessed in a very emphatic way (8) by the surgeon himself, in French, in terms of "editing" ("*mixage*"). On the basis of this editing, an instruction is delivered by the surgeon to the audience ("look," 11), similarly to the previous one.

It is revealing that while the endoscopic camerawork gets complimented, the editing work with the external camera is topicalized only by the surgeon (excerpt 34) or by a colleague prizing his managerial skills but not the image itself (excerpt 33). The relevant video work for the operation is the former: its aesthetic qualities are deeply functional for the safe and efficient unfolding of the operation. Colour (as affected by bleeding, which blurs the image), light, and width of the camera angle (as making difficult places accessible) define the visible conditions of operation and, within them, the practical aesthetics of the camerawork.

6. CONCLUSION

Video has become a routine tool in surgery, both for operating, for example through endoscopic cameras, and for teaching, for example through the use of CCTV and videoconferencing devices. In both cases, video is crucial for the production of the visible intelligibility of the anatomic field and the operating theatre. This chapter has examined some video practices through which surgical teams accomplish this visibility and which constitute video teamwork in surgery.

More particularly, the chapter offered a systematic analysis of actions instructing the camerawork during surgical operations. Two types of action have been studied: directives addressing the endoscopic camera held by the assistant and requests addressing the external camera manoeuvred by the control room. Their sequential organization shows that to comply with directives and requests, the camera operator engages in a situated, moment-by-moment interpretation of both the instructions and of their context. The adequate production of video images relies and depends on the establishment of a praxeological context, which creates a relevant ecology for the directed camera, an intelligible context for the understanding of the instruction, thus making the action granting the directive possible. The camera follows as much the verbal instruction as it does the movements of the surgeon's hook. Requests concerning the external camera establish a visible context for the demonstration: they are recipient oriented towards the trainees and make accessible the surgeon's gesture exhibited for the camera, for the purpose of the demonstration. The images granting both directives and requests can become assessable, but whereas the former are publicly evaluated as an integral part of the surgical procedure, the latter are evaluated in a restricted participation framework that is limited to the team.

The systematic sequential organization of directives and requests governing the instructed camera in the operating room reveals the constitutive role of video in laparoscopic operations and in surgical education; it also demonstrates that the manipulation of the camera is deeply embedded in the moment–by-moment understanding of the ongoing action; finally, it shows how the visibility of the operating theatre is the product of constant, collective, coordinated work.

APPENDIX: TRANSCRIPT CONVENTIONS

Talk has been transcribed according to conventions developed by Gail Jefferson (see Jefferson, 2004).

An indicative translation is provided line per line, in italics.

Multimodal details have been transcribed according to the following conventions (see Mondada, 2007c):

* *	Each participant's actions are delimited by the use of the same symbol.
*--->	Action described continues across subsequent lines.
*--->>	Action described continues until and after excerpt's end.
---->*	Action described continues until the same symbol is reached.
>>--	Action described begins before the excerpt's beginning.
... .	Action's preparation
,,,,,	Action's retraction
os	Participant doing the action is identified in small characters when he/she is not the current speaker or when the gesture is done during a pause.
cam	Camera assistant
im	Image; screen shot
#	Indicates the exact moment at which the screen shot has been recorded.
asp	Aspirator

NOTES

1. In other cases, not studied here, the assistant moves the camera without being asked to do so (Mondada, 2003). Surgeons can control the camera too, especially when the work of the dissection is suspended and they are fully focused on the anatomic exploration, done for the purposes of the operation as well

as for the audience of trainees (Mondada, 2006). In some other cases, the endoscopic camera can even be used by the surgeon to show an exterior detail (Mondada, 2006).
2. For an analysis of the way in which the *completion* of an action granting the directive is controlled in the third turn, see Mondada (2011a).

REFERENCES

Aanestad, M. (2003). The camera as an actor: Design-in-use of telemedicine infrastructure in surgery. *Journal of Computer-Supported Collaborative Work, 12,* 1–20.
Amerine, R., & Bilmes, J. (1988). Following instructions. *Human Studies, 11,* 327–339.
Cekaite, A. (2010). Shepherding the child: Embodied directive sequences in parent–child interactions. *Text & Talk, 30*(1), 1–25.
Curl, T. S., & Drew, P. (2008). Contingency and action: A comparison of two forms of requesting. *Research on Language and Social Interaction, 41*(2), 129–153.
Davidson, J. (1984). Subsequent versions of invitations, offers, requests, and proposals dealing with potential or actual rejection. In J. M. Atkinson & J. Heritage (Eds.), *Structures of Social Action* (pp. 102–128). Cambridge: Cambridge University Press.
Garfinkel, H. (2002). *Ethnomethodology's Program.* New York: Rowman & Littlefield.
Goodwin, C. (1994). Professional vision. *American Anthropologist, 96*(3), 606–633.
Goodwin, M. H. (1990). *He-Said-She-Said: Talk as Social Organization among Black Children.* Bloomington: Indiana University Press.
Goodwin, M. H. (2006). Participation, affect, and trajectory in family directive/response sequences. *Text & Talk, 26*(4/5), 515–543.
Goodwin, M. H., & Cekaite, A. (2012). Calibration in directive/response sequences in family interaction. *Journal of Pragmatics, 46,* 122–138.
Hartswood, M., Procter, R., Rouncefield, M., & Slack, R. (2002). Performance management in breast screening: A case study of professional vision. *Cognition, Technology & Work, 4*(2), 91–100.
Heinemann, T. (2006). "Will you or can't you?". Displaying entitlement in interrogative requests. *Journal of Pragmatics, 38,* 1081–1104.
Hirschauer, S. (1991). The manufacture of bodies in surgery. *Social Studies of Science, 21*(2), 279–319.
Jefferson, G. (2004). Glossary of transcript symbols with an introduction. In G. H. Lerner (Ed.), *Conversation Analysis: Studies from the first generation* (pp. 13–31). Amsterdam: Benjamins.
Keevallik, L. (2010). Bodily quoting in dance corrections. *Research on Language & Social Interaction, 43:4,* 401–426.
Koschmann, T., LeBaron, C., Goodwin, C., & Feltovich, P. (2011). "Can you see the cystic artery yet?" A simple matter of trust. *Journal of Pragmatics, 43*(2), 521–541.
Lindström, A. (2005). Language as social action. A study of how senior citizens request assistance with practical tasks in the Swedish home help service. In A. Hakulinen & M. Selting (Eds.), *Syntax and Lexis in Conversation* (pp. 209–230). Amsterdam: Benjamins.
Lindwall, O., & Ekström, A. (2012). Instructions-in-interaction: The teaching and learning of a manual skill. *Human Studies, 35,* 27–49.
Mondada, L. (2003). Working with video: How surgeons produce video records of their actions. *Visual Studies, 18*(1), 58–72.

Mondada, L. (2006). La compétence comme dimension située et contingente, localement évaluée par les participants. *Bulletin VALS-ASLA, 84,* 83–119.

Mondada, L. (2007a). Operating together through videoconference: Members' procedures for accomplishing a common space of action. In S. Hester & D. Francis (Eds.), *Orders of Ordinary Action* (pp. 51–67). Aldershot, UK: Ashgate.

Mondada, L. (2007b). Bilingualism and the analysis of talk at work: Code-switching as a resource for the organization of action and interaction. In M. Heller (Ed.), *Bilingualism: A Social Approach* (pp. 297–318). New York: Palgrave.

Mondada, L. (2007c). Multimodal resources for turn-taking: Pointing and the emergence of possible next speakers. *Discourse Studies, 9,* 194–225.

Mondada, L. (2011a). The organization of concurrent courses of action in surgical demonstrations. In J. Streeck, C. Goodwin, & C. LeBaron (Eds.), *Embodied Interaction, Language and Body in the Material World* (pp. 207–226). Cambridge: Cambridge University Press.

Mondada, L. (2011b). The situated organization of directives in French: Imperatives and action coordination in video games. *Nottingham French Studies, 50*(2), 19–50.

Mondada, L. (in press). Instructions in the operating room: How surgeons direct their assistant's hands. *Discourse Studies.*

Nishizaka, A. (2011). The embodied organization of a real-time fetus: The visible and the invisible in prenatal ultrasound examinations. *Social Studies of Science, 41*(3), 309–336.

Parry, R. (2004). The interactional management of patients' physical incompetence: A conversation analytic study of physiotherapy interactions. *Sociology of Health & Illness, 26*(7), 976–1007.

Rystedt, H., Ivarsson, J., Asplund, S., Johnsson, A.A., & Bath, M. (2011). Rediscovering radiology: New technologies and remedial action at the worksite. *Social Studies of Science, 41*(6), 867–891.

Sanchez Svensson, M., Heath, C., & Luff, P. (2007). Instrumental action: The timely exchange of implements during surgical operations. In L. Bannon et al. (Eds.), *ECSCW'07: Proceedings of the Tenth European Conference on Computer Supported Cooperative Work* (pp. 41–60). Berlin: Springer.

Schegloff, E.A. (1996). Confirming allusions. *American Journal of Sociology, 102*(1), 161–216.

Schegloff, E.A. (2007). *Sequence Organization in Interaction: A Primer in Conversation Analysis* (Vol. 1). Cambridge: Cambridge University Press.

Schegloff, E. A., Jefferson, G., & Sacks, H. (1977). The Preference for Self-Correction in the Organization of Repair in Conversation. *Language, 53,* 361–382.

Part II
Showing

4 Mundane Video Directors in Interaction

Showing One's Environment in Skype and Mobile Video Calls

Christian Licoppe and Julien Morel
(Télécom ParisTech)

1. INTRODUCTION

With computer-based services (e.g. Skype, MSN, etc.) available on laptops and mobile video communication services on mobile phones and smartphones, there has been what we could call a "mobility turn" in video communication. "Mobility" should be understood here as meaning two things: (1) the way people may themselves be mobile while engaged in a video communication and carrying their terminal with them and (2) the fact that they can independently move the camera and orient it towards various details of their environment. Earlier systems often involved heavy terminals that were very difficult to move. Therefore, most of the initial research done on videoconference-mediated interactions in the 1990s was undertaken mostly from a perspective in which the video communication device was fixed and the participants sitting or moving in front of it (Heath & Luff, 1992; De Fornel, 1994; Dourish, Adler, Bellotti, & Henderson, 1996).

Such a mobility turn in video communication enables participants to show something to their interlocutor. Thirty per cent of mobile video conversations seem to unfold around the intent of one of the participants to show something to the other (O'Hara, Black, & Lipson, 2006), which is probably an underestimate because showing also occurs in video calls that do not have that as an initial goal. From what we observed in the Skype part of our own corpus, the numbers should be much in the same range also for Skype interactions. With the possibility of video communication technologies being able to show something during a call, these at last seem to fulfill their early and heretofore unkept promise that they would allow remote conversationalists to share their environments (Relieu, 2007). A related line of research has looked at "video-as-data," that is, how some part of the ongoing activity could be recorded and made available in real time to provide a shared field of interaction in collaborative situations (Nardi, Kuchinsky, Whittaker, Leichner, & Schwarz, 1996; Whittaker, 2003). In such a configuration, the participants work to articulate video and speech occurrences in a way that is relevant to the unfolding interaction (Mondada, 2007). We will try to show that such an articulation, from which there is no timeout, is also crucial in mobile and Skype video calls.

The aim of this chapter is to study and describe the systematic organization of sequences in which one video conversationalist shows some details of his or her material environment to the other (we will exclude here from the discussion sequences in which other persons—that is, potential interactional partners—are shown because they raise slightly different interactional issues). What characterizes such sequences? How are they initiated? How are the images of the environment relevant to what is said? What kind of reflexive relationship may develop between video-in-interaction and talk-in-interaction? More specifically, we will show how the production of any shot in a showing sequence is a collaborative process and a joint accomplishment.

To show something, video conversationalists must handle the camera. Through their camera motions, show-ers produce video images for the viewer to look at. The show-er thereby becomes a sort of mundane video director. In mundane mobile video recordings, the images produced are usually framed as "point–of-view shots" (Reponen, Lehikoinen, & Implö, 2009). This is also the case for showing sequences in mobile and Skype video calls. However, in these, the images the show-er produces are not meant to be watched later by an audience; they are shot and displayed in the course of a running video interaction, of which they are a constitutive part. This is not just video but video-in-interaction. From a different perspective, video-in-interaction may also be seen as an extreme case of "broadcasting as a social media" (Juhlin, Engström, & Reponen, 2010), in which the production of video images and the utterance of turns-at-talk are completely and unremittingly entwined in the interactional processes that characterize video communication.

Our research is based on the detailed study of a corpus of naturally occurring Skype and mobile video communications. We will first summarize some previous relevant observations in this section, namely that video conversationalists orient towards the maxim put-the-face-of-the-current-speaker-on-screen so that a talking-heads configuration is the default interaction mode in video calls (Licoppe & Morel, 2012). We will use this as a background to discuss how the initiation of showing sequences (which means departing from the talking-heads configuration in an organized and mutually ratified manner) is methodically accomplished, through a particular form of prefatory work. Then we will move on to the showings themselves in Section 3 to describe how the interaction-constituted pair, composed of the show-er and his or her audience, weave together what occurs within the visual and aural semiotic fields as part of their accountable work to sustain a proper video conversation. The video shots produced and displayed in the course of a video call and, more specifically here, those that are achieved when showing cannot be isolated from the talk or attributed to a participant, but they constitute a collaborative and ongoing accomplishment.

The Skype corpus involved ten individual users. The subjects captured and made available to us the video flux of some of their Skype video calls through commercial software such as Camtasia. Our final corpus contains about 100 Skype video conversations. For the mobile video corpus, we recruited ten users on mobile forums, who agreed to make recordings of their mobile video calls. We gave them a mobile phone that video-captured on-screen activities (Morel & Licoppe, 2010) and collected about 100 mobile video calls in this way.

2. THE MULTIMODAL SEQUENTIAL ORGANIZATION OF SKYPE AND MOBILE VIDEO CALLS

A common feature of Skype and mobile video calls is the ability to orient the camera, either because the camera itself is mobile (as with separate webcams) or because, though the camera is fixed, the device itself is mobile (e.g. laptops and mobile phones). This enables video conversationalists to show various features of their environment when they deem such an action relevant. There is, however, a distinctive organization to the production of images in video conversations, as evidenced in some observable features of video calls:

1. Most video calls open in a talking-heads configuration in which both participants show as much of their face as possible.
2. Mobile and Skype video calls are patterned, often alternating between a talking-heads arrangement in which both participants are on screen and facing the camera and moments in which they are producing various shots of their environment in line with their current interactional purposes.
3. The video images on each side are ceaselessly produced and expected to be scrutinized with respect to their relevance to the ongoing interaction, with a particular emphasis on the moments at which one participant or the other departs from the talking-heads format.
4. The talking-heads arrangement is oriented to as a default mode of interaction, with the implication that when there is nothing else relevant to show, the participants should show themselves on screen.
5. In multiparty interactions, the party who is handling the video communication apparatus has an obligation to put other speakers on screen when they talk; video conversationalists orient to their appearance on screen as making relevant a distinctive participation status and as an interactional move in itself, also making relevant a response on their part in the next available slot.

We have shown that these phenomena are not separate issues but rather integral components of the interaction order specific to "video-in-interaction" (Licoppe & Morel, 2012). They can all be seen to derive from the common-sense orientation of video conversationalists towards a single foundational maxim that provides a kind of "simplest systematics" to the organization of video calls: put the face of the current speaker on screen. It accounts for why the talking-heads arrangement is treated as a default configuration: whenever there is no reason to show anything in particular, an orientation to the maxim makes it relevant for participants to put their faces on-screen and therefore to produce a talking-heads arrangement. During openings, before any reason for the call has been provided, there is no ground for showing anything in particular, and so the default talking-heads arrangement is expected. Finally, it accounts for the fact that in multiparty settings, the camera holder is expected to show whoever may be understood as the current speaker on screen and that the parties to video calls behave as if they had special interactional rights and obligations when they appear on screen.

One of the consequences of an orientation towards the put-the-face-of-the-current-speaker-on-screen maxim is that participants will be held accountable for the images they provide all the time and not only in the opening stage of video calls. When one party shoots something other than his or her own face, such images are available for monitoring and are scrutinized by the recipient with respect to their "gazeworthiness" and relevance to the ongoing interaction. Irrelevant images, the production of which is often unavoidable in the course of the routine action of showing something during a video call, will have to be attended to in specific ways. In such situations, show-ers will be expected by participants to behave as mundane video shooters, producing images that are treated as meaningful with respect to the current circumstances and for the relevance of which they are held accountable on a moment-by-moment basis.

We will now focus on situations in which one participant tries to show the other something in his or her physical environment. In the next section, we will analyse how the video conversationalists manage to depart from the talking-heads configuration so as to initiate a so-called showing sequence.

3.   STARTING TO SHOW SOMETHING: THE SEQUENTIAL ORGANIZATION OF THE BEGINNING OF SHOWING SEQUENCES IN SKYPE AND MOBILE VIDEO CALLS

The focus in this section will be on how video conversationalists initiate a showing sequence as a methodically organized and collaborative accomplishment that displays recognizable sequential concerns. Video conversationalists about to show something actually face problems akin to those of face-to-face conversationalists about to engage in storytelling or, more generally, in the production of extended turns-at-talk. Following up on Harvey Sacks' seminal analysis (Sacks, 1992), storytelling involves a suspension of the usual turn-taking organization and a suspension of the type of obligation to listen that it embeds. Storytellers usually manage this through the initiation of story prefaces (Sacks, 1992; Jefferson, 1978). The preface to the story acts as a metapragmatic move orienting the ongoing interaction towards this particular conversational format, while offering a slot for the potential recipient to commit to such a development. Moreover, the design of the preface provides resources for the recipient to recognize when the story (and therefore the particular turn-taking format that characterizes the storytelling sequence) is about to come to its point (and therefore its end), so that the transition to a next sequence becomes a relevant concern for the participants.

The parallel lies in the fact that a video conversationalist about to show something is likely to produce unintelligible or irrelevant images for a short lapse of time while he or she rearranges the video communication device. This will require a temporary suspension of the normative expectations regarding the accountability of the video images, these expectations being central to the sequential organization of video calls. The launch of a preface sequence somehow announcing that he or she will show something then becomes an efficient and effort-saving solution to such a practical concern. As in the case of storytelling, it offers a slot for recipients to agree to the ongoing move, and it prepares them to view strange images for a short time and to refrain from noticing or commenting on their irrelevance on the basis of the usual video accountability demands. The design of the preface may be shaped so as to constitute a powerful resource to provide the viewer with some clues (1) to recognize when a candidate image to be viewed may have been produced by the show-er and when relevance requirements may be enacted anew; (2) to anticipate what kind of camera motions might be performed (as we will see, these expectations are different when what is at stake is for show-ers to provide evidence that they are, for instance, at the beach or to give recipients a tour of her newly refurbished flat).

3.1.   Case 1: "Shall I Give You a Tour of the Flat?"

Our first instance occurs during a mobile video call. The caller and the call recipient are two close friends and regular partners in mobile video calls, and until the start of the extract they have been discussing various topics in a talking-heads configuration.

C is the caller, and R is the call recipient. Hashes are used to mark the moment at which the screen captures shown in the figures were taken.

(1a)

```
01 REC:   qu'elle s'mé- (.) qu'elle se méprenne pas ou autre
          that she shouldn't mis- (.) misunderstand or something
02 REC:   chose tu vois#
          else you see
   fig                    #fig.1
```

Figure 1   The talking-head format of their current conversation. The caller appears in the small control image at the top, and the called party is in the larger picture.

```
03          (0.2)
04  CAL:    ah bah ouais
            ah bah yeah
05          (0.4)
06  CAL:    non (.) t'as eu raison hein
            no (.) you were right eh
07          (0.5)
08  CAL:    bon bin c'est bien
            well then it's fine
09          (1.0)
10  CAL:    bon (.) j'te fais visiter l'appart
            well (.) let me give you a tour of the flat
11          (1.0)
12  REC:    comment?
            what?
13          (0.1)
14  CAL:    j'te fais visiter l'appart?
            shall I give you a tour of the flat?
15          (0.7)
16  REC:    ouais: vas-y (.) fais-moi visiter.
            yeah go on (.) give me a tour.
17          (.)
```

The extract displays a sense of the exhaustion of a prior topic (lines 1–10), and this forms the context for the caller to self-select and introduce a new topic, namely an offer to show his newly refurbished flat ("Shall I give you a tour of the flat?," 14). It is uttered with a rising tone at the end, which turns it into a question. After a short repair sequence (12–14), the call recipient answers by accepting the offer by giving it a kind of go-ahead, which displays his anticipation of a rather extended showing sequence and the kind of camera handling this might entail (16). The adjacent pair offer/acceptance has a prefatory and even a presequential character with respect to the initiation of a showing sequence.

In this case, the offer is not an offer to show any item in particular but rather the flat as a whole. Any recognizable image of the furniture or the apartment may constitute a potential candidate as a proper "showable" thing in such a context. This provides the recipient with an interpretive scheme from which to infer when something is being shown, especially when the caller actually starts to show the flat. It is an important clue because to show something, the caller must perform some preliminary handling, during which he must unavoidably send unintelligible or irrelevant images for a short lapse of time. So the design of the offer also has a prefatory function in providing clues for the viewer to guess when the showing will start, that is, when a relevant shot is first produced and therefore when he should resume paying attention to the screen and scrutinize the images there with respect to their relevance to the ongoing activity.

Finally, such a preface initiates a particular type of showing sequence, of which we have several instances in our corpus. It aims towards giving a visual tour of one's surroundings that makes relevant, for the show-er, two different membership categories: host and director. It also acts as a metapragmatic move, which cues in a particular genre of showing sequence.

(1b)   (continued)

```
18 CAL:     #allez go
            go go
    fig     #fig.2
```

Figure 2   The screen ceases to show the environment as the caller starts to switch the camera.

```
19          (0.3)
20 CAL:     attends
            wait
21 REC:     (   )
22          (0.2)
23 CAL:     attends
            wait
24          (1.8)
25 CAL:     ho::p
26          (1.0)
27 REC:     (   ) #(rasé) aujourd'hui
            (   ) (shaved) today
    fig         #fig.3
```

Figure 3   The first recognizable image produced after the camera switch, a shot of the door. It is held in a relatively stable way throughout the turns at lines 27–28.

```
28 CAL:    alors tu vois quelqu'chose  là (.) c'est bon?
           so can you see anythin' there (.) is it okay?
29         (0.9)
30 REC:    ouais (.) c'est bon (0.1) mais t'es pas rasé# là
           yeah (.) it's ok (0.1) but you haven't shaved there
   fig                                                     #fig.4
```

Figure 4   The camera lingers around the door (the handle is still slightly visible in the bottom left-hand corner), but the camera is still moving about, and the shot is not stable.

At the moment the caller departs from the talking-heads configuration and starts to produce images that are no longer intelligible (Figure 2), he utters an instruction to wait (line 20), which he repeats (23) in what is probably a repair sequence. What does such an instruction do exactly? Because it accompanies the production of dubious, unintelligible images, it seems that it might be related to that. That this is the case is made retrospectively clear by the fact that, first, the call recipient tries to introduce another topic, a noticing on the facial appearance of the caller, which points back to the previous talking-heads configuration and overtly displays its disjunction from the images being produced and thus an orientation towards complying with the instruction. Second, the caller himself verbally marks the moment he starts producing recognizable images (and therefore the end of the camera-switching phase) through his yes/no check-up question (28; Figure 3).

The generic design of the question ("can you see something there?," 28) marks a resumption of the intelligibility of the images and shows that the visual tour of the flat has not started yet. It frames the way the following images are to be considered, that is, as intelligible but not yet available to be scrutinized for relevance. The call recipient collaborates by making another try at introducing the same topic related to the caller's visual appearance, the discussion of which proceeds as the images are being produced (30–35). The check-up question of the caller at line 28 therefore marks a first step in the initiation of the showing sequence, namely the resumption of the production of intelligible images of the environment (but not yet the production of an image that may count as the first one in a "visit"). The instructions at lines 20 and 23 to wait may retrospectively be seen as an attempt to block visual sense-making activities on the part of the recipient, which would otherwise have been warranted by the sequential organization of video calls (since it embeds a requirement to scrutinize images for relevance in this type of situation).

(1c)   (continued)

```
31          (0.2)
32 CAL:     h.h. non:: bah tu sais moi l'week end euh:::
            h.h. no well you know me during the weekend er
33 CAL:     #j'm'en fous (0.2) j'm'en fous mon rasoir
            I don't care. (0.2) I don't care my razor
   fig      #fig.5
```

Figure 5   The image produced by the caller moves to the right of the door to show the wall.

```
34 CAL:     i marche que la s'maine (.) i marche pas
            it only works during the week (.) it doesn't work
35 CAL:     le week end
            on the week end
36          (.)
37 REC:     par contre ça coupe vachement::#
            on the other hand it cuts a lot
   fig                                    #fig.6
```

Figure 6   The camera moves left and briefly shows the door handle again.

```
38          (0.3)
39 CAL:     hein?
            uh?
40          (0.8)
41 REC:     ca n'arrête pas de couper#
            it keeps cutting off
   fig                      #fig.7
```

Figure 7   The camera is lowered so that it now shows part of the floor.

```
42              (0.1)
43  CAL:        ouais ouais (.) ça::: apparement ça:::::
                yeah yeah (.) it apparently it
44  CAL:        déconne un peu là (.) (mais bon) on va
                breaks down a little there (.) (but well) we will
45  CAL:        essayer d'faire euh:: avec
                try to make do er with that
46              (0.4)#
    fig           #fig.8
```

Figure 8   The camera stabilizes on what turns out to be the entrance door.

```
47  CAL:        donc ça c'est l'entrée::
                so this is the entrance
48              (0.8)
49  REC:        la porte d'entrée (.) blindée::?
                the entrance door (.) steel security?
```

The shaving topic elicits a response and a justification (33–36), after which the call recipient complains about the poor quality of the communication channel (41), which the caller acknowledges (43–45). During all this, the camera moves so that it produces recognizable images related to the environment (Figures 4–7) but not yet to be treated as relevant to the announced tour of the flat, as shown by the disjointed talk that proceeds meanwhile.

After acknowledging the technical problems, the caller announces that he and the call recipient will override the difficulties, and after a short pause he produces a rather stable and recognizable shot of a door (Figure 8). The relative stabilization of the camera (at least with respect to what has been going on before) is a first clue that this shot has a special significance. This is also marked in the talk, for the caller simultaneously utters a comment referring to "the entrance," which is a likely point to start a visit in copresence. The turn is introduced with a conjunction device, the "*donc*" (47), that separates the reference to the entrance door from what immediately preceded it. So the design of the visual field and that of the talk-in-interaction are shaped so as to convey together that this particular image can be taken as the first one relevant to the visit. The call recipient clearly picks up on this in his response by repeating the reference to the image as being that of the entrance door and furnishing it with a candidate attribute, thus composing a question about the type of entrance door it is. He thus displays his collaboration towards treating the image shown as the first one relevant to the visit and treats it as making available potential items to be referred to or noticed as a visitor.

The whole sequence displays the kind of interactional work that is needed to start showing something in a video call: (1) a two-part preface sequence is produced, with the design of the initial turn providing clues to recognize a possible first relevant image with respect to the kind of showing it projects. The preface also marks the images produced during the necessary lapse of time needed to move the camera away from the talking-heads configuration and towards this first candidate image as potentially unintelligible or irrelevant to the stated showing project (though such a projected frame of interpretation has to be jointly accomplished all along the camera motion itself, for instance by the recipient not providing any kind of noticing). Such a suspension of the kind of normative orientation towards the images characteristic of video-in-interaction in ordinary video calls can be further underlined by the use of additional blocking injunctions such as "wait" (Balthasar, Bruxelles, Mondada, & Traverso, 2007). The kind of video work required to depart from the talking-heads configuration and produce a relevant first image involves a suspension of the obligation to watch embedded in the sequential organization of video-in-interaction, which has to be collaboratively managed. Preface sequences are an efficient and routine way to achieve this.

3.2. Case 2: "I Want to Show You the Bedroom"

A second example also deals with the showing of visible details of the built environment. The caller is the son. He is calling his mother to inquire about her car, as will transpire later during the call.

(2a)

```
01          ((ring)) ((ring)) ((ring)) ((ring))
02          (4.0)#
     fig          #fig.9
```

Figure 9   Image at connection.

```
03 REC:     Δoui:
            ye:s
    rec     Δwalks
04 CAL:     b'jour maman
            good morning mom
05 REC:     oui::
            yes
```

```
06 CAL:    ça va bien?
           are you well?
07 REC:    je te vo- tu me vois?
           I can see y- can you see me?
08 CAL:    oui je te vois (.) ça va?
           yes I can see you (.) are you okay?
09 REC:    bon bah moi aussi je te vois
           well bah I can see you too
10 CAL:    bo:n
           okay:
11 REC:    et je t'ai j'étais à la chambre je voulais
           and I I was in the bedroom I wanted
12 REC:    te faire voir la chambre
           to show you the bedroom
13 CAL:    ah vas-y=
           ah go ahead=
14 REC:    =attends
           =wait
15 CAL:    m- montre-moi
           sh- show me
16 REC:    Δ#attends (.) *#je te montre hein
           wait. (.) I'll show you huh
    rec    Δstops after a threshold
    rec                      *gets close to the screen
    fig    #fig.10           #fig.11
```

Figures 10–11　Starting to switch camera orientation.

```
17 CAL:    d'accord
           okay
18         Δ(5.0)
    rec    Δmanipulates the terminal to show the room
```

The turn at line 11 works as the first part of the kind of preface sequence (to the showings) with which we are now familiar. Its placement is significant: during the opening sequence, just after the initial greetings and audio/video connection checks and before the caller has volunteered a topic that might be recognized as a reason for the call. In the way she latches her offer to her previous utterance through the initial "and," there might be an indication that she is rushing to get her offer in. The preface itself is so designed to open as a justification ("I was in the bedroom," 11), which precedes the offer to show her bedroom itself, phrased in a way that might suggest a prior reference and an already existing project ("I wanted to show you the room," 11–12). The son responds with a go-ahead (13), and she follows up by uttering an injunction for him to "wait" (14), to which he explicitly agrees in a way that confirms his ongoing alignment with her showing project ("show me," 15). All of this occurs while she is still walking towards her bedroom and speaking as a talking-head. So the injunction seems less oriented towards the fact that she will soon be switching the camera focus than it is to block a possible slot (marked by the pause and the fact that they are both in a talking-heads configuration), which, at this stage of the opening, he might use as an opportunity to volunteer a first topic. This interpretation is retrospectively reinforced by the fact that the mother repeats her injunction to "wait" while marking it as different by following it with a statement that makes her project salient again ("I'll show you huh," 16). This coincides with the moment at which she moves her face close to phone and switches the orientation of the camera from front to back (Figures 10–11). The initial instruction at the start of line 16 ("wait") does a different job than the prior and similar one did at line 14. It does the usual work in showing prefaces of getting the recipient to momentarily suspend his or her interpretive orientation towards the images he or she produces. The caller agrees to do this (17) and displays his compliance by remaining silent during the several seconds she takes to produce a recognizable image of the bedroom. Refer to extract 2b and the following discussion.

(2b)   (continued)

```
19 CAL:    #est ce que tu vois?#
           can you see?
    fig    #fig.12                #fig.13
```

Figure 12   The image of the right corner of the room that she produces just as she starts her check-up question (line 19).

Figure 13   The window shot she produces at the end of the same turn after a short movement of the camera to the left.

Looking at the similarities between both extracts, both sequences clearly display the kind of multimodal and interactional work that is routinely done to initiate showing sequences: first, there is the production of prefatory sequences (preface plus go-ahead), with the design of an initial prefacing turn projecting visual clues to determine when a possible first image relevant to the showing project has been produced. The turn also orients the recipient towards disregarding the images produced during unavoidable device manipulations and camera motions (required to move away from the initial talking-heads configuration) and treating them as irrelevant with respect to the showing project initially announced. This suspension of the scrutinizing attitude towards images, which is characteristic of the sequential organization of video-in-interaction, can be reinforced by instructions on the part of the show-er such as "wait," which can be used to block various actions or interpretive processes according to the contingencies of the current situation. The production of the first recognizable and relevant image is marked and highlighted in the talk, for instance with a check-up question aiming at an explicit confirmation on the part of the recipient that he sees it and sees it precisely in such a light.

Among the Skype and mobile video calls that include well defined showing sequences, some include just one, while others involve several. When this is the case, the preface work is usually well developed to initiate the first showing, but, though an orientation towards doing a preface remains, it might be accomplished more cursorily after the first instance of showing. As to the first instance, its accomplishment is sensitive to the interactional contingencies of the situation in which it is performed. As we have seen, blocking instructions are, for instance, particularly frequent when the show-er tries to get the showing under way while other interactional opportunities are salient. We will focus now more specifically on the ways in which participants exploit different interactional resources and collaborate to produce relevant images during a showing.

4. PROVIDING VIDEO SHOTS OF THE ENVIRONMENT AS MULTIMODAL AND COLLABORATIVE INTERACTIONAL ACCOMPLISHMENTS

In this last section, we will focus on what happens next in this sequence and particularly in the kind of mutual elaboration of camerawork and talk involved in the production of the first relevant images after the preface sequence.

4.1.   "I Wanted to Show You the Bedroom"

(2c)   (Continued)

```
20 CAL:    ouais très bien
21         (1.0)
22 CAL:    bon alors nouveau papier Δpeint:/
           so then new wallpaper
    rec                              Δpans right (fig.14)

23 CAL:    nouΔveaux rideaux:/ Δ
           new curtains
    rec        Δmid pan (fig.15)Δend of pan (fig.16)
```

Figures 14–16   The images produced by the call recipient during the caller's noticing turn (lines 22–23) as she pans the camera to the right from the window to the wall.

```
24        (1.Δ0)
   rec        Δ((pans left until end of line 30))
25 CAL:   c'est beau hein
          it's nice uh
26        (1.0)
27 REC:   voilà
          There
```

Figures 17–22   The successive images produced by the call recipient as she pans back to the window (lines 23–25).

The visual confirmation check at line 19 ("can you see") in excerpt 2b occurs at the same time as the actual production of a recognizable image of her bedroom (Figure 12). It can be heard as closing the interpretive suspension opened earlier by the waiting instruction and is treated as such because the caller first confirms he can see (20) and then provides a noticing related to the images that his mother is producing (22–23). The question check therefore marks the end of the prefatory work. However, while the call recipient is producing her question, she slightly moves the camera to the left, such that, at the end of the question, the image is that of the window.

After her question, there is a significant lapse of time during which she neither moves the camera nor says anything, i.e. a multimodal pause (21). The recipient/viewer self-selects to produce a new utterance, composed of two successive noticings (22–23) of recognizable things he saw during the initial camera motion (during line 19) in the same order in which they were made available to him at the time. The objects he notices are at the same time things he may have fleetingly seen and been able to identify and pieces of furniture relevant to notice in a refurbished room, that is, the "new wall paper" and "new curtains." His noticings retrospectively transform the meaning he had given to his mother's prior camera motion by treating it not just as a first intelligible image (and therefore as a starting point for her to initiate the showing) but as the showing itself. He may have been feeling slightly uncertain at this point after the pause in line 21. Indeed, his noticings could be taken as a kind of repair of his previous turn, marking the inadequacy or incompleteness of his earlier assent. This hypothesis is supported by the fact that, instead of assessing the items noticed in the room, as he might have done if he thought she was giving him a tour of her new bedroom at that point, he simply names the items, thus providing candidate assessables.

What makes possible the inference that the initial camera motion of his mother might have been both a start and an end to the showing itself is the fact that she moved the camera in a way that allowed him to see at least two different relevant features of the room, in two different locations, which constitutes a kind of minimal tour of a room, in addition to the pause itself, opening up the possibility that she might have been done with showing after all. This provides direct evidence that he is interpreting what goes on both in the talk and on-screen as potentially meaningful actions, interweaving occurrences in both semiotic fields (Goodwin, 2000) as a relevant context for his own utterance to display proper understanding.

The caller's mother does not stand still while he finishes uttering his first noticing in line 22. As evidenced by the changes in the video shot, she starts to move the camera to the right, until a large segment of the wall (and therefore of the wallpaper) becomes visible. The motion stops just as the caller finishes his turn. Then, in the middle of the pause that follows, the camera motions resume, this time leftwards, back towards the window. In the first camera motion, the mother appears to orient to her son's developing turn and more particularly to his naming of the wallpaper as a request to show: her first camera motion provides a good view of the wall. Similarly, the second camera motion appears to be a response to his mentioning the window, treating it in effect as a request to be shown. She moves the camera back so as to provide a good view of the window. With her two successive and opposite pans (Figures 14–16), she thus manages to provide adequate views of the things he is mentioning and in exactly the same order he is naming them. The kind of reading she thus displays of his ongoing noticing turn somehow retrospectively suggests that what she had initially shown, when she had begun to produce intelligible images of the room again in line 19, is inadequate to account for them and was not to be taken as a proper showing of the room. In this context, his later naming of the wallpaper and the window may be heard requests to show these items.

The caller/viewer responds to what his mother is now doing with the camera with a direct and positive assessment ("it's nice uh," 25) as she is still panning back left. Through such a generic appreciation, he behaves as if he is being shown the room, here and now, and adequately so. Her next turn, uttered as she finishes the camera motion and produces a shot of the window, is the conclusive "*voilà*" (27), which marks that something has been completed. With respect to the visual semiotic field, it coincides with the end of her two-part camera sweep to the right side of the room, in which she had shown the items of the room he had picked as relevant. With respect to the talk, it comes after he has produced a positive generic assessment of the images he has been shown, a potential reason to infer that he has been satisfactorily shown the bedroom. So her turn can also be heard as marking a potential completion point for the ongoing showing activity.

The analysis of this showing sequence and the ambiguities that emerge within it gives us an understanding of how such sequences are organized with respect to concerns regarding multimodality and interactional asymmetries. Ordinary phone calls have been argued to make relevant "turn-generated categories" in the course of their production, such as caller and call recipient (Sacks, 1992; Watson, 1997). By analogy, showings in Skype and mobile video calls make relevant some other emergent paired categorizations such as show-er and viewer, as sketched, for instance, in preface sequences. Show-er and viewers do not have access to the same set of resources. Available and relevant to the viewer on a moment-by-moment basis are the speech turns and video shots accomplished by the show-er. What is available and relevant to the show-er is mostly the talk produced by the viewer and to a lesser extent his facial expressions (as he interacts in the talking-heads format). Both parties orient to multimodal resources, namely the fact that the things the show-er says and shows are mutually elaborative and relevant semiotic fields and that what the viewer says can be heard as displaying his understanding—for which he is accountable—of what goes on in these relevant semiotic fields (which allows for various sorts of potential mismatches). As to the show-er, the parties orient towards an expectation that they will provide a relevant combination of talk and video with respect to (1) the unfolding interactional context, particularly the displays of understanding that the viewer produces, and (2) the project announced and ratified in the preface. These are all things that should contribute to an evolving context for the various relevancies of the viewer's actions, particularly the images that the show-er may produce.

More generally, video shots of the environment must be understood as fundamentally multimodal and collaborative accomplishments in Skype and mobile video calls. They are multimodal in the sense that they involve a reflexive and emergent relationship between video shots and turns-at-talk, a dynamic combination that acts as a resource for participants who produce recognizable and meaningful actions. They are collaborative in the sense that every video shot can and must be understood within the unfolding dynamics of the ongoing interaction. We could speak here of a video "contextual configuration" (Goodwin, 2000) involving the subtle articulation of video-in-interaction and talk-in-interaction.

4.2. Camera Motions as Sequence Shots with a Discoverable Coherence

The extract we will analyse now is taken from the Skype corpus. At the start, the call recipient, who has recently moved to another European capital and is just settling into his new flat, is finishing telling the caller, his sister, a story about his new roommate.

(3a)

```
01          (0.7)
02   REC:   donc y a des nanas qui viennent
            so there are girls who come
03          (0.7)
04   REC:   il est marrant#
            he is fun
     fig                       #fig.23
```

Figure 23   The brother, who is the call recipient.

```
05          (1.0)
06   REC:   donc (.) faudra que j'te montre à côteerrzzz: mais là chuis
            so (.) I'll have to show you the rest but right now I'm
07   REC:   chuis: (.) j'ai un peu la flemme (   ) chuis pieds nus
            I'm. I'm a bit lazy. I'm barefoot
08   REC:   (.) fait froid au sol=
            (.) the ground is cold
09   CAL:   =fais voir ta chambre déjà
            =show me your room to begin with
10          (0.7)
11   REC:   ra:[::::: (   )
12   CAL:      [fais juste tourner ton ordi
               [just turn your laptop
13          (0.5)
```

After the pause that marks the exhaustion of the previous topic at the beginning of line 3, the call recipient introduces another issue with the assertion that he will have to show the caller the flat. Such an obligation rests on categorization work. It makes relevant an additional "standard relational pair" (Hester & Eglin, 1997) besides brother–sister (that is, host–guest) and, more specifically, newly arrived host/first-time guest (in the sense of having visual access to the place for the first time). What is important here is that a "category-bound activity" is associated with this "relational pair," that is, a "visit" of the place, a video tour of the premises accomplished together with special obligations attached to the host. Because this turn evokes a future showing sequence, it also makes relevant such an activity and its associated relational pair (show-er–viewer). But such an action is put off until later, and the possibility of doing it now is even dismissed with an excuse (lines 6–8). So the speaker eludes showing the caller his flat and acting the part of show-er here and now.

The caller responds with a request (9), in which she asks him at least to show her his room. This request is finely crafted. It picks up on his prior categorization work for its relevance (since he has made the category-bound activity of showing her the premises a salient topic in the current conversation and she belongs to the category of persons with respect to which a tour of the premises is relevant, she is entitled to ask for it). Indeed her use of "*déjà*" (meaning here "to begin with") after her request suggests that showing her the room would be a start to fulfilling his self-avowed obligation to show her his premises. She sidesteps any direct reference to his previous excuse by an artful design of her request which delineates the kind effort he would have to do or, rather, not have to do: her request presupposes that if he limits what he shows her to the room he is lying in, he might not have to get up and get his feet cold. He produces a kind of "response cry" in line 11 (Goffman, 1981), which she treats as an expression of resentment and an indication of her request in line 8 being problematic, for she reformulates it as an instruction to "just" turn his laptop (12). Such a repair accomplishes several things: (1) It provides a practical procedure to satisfy her request that requires a minimal effort (which orients to the reluctance that might be interpreted from his response cry). (2) It provides the additional justification that he would not have to move to do this, which addresses his earlier excuse in lines 6–8 more overtly than her request in line 8, a corrected form of the request that also treats retrospectively the potential reluctance contained in his response cry. (3) "Turning the laptop" may thus briskly be associated with "giving a tour of the room" in a way that minimizes his agency (in view of his prior dismissal).

Finally, this initial negotiation, which stands as a preface for the negotiated visual tour of the flat, also shapes in advance the kind of shot that will be produced. The camera motion itself is prefigured as a complete rotation that will allow a gradual unveiling of his room environment, that is, as the particular form of camera motion that is category-bound to the activity of a "mobile video tour of the premises": a 180° pan sequence shot, produced so as to gradually unveil "discoverable" and "mentionable" features of the room. Like some of our previous examples, it will look like a point-of-view (POV) shot, providing the kind of general impression that someone present in the room would have when turning around to "discover" it. It is expected to be done here within an interactional arrangement in which the show-er complies (somewhat grudgingly) to a request on the part of the viewer and is expected to turn the camera to provide a semicircular sequence shot for the viewer to discover features relevant to her project of being given a tour of the room.

Looking more closely at how the conversation itself works out, the caller has just asked the call recipient to show her his room by turning his laptop around. The call recipient complies with the request and begins to move his laptop and webcam around.

(3b)   (Continued)

```
    rec    starts to move the camera
14  REC:   ssss ça c'est:: # la:: c'est donc le mur
           this this its's the::  so that's the wall
    fig                       #fig.24
```

Figure 24   After he has started to turn the laptop around, he shows and stabilizes the image of his bed corner.

```
15  REC:   de: not'chambre#
           of our room
    fig                       #fig.25
```

Figure 25   As the turn proceeds he starts to rotate the laptop.

```
16          (1.3)
17  CAL:    d'accord:# elle est bleue (0.3) j'vois:: donc la lampe
            Okay: it's blue (0.3) so I see the lamp
    fig              #fig.26
```

Figure 26   While he turns the laptop the camera drifts up, providing a glimpse of the ceiling lamp.

```
18  CAL:    maintenant #(.) >tu m'fais voir l'plafond< pete#
            now (.) you are showing  me the ceiling Pete
    fig              #fig.27                      #fig.28
```

Figure 27   Pete carries and rotating the laptop slowly but the camera is up, so that he shows part of the ceiling.

Figure 28   Pete treats her mention of this as a request to lower the video frame which makes him show the foot of his bed.

```
19  CAL:    [baisse  baisse
            [down    down
20  REC:    [°là?°
            [there?
21  REC:    là?
            there?
```

The accomplishment of the visit has been the object of a negotiation, with the potential guest/viewer eventually having to request it to elicit compliance from a slightly reluctant potential host/show-er. This initial negotiation is also treated retrospectively as a preface, as shown in lines 14–15, in which the caller signals the resumption of the intelligibility and accountability of the images he is currently producing: he thus proposes the image in Figure 24 as a candidate starting point for the showing sequence and brackets what has just been shown in his initial motion as irrelevant. However reluctant the call recipient may have appeared (or tried to appear) to show his room, he displays here the kind of collaborative conduct that is characteristic of showing sequences, through his concern to produce relevant images for the viewer to look at and the care he takes to manage moments in which he must necessarily produce unintelligible or irrelevant images.

As he is finishing this turn on line 15, he starts to rotate the laptop slowly again so that the video image moves right along the wall (Figure 25). This motion goes on while the caller responds (17). Her reply starts with an agreement token and a first noticing, namely that the room is blue. The combination of these verbal items provides the show-er with token evidence of the intelligibility of the images he is producing, from her point of view. While she is uttering this, the camera moves up and right, so that the ceiling and ceiling light become visible. This occasions a new noticing on the part of the caller, of the lamp, which displays another kind of understanding and stance with respect to what her brother is showing her. In this case, her stance may be slightly ironical, for the lamp is an uninteresting feature and her noticing is uttered with a complaining undertone. This is further highlighted by the fact that, when he keeps on showing the ceiling (Figures 26–27), she mentions that fact directly (18) and then quickly following that by a direct request to lower the camera. Once more, the show-er displays his orientation towards providing her with adequate images by immediately treating the reference to his showing the ceiling as a request, even anticipating the completion of the turn unit: he begins to lower the camera as she is uttering the word "ceiling." Later on he even checks that she is satisfied with the resulting image (Figure 28), first in overlap with her explicit request and then a second time (20–21).

He is thus making visible the fact that he is hearing her successive noticings as a kind of running commentary to the images he produces, which displays her evolving understanding of whatever he is showing as well as her particular stance towards it. Her utterances constitute a resource for him to decide in which direction to orient the camera now and to project further camera moves in a way that is relevant to her comments. Her verbal noticings are thus treated, according to their design and prosody, as accomplishing various actions related to the orientation of the camera (e.g. requesting a shot, suggesting a change, complaining about an orientation, etc.). And in hearing them precisely in this way he makes visible his concern with the provision of suitable images and therefore his cooperativeness to their joint production of a proper tour of his room. This form of cooperativeness is endogenous to the organization of the showing sequence.

The production of a given video image at a given time appears as a collaborative accomplishment that relies on an artful weaving together of visual and verbal resources in which talk-in-interaction, video-in-interaction, and activities (e.g. giving a tour of new premises to a sibling) are mutually elaborative. Such a format may recall Douglas Macbeth's analysis of the "long shot" in ethnographic films documenting complex scenes (Macbeth, 1999). However, the situation here is unlike an ethnographic film in that the sequence shot is produced with an audience able to watch the video sequence unfold moment by moment in real time and to comment upon it as it proceeds, thereby collaborating in its production with an involved "director."

5. CONCLUSION

The increasing use of mobile cameras and mobile terminals provides a resource for the development of sequences in mobile and Skype video calls where participants show something other than their own faces. We have analysed the organization of sequences in which one participant shows the other some material detail of her environment (as opposed to, for instance, showing another person). We have shown how such showing sequences are embedded in a more general organization of video calls in which participants orient towards the normative requirement of putting the face of the current speaker on-screen. An important consequence of such an orientation is that participants who stray away visually from a standard talking-heads format are held accountable for the relevance of the images they produce and that the recipients are expected to scrutinize such images on a moment-by-moment basis with respect to their relevance to the unfolding interaction. Hence the initiation of a showing sequence, the purpose of which is precisely to show something other than the face of the current speaker, has to be accomplished methodically.

We have shown how a common method to launch a showing sequence involved prefatory work, particularly when the showing sequence is the first one in the ongoing video call. The showing is somehow announced (by the show-er) or requested (by the potential audience). This constitutes the first turn of a preface structure, which offers a slot for the other participant to ratify the project. Such a preface is attending to the fact that, as the show-er starts to move his device, he will necessarily produce images that are potentially unintelligible and/or irrelevant with respect to the project to show stated in the preface. He would be held accountable for producing these immaterial images if the preface did not precisely act to temporarily suspend the scrutiny and assessment of the images with respect to their local and immediate relevance. Moreover, through its design, the preface (1) provides clues to recognize when a candidate first image for the showing is being produced (this being often explicitly signaled verbally by the show-er to initiate a resumption of the evaluative scrutiny of the video shots); (2) frames the kind of camera motion that may be expected for a proper showing to proceed. As we have seen, showing the beach and giving a tour of one's room do not forecast the same kind of camerawork: for the former, a single recognizable shot of the beach may suffice, whereas for the latter, some amount of camera motion and noticing are unavoidable.

Participants in Skype and mobile video calls attend to the images and talk as mutually elaborative semiotic fields composing a kind of video contextual configuration, characteristic of video communication. However, within showing sequences, participants are constituted as an interaction-generated relational pair, show-er and viewer, with asymmetric resources and concerns with respect to the production of video image and talk-in-interaction. The show-er combines the resources of speech and video to produce intelligible images, with a constant concern for their relevance to the viewer with respect to the unfolding interaction and the showing project under way. Then the talk and facial expressions of the viewer (when visible) are produced (by the viewer) and treated (by the show-er) as potential displays of understandings of the show-er's previous interactional moves (which can involve both speech utterances and camera motions). So the moment-by-moment production of video images in mobile and Skype video communication is a collaborative and joint interactional process. It is not just a matter of A showing her flat to B and becoming thus a mundane video director through the mobile turn of videoconference technologies, but of both participants becoming skilled video conversationalists and codirectors, collaborating constantly to produce relevant images as a joint accomplishment. An interesting question for further research would be to investigate whether such interaction-embedded video work leads to the emergence of a shared vocabulary and syntax of camera motions and how these might be related to professional video practices.

Finally, several of our examples are relevant to a particular subgenre, that of a showing sequence in which one party shows his or her new home environment to the other. Such sequences make relevant other categories as well, such as host and remote guests. Because this also means giving visual access to the privacy of one's home and behaving as if any change warranted showing one's home to this particular recipient, such showings index personal relationships. Through the way they are performed and their agency is distributed, in doing being a mother–son pair (and, more specifically, doing being a mother in a rush to show her new room to a compliant son), or doing being siblings (and more specifically doing being a brother who grudgingly agrees to show his new flat to an involved sister), complex personal histories as well as various intimacies are reenacted in the contingent way in which the showing is performed.

REFERENCES

Balthasar, L., Bruxelles, S., Mondada, L., & Traverso, V. (2007). Variations inter-actionnelles et changement catégoriel: L'exemple de "attends." In M. Auzanneau (Ed.), *La mise en oeuvre des langages dans l'interaction* (pp. 299–319). Paris: L'Harmattan.

De Fornel, M. (1994). Le cadre interactionnel de l'échange visiophonique. *Réseaux*, *64*, 107–132.

Dourish, P., Adler, A., Bellotti, V., & Henderson, A. (1996). Your place or mine? Learning from long-term use of audio-video communication. *Computer Supported Cooperative Work*, *5*, 33–62.

Goffman, E. (1981). *Forms of Talk*. Philadelphia: University of Pennsylvania Press.

Goodwin, C. (2000). Action and embodiment within situated human interaction. *Journal of Pragmatics*, *32*, 1489–1522.

Heath, C., & Luff, P. (1992). Media space and communicative asymmetries. Preliminary observations of video mediated interactions. *Human Computer Interaction*, *7*, 315–346.

Hester, S., & Eglin, P. (1997). *Culture in Action. Studies in Membership Categorization Analysis*. Washington DC: International Institute for Ethnomethodology and Conversation Analysis/University Press of America.

Jefferson, G. (1978). Sequential aspects of storytelling in conversation. In J. Schenkein (Ed.), *Studies in the Organization of Conversational Interaction* (pp. 219–248). New York: Academic Press.

Juhlin, O., Engström, A., & Reponen, E. (2010). Mobile broadcasting. The whats and hows of live video as a social medium. In *Proceedings of Mobile HCI 2010* (pp. 35–44). New York: ACM Press.

Licoppe, C., & Morel, J. (2012). Video-in-interaction: "Talking heads" and the multimodal organization of mobile and Skype video calls. *Research on Language and Social Interaction*, *45*(4), 399–429.

Macbeth, D. (1999). Glances, trances, and their relevance for a visual sociology. In P. Jalbert (Ed.), *Media Studies: Ethnomethodological Approaches* (pp. 135–170). Lanham, MD: University Press of America.

Mondada, L. (2007). Operating together through videoconference: Members' procedures for accomplishing a common space of action. In S. Hester & D. Francis (Eds.), *Orders of Ordinary Action* (pp. 51–67). Aldershot, UK: Ashgate.

Morel, J., & Licoppe, C. (2010). Studying mobile video telephony. In M. Büscher, J. Urry, & K. Witschger (Eds.), *Mobile Methods* (pp. 164–182). London: Routledge.

Nardi, B., Kuchinsky, A., Whittaker, S., Leichner, R., & Schwarz, H. (1996). Video-as-data: Technical and social aspects of a collaborative multimedia application. *Computer Supported Cooperative Work*, *4*(1), 73–100.

O'Hara, K., Black, A., & Lipson, M. (2006). Everyday practices with mobile video telephony. In *Proceedings of CHI 2006* (pp. 871–880). New York: ACM Press.

Relieu, M. (2007). La téléprésence, ou l'autre visiophonie. *Réseaux*, *144*, 183–223.

Reponen, E., Lehikonen, J., & Implö, J. (2009). Mobile video in everyday social interactions. In A. Marcus, A. Roibas, & R. Sala (Eds.), *Mobile TV: Customizing Content and Experience* (pp. 67–80). Berlin: Springer.

Sacks, H. (1992). *Lectures on Conversation*. Cambridge: Cambridge University Press.

Watson, R. (1997). Some general reflections on "categorization" and "sequence" in the analysis of conversation. In S. Hester & P. Eglin (Eds.), *Culture in Action. Studies in Membership Categorization Analysis* (pp. 49–75). Washington, DC: International Institute for Ethnomethodology and Conversation Analysis/ University Press of America.

Whittaker, S. (2003). Things to talk about when talking about things. *Human Computer Interaction, 18*(1), 149–170.

5 The Use of Video in Dental Education

Clinical Reality Addressed as Practical Matters of Production, Interpretation, and Instruction

Oskar Lindwall, Elin Johansson, Hans Rystedt, Jonas Ivarsson (Department of Education, Communication and Learning, University of Gothenburg)
Claes Reit (Department of Odontology, Sahlgrenska University Hospital)

1. INTRODUCTION

Performing a root canal treatment has been described as working within a "black hole" (Castelucci, 2003: 29). Everything within the tooth is tiny, and it is hard to provide light in the inner structures of the teeth. This poses challenges not only to the practising dentist but also to the student of dentistry. For someone watching a root canal treatment from the side, visual access to anatomical structures, pathological features, and embodied procedures is very restricted. Traditionally, it has therefore been hard or impossible to demonstrate what the professional dentist does or sees during an endodontic procedure. With the recent introduction of the operational microscope, however, the conditions for both doing and demonstrating such procedures have changed. The combination of magnification and coaxial illumination makes it possible to see details that were previously out of sight. By connecting a camera to a microscope, it also becomes possible to record and broadcast the visual field of the dentist. The study reported in this chapter explores how this technological configuration is used in an endodontics course. More specifically, it investigates how relations between what the recordings show and what is actually seen and done in the dentist's surgery are addressed as practical matters of production, interpretation, and instruction. In interviews, instructors, as well as students, expressed that the use of video was "great" because it showed "how it really looks like," "what actually happens," and "how it is done in reality" (cf. Rystedt, Reit, Johansson, & Lindwall, 2013). In the actual demonstrations, however, differences between what appears in the recordings and what the dentists really see and do were recurrently raised.

General questions about how media—such as film, video, and television—stand in relation to the events they depict have, of course, been dealt with extensively in the literature. The distinction between appearance and reality, with its strong ties to central philosophical issues, has been one of the main themes in media and film theory from their inception and has encompassed a wide range of positions. Still, for someone who works with video and for whom video constitutes a basis for decisions made and actions taken, general positions and theoretical arguments might not be that relevant. Instead, work-specific considerations on what is seen in the recordings in relation to what is actually there or going on are raised as practical matters embedded in and tied to the business of the setting. Within laparoscopic surgery, for instance, video images of the inside of the patient's abdomen constitute the visual basis on which the surgeons act (Koschmann, Lebaron, Goodwin, & Feltovich, 2011; Mondada, 2003, 2009, Chapter 3 in this volume). During a clinical procedure, it is therefore crucial to be able to distinguish the anatomical details seen in the recordings—whether what appears on the monitor is some loose tissue that should be dissected or it is really something else and dissection therefore would be harmful. The frequent use of closed-circuit television (CCTV) in surveillance and control centres provides another case where video recordings form a basis for professional conduct (Goodwin & Goodwin, 1996; Heath & Luff, 1992, 1996; Heath, Luff, & Sanchez Svensson, 2002); here, classifications of acts and activities shown in the recordings—such as instances of pickpocketing, crowding, and so on—are central for managing events that take place outside the control centres, sometimes even outside the view of the cameras used. In the broadcast of live television talk shows (Broth, 2008, 2009, Chapter 2 in this volume; Mondada, 2009) and sports events (Engström, Juhlin, Perry, & Broth, 2010; Chapter 9 by Perry, Juhlin, & Engström, this volume), the production team must work to show what is going on so that it can be seen, understood, and appreciated by the audience; when a referee signals for a foul in a hockey game, the replay operator has to search for the event leading up to the decision, thereby providing the commentators and the viewers with the visual grounds to see and assess what actually caused the whistle to blow.

In the case reported here, as well as in other instructional settings (e.g., Mondada, 2003), the relation between the recordings and what is recorded takes on yet another significance. Whereas CCTV and live television are produced so that viewers can see and follow the actions and events taking place, the aim of the instructional videos is for students to learn how to classify anatomical and pathological features and ultimately be able to reproduce the demonstrated procedures. To adapt an expression by Mondada (2006: 51), this puts particular demands on how the recordings preserve and configure the phenomenal features of actions and material structures. The students must see not only what procedure is done but also the relevant details of how it is done. To achieve its instructional purpose, the video also needs be complemented with commentaries, descriptions, and explanations. Although the broadcast might show how a procedure is done, the images alone do not say what procedure it is or why it is performed. In addition, technological and practical constraints set limits to what can be shown. The endodontic scene looks different in the dentist's surgery compared to the seminar room, and some events take place outside the camera frame. This chapter aims to explore how relations between video recordings and endodontic scenes are addressed as practical matters of production, interpretation, and instruction; on the one hand, how the video is produced to capture what the dentist does and sees and, on the other, how discrepancies between what is seen on the video and in the dentist's surgery are raised and handled.

2.   THE SETTING OF THE STUDY

The study is based on video recordings of a five-week endodontics course that took place in the sixth semester of a Swedish dental education programme. As in many other medical fields, endodontics is both an academic domain and a clinical practice; it refers to scientific knowledge about the pulp and the tissues surrounding the root canals, as well as the practical work of diagnosing, preventing, and treating diseases and injuries. As noted by the editors of a recent volume on endodontics for students, "there is a massive body of epistemic knowledge within endodontology, for example, on the biology of the pulp, the microorganisms that inhabit root canals" (Reit, Bergenholtz, & Hørsted-Bindslev, 2010: 1). Still, this body of knowledge does not account for everything there is to know about endodontics; to become competent in the field, "observing a good clinical instructor, watching other dentists at work, performing the procedures oneself and reflecting on what has been learned are all important" (ibid.).

Figure 1   An overview of the seminar room and the dentist's surgery.

The organization of the investigated course could be seen as reflecting the dual nature of the field; besides reading textbooks and taking part in lectures, the students were also doing practical laboratory assignments and observing patient demonstrations. This chapter focuses on the patient demonstrations, where groups of students followed a series of live broadcasts of dental treatments that took place in an adjacent room (see Figure 1). For the purpose of these demonstrations, three video cameras had been installed in two of the rooms at the teaching hospital (see Figure 2): one camera was connected to a microscope and could therefore show a magnified view of the inside of a tooth; the second was fastened to the operatory light and was commonly used to record and display a patient's face and mouth; and the third was placed on the wall and thereby gave a broad overview of the dentist's surgery. In the seminar room, a projector displayed the chosen camera view, while another projector displayed X-ray images and other information that were found in the patient's record (see Figure 1). The dentist performing the treatment could switch from one camera to another using a panel on the wall, whereas the seminar leader had control of the view of the other projector through a computer interface. By using a system of headsets, microphones, and speakers, the seminar leader and the dentist who performed the treatment could talk to each other. The voice of the dentist in the surgery was broadcast by a set of speakers in the seminar room, making it possible for the students to follow this communication. Since only one microphone was used in the seminar room—either a headset or a wireless handheld device—the dentist was able to hear only the seminar leader but not the students. Moreover, since the dentist was wearing a headset, the patient and the nurse could hardly be heard in the seminar room and what was said in the seminar room was not audible to them. Throughout the seminar, this setup provided for different interactional organizations and educational formats: the dentist made online commentaries (Heritage & Stivers, 1999) on what she or he was currently doing, seeing, and tactilely sensing; the seminar leader used the video as a starting point for minilectures on certain topics; and the students posed questions to the seminar leader on what was said and shown (Lindwall & Lymer, 2014).

For this study, the course was followed for two consecutive academic years. To capture the interaction in the seminar room, two high-definition cameras were used. One of the cameras recorded the front of the seminar

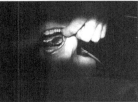

Figure 2   The views of the three cameras. Left: the overview camera; center: the camera fastened to the operatory light; right: the camera connected to the microscope.

room, including the two screens and the seminar leader, whereas the other camera captured the students. Additionally, the video streams from the surgery were captured and stored. For both student years, the space of the seminar room did not allow the whole class to attend the patient demonstrations simultaneously. During the first year, a class of about 25 students was therefore divided into two groups. In the second year, there were almost 40 students, and the class was divided into four groups. Sixteen patient demonstrations were organized for both years, which meant that the students had the possibility to attend eight demonstrations during the first year and four demonstrations in the second one. In an effort to rationalize the organization of the course, only half of the demonstrations in the second academic year were based on live broadcasts; half of the class watched the treatment live, while the other half watched the recordings immediately after the treatment.

3. PRODUCING VIDEO AND INSTRUCTING STUDENTS

The empirical part of the chapter is divided into two parts. The first part addresses issues connected to video production, particularly how switches among different camera views are reflexively related to the procedural organization of the activity. The endodontic treatment unfolds as a number of consecutive steps, where each step has its own specific centre of attention. Switching between cameras thus becomes a way to display changes in the phenomenal field of the practising dentist. Still, what the students see is not identical to what the dentist sees—something that is recurrently turned into a topic of instruction. The second part concerns instances where technological transformations of different sorts are addressed and managed. For instance, there is a significant difference between the optically enhanced stereoscopic view provided by the microscope and the digitally down-sampled, two-dimensional images presented to the students. Relevant events also take place outside the camera views. When instructing the students, it might thus be relevant to distinguish what "really happens" and what things "really look like" from what is shown on the video.

3.1. Showing What Is Seen and Done: The Production of the Instructional Video

In a study of the work of professional film editors, Laurier, Strebel, & Brown argue that "editing is not concerned with recovering what actually happened during any particular event . . . the concerns film editors are orienting to as they assess footage, set edit points and so on are of a *filmic* order rather than an *epistemic* one" (2008: paragraph 9). Even though the operating dentists in the investigated setting are switching camera views and in this sense are involved in some kind of editing, it is clear that the dentists' concerns are different from those described in the quote. The idea is not that the students should enjoy "the pleasures and fascination of film as spectacle" (Cowie, 2011: 3) but that they should see, understand, and learn how to perform root canal treatments. In this respect, the concerns that the dentists are orienting to when producing the video reflect an epistemic order, not a filmic one. The decision to shift from one camera to another is intertwined with the step-by-step nature of the endodontic treatment and the ways in which the continually changing phenomenal field of the dentist makes certain points of view instructionally relevant. As will be demonstrated, however, this does not mean that the edits are perfectly matched with the phases of the activity or that the students see exactly what the dentist sees.

Figure 3 illustrates when and the amount of time that each of the three cameras (cf. Figure 2) is used. Although the uses of the camera in the 22 investigated treatments clearly differ from each other, all cases share some similarities regarding the order of use. A typical demonstration begins by showing an overview of the surgery, thereby providing the students with a view of the whole dentist–patient situation. Displaying a context for what comes next has some parallels to the establishing shot found in many films. Rather than trading on the conventions of film-making, however, the opening shot is contingent on the dentist's initial orientation towards the context of the case. During the first minutes, the dentist talks to the patient about the problems and investigates case files and radiographs. Even though the students are not able to discern the details of what the dentist sees, the overview camera at least lets them get a sense of the dentist's position in the room and his or her general orientation. After interviewing the patient and starting the clinical examination of the tooth, the dentist switches to the camera on the operatory light to display a close-up view of the patient's mouth. Because the instructional and clinical activities are not always perfectly synchronized, the students sometimes miss the initial phases and the

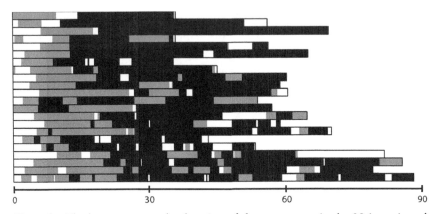

Figure 3   The bars represent the duration of the camera use in the 22 investigated treatments: the white parts represent the overview camera; grey, the camera fastened to the operatory lamp; and black, the microscope camera.

demonstrations starting with this view (this is, for instance, the case in the treatment represented by the uppermost bar in Figure 3). The majority of the remaining work is then filmed with the microscope camera, with various numbers of shorter or longer clips intersected from the other two cameras. During the actual root canal treatment—which includes the preparation of the tooth; the cleaning, shaping, disinfection of the root canal system; and the use of obturation materials—the camera connected to the microscope is used to record a detailed view of the inner structures of the tooth. Although most of the action in this phase takes place within the limited space of the microscope, relevant actions and events also occur outside this view. At times, it might therefore be relevant to switch temporarily to another camera view, for instance, when taking radiographs, preparing the obturation materials, or determining the length of root canals using an apex locator. Most broadcasts are terminated when the treatment reaches its final stages or when it is decided that "nothing more of interest will happen." When the broadcast continues until the patient leaves the room, the last part is usually recorded with the overview camera.

In relation to film and television productions, it is sometimes argued that the best edits are those that the audience does not recognize—the so-called invisible cuts. Whether or not this is true, it is safe to say that the cuts found in the instructional broadcasts are far removed from this ideal. Rather than having a studio crew working behind the scenes (such as in a live TV production; cf. Broth, 2008, 2009) or a technician in a control booth (such as other medical demonstrations; cf. Mondada, 2003), it is the dentist whose actions are being recorded and who also operates the cameras. Each switch takes a couple of seconds to perform because the dentist needs to turn away from the patient and press a button on a panel on the wall. Switching cameras thus creates a small but noticeable disruption in the broadcast of the clinical activity. Given that the dentists are regularly commenting on what they are doing, the camera operation becomes yet another set of actions that their online commentaries address—either through explicit statements (excerpt 1, line 4) or by marking a switch as upcoming or achieved (e.g., the use of "*så*" (12); cf. Andrén, 2012). Moreover, and as illustrated in excerpt 1, any discussions or deliberations concerning the selection of a camera and appropriateness of a given view necessarily become issues to be handled front stage.

(1)   *Microscope camera* [END101021 00:17:50–00:18:32]

```
01 De:    då ska vi se om vi kan bestämma re:nsdjupet
          then we'll see if we can determine the working length
02        mä en sån här foramenlokalisator. då ska vi se om vi
          with this kind of apex locator. then we'll see if we
03        får nåt utslag här då om vi sätter in den (1.7)
          get any response here then if we put it in (1.7)
04        då tar jag ja översikten igen där.
          then I take the overview again there.
05        ((microscope camera -> overview camera))
```

```
06          som ni ser då, sätter ja in den här (0.4)
            as you can see, then I put in this here (0.4)
07          umph (1.1) dä:r (0.7) så: (1.9) åsså ska vi (3.0)
            umph (1.1) there (0.7) like that (1.9) 'n'then we (3.0)
08 SL:      Tom har du lust å å ta via:: op-lampan där
            Tom would you mind to to take it through the op-lamp there
09          istället. bara för å visa [hur man] krokar på den på filen
            instead.  just   to   show  [how you] attach that on the file
10 De:                                 [m:hm    ]
                                        [m:hm    ]
11          ((overview camera -> OL camera)) (0.8)
12 De:      s::å (1.2) och då ska vi se här
            that's it (1.2) 'n'then we'll see here
```

Throughout the dentists' online commentaries, condensed remarks regularly project what they are going to do and show. In excerpt 1, the overall project of determining the working length with an apex locator is introduced and then further specified in terms of the practical actions involved (lines 1–3). Both the overall characterization and the specification are prefaced with "*då ska vi se*"/"then we'll see." On the one hand, this marks the actions to come as a next step, and on the other hand, it makes it relevant for the students to look for what "we'll see." Perhaps realizing that his use of the apex locator takes place outside the view of the microscope, making it impossible for the students to see, the dentist switches to the overview camera before he continues with the procedure. Even though his actions are now inside the camera's frame and despite his "as you can see" (6), the view from the selected camera does not allow the students to visually discriminate the details of what the dentist's indexical "this," "here," "there," and "like that" (6–7) actually refer to (cf. Figure 2). If the demonstration aims not only to let the students get a general sense of clinical procedures but also to allow access to the reproducible details of these procedures, the broadcast view is not sufficient. In contrast to the students, the seminar leader—being a competent dentist herself—does not have any problems following what the dentist is doing; for her, knowing that the dentist uses an apex locator is enough to know the practical steps involved. Since she is looking at the same broadcasts as the students, it is therefore possible for her to monitor the instructional relevance of the recordings and direct the dentist if she thinks there is a better view.

As shown in Figure 3, the number of switches between cameras varies a lot among the cases: although there are only three in the treatment represented by the uppermost bar, there are 25 changes in the treatment represented at the bottom of the figure. Generally, and as exemplified by excerpt 1, one of the three views might be considered better than the others to show a certain step or procedure. It therefore makes sense to stay with that view until a new step or procedure makes another view relevant. Because switching cameras takes some time, the dentist also has to decide whether it is worth leaving one view just to show something quickly from another view. There are also other ways in which the camera edits are tied to and limited by the clinical activity. The amount of camera use is outlined in Figure 3. The two bars at the top of the figure represent the less frequent surgical treatment of an inflammatory lesion around the apex of the tooth (periapical periodontitis). In contrast to conventional orthograde root canal therapy, surgical treatments require aseptic techniques. The dentist and the nurse therefore need to set up a sterile field before the treatment begins. In these two cases, the dentist chooses to show how setting up a sterile field is done by switching to the overview camera after completing the examination (represented by the relatively long white sections after the initial grey in the two uppermost bars in Figure 3). Another result of the aseptic techniques is the continuous use of a single camera during the actual treatment. As pointed out in excerpt 2, switching between cameras without taking extra measures might contaminate the sterile field.

(2)   *Overview camera* [END101028 00:15:40–00:16:01]

```
01 De:   nu blir de ju så att de blir (.) lite svårt att växla
         now it will (ju) be (.) a bit hard to switch
02       mellan dom dom olika kamerorna där, så att ja gör så
         between the different cameras there, so I do it so
03       att jag (0.5) tar å kopplar in mikrosko:pet.
         that I (0.5) connect the microscope.
04       (0.6)
05 SL:   okey¿
         okay¿
06 De:   å så kommer ni:: å::, a du vet problemet där va mä:
         'n'then you will and::, yeah you know the problem there
07       å: (.) trycka på (.) väggen¿
         with (.) pushing on (.) the wall¿
08       (0.7)
09 SL:   vi vi skulle ju kunna:: tejpa upp en steril liten
         we- we would (ju) be able to tape a small sterile
10       plastpåse   [över (.) om ja    ]
         plastic bag [over (.) if I     ]
11 De:               [>ja men jag tror  ] att annars< vi
                     [>yea but I believe] that we otherwise< we
12       kommer att se det mesta i mikroskopet där.
         are going to see most of it in the microscope there.
13 SL:   okey¿
         okay¿
```

Primarily addressing the seminar leader, the dentist explains the rationale for the upcoming and sustained use of the microscope camera (lines 1–3 and 6–7). On the one hand, this rationale marks the decision as something less than ideal, which the dentist is or could be held accountable for. On the other hand, through the inclusion of the epistemic particle *"ju"* (1; cf. Heinemann, Steensig, & Lindström, 2011) and the nonidiomatic use of *"du vet"*/"you know" (6), the dentist's comment implies that the seminar leader already understands or perhaps should understand the reason for the dentist's decision. Without questioning the need for a sterile environment, the seminar leader does not agree with the implications proposed by the dentist. As she points out, it is possible to set up the sterile field so that switching cameras would not contaminate it (9–10). The dentist, who does not comply with the seminar leader's suggestion, provides a new account for staying with just one camera: that they "are going to see most of it in the microscope." In the end, it is the dentist who operates the cameras and conducts the surgical procedure. As a practical matter of ongoing workplace performance, it is he who must balance the requirements of the demonstration with those of the patient's treatment. The account also indicates the special status of the view from the microscope. Of the three camera views, it is the only one that is able to capture anatomical and pathological details and the procedures taking place inside the tooth. Still, as illustrated by excerpt 3, it is not just what the camera shows that is important; the chosen point of view might also say something about the dentist's orientation and the procedures involved.

(3)   *Operating light camera* [END101011#1 00:17:50–00:18:32]

```
01 De:   ska ja byta litegrann till mikroskopet så att ni ser lite
         shall I switch a bit to the microscope so you'll see some
02       (1.0) ((OL-camera -> microscope-camera)) (0.4)
03 SL    .h då har vi en knapp på sidan så nu väljer han att
         .h then we have a button on the side so now he chooses to
04       visa via mikroskopet istället då va så så växlar vi (.)
         show via the microscope instead then so so we switch (.)
05       på väggen där (8.3) så blir de ju lite speciellt också
         on the wall there (8.3) so it becomes a little peculiar
06       när man e:hm (.) när man arbetar såhär för
         also when one e:hm (.) when one works like this because
07       nu få- vill man ju göra så mycke som möjligt i mikroskop
         now ge- one wants to do as much as possible in microscope
08       även sånt som vi kanske normalt sett inte gör i mikroskop,
         even things we perhaps normally do not do in microscope,
09       för då vet man att ni ser bättre härinn:e
         because then one knows that you can see better in: here
10       (.) så ibland kan de bli lite bakvänt öh då då
         (.) so sometimes it can be a bit upside down uh then
11       (1.9) för just ta bort täckförbandet de gö- de gör
         (1.9) because just removing the temporary sealing we do-
12       vi inte under mikroskop utan de gör vi ju (.) genom att
         we do not do under microscope but we do that you know (.)
13       bara (.) vanliga ögon eller luppar så
         by simply (.) plain eyes or loupes like that
```

In contrast to the fly-on-the-wall or "zero focalization" (Genette, 1988) perspective of the overview camera, broadcasting from the camera attached to the microscope strongly suggests that actions and events are seen from the same point of view as that of the dentist. Although the overview camera broadcasts the dentist's bodily orientation, the camera connected to the microscope rather presents the whole scene as an "oriented," "lived," and "bodily space" (Merleau-Ponty, 1962: Ch. 3). However, as the seminar leader points out in excerpt 3, that the "dentist chooses to show via the microscope" does not necessarily mean that the demonstrated procedure is one for which the microscope is being or should be used. Neither does it mean that the dentist himself is looking through the microscope. In this case, it is most likely that the dentist uses only "plain eyes" (13) because that is how dentists normally do it and the broadcast image of the relevant tooth is almost outside the frame. Besides accounting for the less than perfect technical quality of the image, the seminar leader thereby points out that procedures and the way they appear on the screen are affected by how the recordings are produced. Despite the illusion of sharing a perspective, what the dentist sees and what is shown in the seminar room are not the same.

3.2. Seeing What Is There to Be Seen: The Instructional Analysis of the Video

The video is a necessary but not sufficient or self-explicatory constituent of the seminar as a whole. For the students to find and comprehend the significant details, additional instructional and interpretational work is needed. The commentaries of the dentist and the seminar leader are thus crucial in providing the video with a narrative and disciplinary sense. Without these commentaries, it would in many cases be hard or impossible for students to recognize and localize the relevant anatomical structures, pathological features, or more unspecific visual features. The commentaries are also central if the students are to see formal procedures in the details of the particular and concrete. Despite having visual access to the dentist's actions and having read about the procedure that the dentist performs, the students often need help to see the procedure in and as the dentist's actions (cf. Lindwall & Lymer, 2014). Also, critical issues are tied to the differences between what is seen on the screen and what is going on in the surgery. As demonstrated in the previous section, the camera view does not portray all the relevant actions. One thing that the seminar leader can do is to introduce what is "specifically missing" (Livingston, 2000: 252) in the video—things that are done and relevant to the unfolding procedures but that did not appear on the screen and that therefore risk being overlooked by the students.

(4) *Microscope camera* [END100316 00:26:45–00:27:08]

```
01 SL:   å de som har hänt, som vi kanske inte fick se här nu de e
         and what happened, what we maybe did not get to see here
02       ju att nu har dom ju bytt (.) från a-brickan
         now is that now they have (ju) changed (.) from the a-tray
03       (0.7) då (1.2) till: b-brickan (0.8) de koppla dom nog
         (0.7) there (1.2) to: the b-tray (0.8) they probably never
04       aldrig om när dom gjorde. för att nu e de ju bara
         switched there when they did. cause now it is (ju) only
05       sterila instrument som e: nere (.) å de kan man
         sterile instruments that's down there (.) and that you
06       framförallt se på sugen som sköterskan har, för
         can primarily see on the suction that the nurse has, cause
```

```
07        när hon (.) går på: arbetsfältet me: den här vita
          when she (.) goes into the work space with: that white
08        sugen som e steril (.) då vet vi att då-
          suction that is sterile (.) then we know that then- then
09        e (0.7) allt sånt bytt (1.7) de e ju svårare för oss
          are (0.7) all such things changed (0.7) it is harder for
10        oss här å följa me när man e på rummet själv
          us here to follow than when one is in the room
```

Heath, Luff, and Sanchez Svensson have investigated how supervisors at the London Underground "are able to use the CCTV equipment to discover problems and events which are occurring beyond the scope of the camera" (2002: 186)—how they "rely on what they can see to interpret what is happening in the world beyond" (ibid.) Similarly, the seminar leader in excerpt 4 tells the students "what happened" and what they "did not get to see" and then explains the visual basis for her knowing that. Before the episode, the seminar leader has been talking with her back turned towards the screen for a while, and now she expresses uncertainty whether the dentist has switched the camera to show this event or not ("*kanske,*" "maybe," line 1; "*nog,*" "probably," 3). In contrast, there is no doubt when it comes to the events taking place outside the camera; her description is not presented as a guess or a personal interpretation but as something that any competent member could deduce from what is currently shown (4–9). At this stage, the procedures require the dentist to change from the instruments on the a-tray to the sterile instruments on the b-tray. Her concluding comment, "it is harder for us here to follow than when one is in the room"—even though she talks in terms of a first-person plural and a generic "*man*"/"one"—actually works to acknowledge the difficulties that the students encounter rather than any problems on her behalf. Even though the teacher and the students are in a similar physical position, thereby making up an "us here" (9–10) in contrast to any real or hypothetical person "in the room" (10), what they see in the recordings differs extensively (cf. Goodwin, 1994). In this respect, the instructor might have more trouble seeing what the students see and do not see than following what the dentist sees and does.

Several things can be noted from looking at the video-recorded image in Figure 4. At this point in the treatment, the dentist uses a retractor to push the lip up so that he can prepare for the upcoming retrograde root canal treatment. The view of the patient is upside down, displaying the tip of his nose at the bottom left of the image, and the dentist is standing on the right side of the patient with the nurse on the left. From the seminar leader's viewpoint, these issues are not problematic. Up to this point, nothing has indicated that anyone else other than the dentist is holding the retractor or that the dentist and the nurse have switched positions. Moreover, given the procedure that the dentist is about to perform, the reasons for his use of the retractor are evident. Nonetheless, the image in itself does not show how the hook is held, nor are the motives or reasons accessible to everyone.

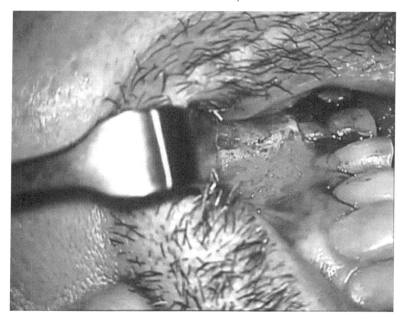

Figure 4   The dentist holding the patient's upper lip with a retractor.

(5)   *Microscope camera* [END100329 00:23:23–00:23:43]

```
01 S1:   håller han hela tiden i den dära (.) spaken?
         is he holding all the time that (.) lever?
02       (1.2)
03 SL:   ja de: e ju så:rhaken      [där  ]
         yes that is (ju) the retractor [there]
04 S1:                                 [ja   ]
                                       [yes  ]
05 SL    =öh för å hålla undan kinden ja för annars ser han
         =uh to keep away the cheek yeah because otherwise he sees
06       in[te läppen går ju                     ]
         no[thing the lip is                     ]
07 S1:     [ja (.) men den håller han i          ]
           [yes (.) but that one he is holding]
08 SL:   han håller i [den ] ja precis själv=
         he is holding [that] yes precisely by himself=
09 S1:                 [ja  ]                    =mhm
                       [yes]                     =mhm
10 SL:   så man ä som en enarmad bandit [ja ] précis ((skrattar))
         so one is like a slot machine  [yes] exactly ((laughter))
11 S1:                                   [ja ]
                                         [yes]
12 SL    ibland kan man naturligtvis be sköterskan om man känner
         sometimes one can of course ask the nurse if one feels
13       att man behöver båda händerna [men] oftast har man mer
         that one needs both hands     [but] usually one has more
14 S1:                                 [mhm]
15 SL:   kontroll själv om man kan hålla undan
         control by oneself if one can keep away
```

Although the yes/no interrogative of the student receives an affirmative answer, the embedded correction (Jefferson, 1987), together with the following expansion, leaves open whether the dentist's reply actually addresses the issue asked. For the seminar leader, it is perhaps not clear what the student means by "holding all the time," and calling the retractor a "lever" also makes further instruction on the instrument's function relevant. Besides the seminar leader's "yes" (line 3) in turn-initial position, nothing in her answer confirms that the dentist is actually holding the retractor, only that it is used for him to see. Overlapping the teacher's utterance, the student's yes/no declarative question indicates that she is not fully satisfied with the instructor's response; an answer to her question has been implied, but it needs confirmation (cf. Raymond, 2010). After having provided an explicit verification (8) and having made some sort of joke, the instructor moves from the concrete situation and talks about the procedure in general terms—what one could do and why holding the retractor oneself is usually a good thing to do. Similar to the previous episode (excerpt 4), talking about how things are done in this case gives the students interpretative resources to see and follow what is not really shown; more importantly, however, it provides the students with resources to see the video in terms of the professional procedures that the seminar aims to demonstrate. As has been repeatedly argued, the video is the central instructional resource in the seminar but at the same time does not perfectly show things as they are done or seen by the dentist. Not everything is recorded, and as the seminar leader points out in excerpt 6, what is recorded looks different from the view of the dentist in the surgery.

(6) *Microscope camera* [END100316 00:36:44–36.55x]

```
01 SL:  de e ju lite annorlunda när man tittar för att (0.5) när
        it's a bit different when one looks 'cause (0.5) when
02      vi tittar ner i mikrosko:pet inne på: rummen, så e de ju
        we look down in the microscope in the: rooms, it is
03      faktiskt en två: eller vi ser ju i stereo (0.7) så man får
        really a two: or we see (ju) in stereo (0.7) so one gets
04      en mycket större djupkänsla när man tittar ner, här
        a much better feeling of depth when one looks down, here
05      blir ju bilden lite platt. (0.8) men ja kan lova att
        the image is (ju) a bit flat. (0.8) but I can promise
06      att han e väldigt långt ne:r å jobbar i den här kanalen nu
        that he's working very deep down in this canal right now
```

On the one hand, the seminar leader in excerpt 6 is instructing the students on how they should understand this particular treatment and its associated images: that she can "promise" that the dentist is very deep down, working in the canal even though this might be hard to see from the images alone (lines 5–6). On the other hand, she is raising general concerns about the difference between what they see and what anyone using the microscope would see: that the image in the microscope is stereoscopic, has a feeling of depth, and thereby is not as flat as the image shown on the screen (1–5).

The distinction between two and three dimensions is just one of several differences between what the dentist sees under the microscope and what is shown in the seminar room. The quality of the projected image is dependent on the resolution of the video stream sent to the projector—which in this case is 720×576 pixels or the same as a European DVD—whereas what is seen under the microscope is not digitized, and the resolution is therefore affected only by the optics. There are also a number of transformations of the image on its way from the dentist's surgery to the seminar room. Besides the optical quality of the camera lens, the chosen depth of field, focal length, and exposure all affect how the image is recorded and displayed. Because cameras have problems handling situations where the distribution of light is strongly unbalanced, for instance, the camera placed on the operatory lamp produces images having the most illuminated parts overexposed, while everything else is heavily underexposed (cf. Figure 2). Further transformations are results of the digitalization, distribution, and projection of the recording. In addition to differences in size, resolution, and the loss of the third dimension, these transformations have impacts on the hue, luminance, and saturation of the image. These results, in turn, might influence the ability to see and differentiate anatomical, pathological, and other significant visual details.

(7)   *Microscope camera* [END101028_2 00:35:23–00:35:53]

```
01 S1:   va ä dom skruvpiggarna som sticker ut mellan tänderna (.)
         what are those screws sticking out between the teeth (.)
02       där?
         there?
03       (1.0)
04       ä de metall som sticker ut?
         is that metal sticking out?
05       (1.1)
06 SL:   nu vet ja inte riktigt va du [menar   ]
         now I am not sure what you    [mean    ]
07 S1:                                 [från    ] två-tvåan
                                       [from the] twenty two
08       asså (.) apro- aproximalt där
         like (.) prox - proximal there
09       (0.9) ((the seminar leader walks to the screen
         and points to an area on the projection))
10       där menar du eller?
         there you mean or?
11 S1:   a dom
         yeah those
12 SL:   a de tror jag   [bara ä:: blänk i ] i (.) i
         yeah that I think [is:: just glare in] in (.)
13 S2:                   [blod (.) blod     ]
                         [blood (.) blood   ]
14 SL:   vätskan där
         in the liquid there
15       (0.4)
16 S1:   för de   [på den    ] e:h (1.3) a-ah
         since that [on it    ] e:h (1.3) a-ah
```

```
17 SL:                [som blir ]
                      [that gets]
18        hja (0.6) de blä- de ä blänk (0.7) vae- vätskeblänk
          yeah (0.6) it gla- it is glare (0.7) wa- liquid glare
19        som blir (.) i en effekt i bilden (.)
          that gets (.) in an effect on the image (.) with the
20        mä blodet (.) lampan (.) som lyser i (.) vätskan
          blood (.) the light (.) that shines in (.) the liquid
```

Not receiving any immediate answer, the student's initial "what are those screws sticking out" is rephrased to "is that metal sticking out?"; the things that were seen as some curious screws are thereby reduced to some unspecified metal. Despite this revision, the objects referred to might still pose a problem to the instructor because there are no screws or metal sticking out between the patient's teeth. Instead of further characterizing the unknown thing being seen, the student begins to locate its position, using anatomical and numerical terms for the locations of known objects as reference points. When the two parties come to an agreement on where to look, it is notable that what is a "there" for the instructor is still a "those" for the student (10–11). The instructor then starts to explain what is seen and how it comes to be seen as such. As a collection of pixels, shining metal and glaring liquid might look identical. However, with the seminar leader's experience, it is in many cases apparent whether the glare should be interpreted as metal or liquid. In some cases, the distinction between the two is central, for instance, when the dentist attempts to remove broken instruments inside the root canal. Nonetheless, in the case of excerpt 7, the dentist might not even notice the liquid; it is not relevant to the procedure in any way, and what is seen can therefore be discarded as "just glare" or "an effect."

4. CONCLUSION

The aim and interest of this chapter have partly been motivated by a series of interviews conducted in relation to the investigated course. In these interviews, students repeatedly compared the demonstrations with more traditional formats such as textbooks and lectures. In contrast to their experiences of the latter, the video recordings were said to show how endodontic procedures "looked like in reality." In the words of one of the students, "you have now seen someone doing it, and really for real, and it almost feels like I have done it myself." Following this, one might argue that the video or, more generally, moving images have some clear advantages over other media when it comes to the depiction of actions and events. As argued by Cowie, "Film—as images and sounds in time and space—is mimetic, like photography from which it derives; but it is also, like drama, mimetic in its showing of performed actions and events in time and space" (2011: 29). The video introduces temporality in a way that textbooks and lectures cannot.

For instance, it is hard to get a sense of the tempo, duration, and movement involved in the competent preparation of a tooth if the technique is represented only by text and still images. In the video demonstrations, the students can see how fast, for how long, and in which way the dentist's fingers move when preparing the tooth.

Notably, however, it was not just actions, techniques, and procedures that came across as "more real" in the interview accounts. Several students also mentioned the difference between looking at anatomical and pathological features in textbooks and watching these features as part of the video demonstrations: "[O]ne has seen images of it [spongy bones] many times, but it does not look the same when one sees it in reality" (Rystedt, Reit, Johansson, & Lindwall, 2013). Thus, even in this case, when a high-resolution printed image arguably would do a better job in depicting the anatomy than the low-resolution video footage, the student contrasts the images that she has previously seen with how the spongy bones look "in reality." The distinction here should not be reduced to one of different media. As part of the recorded demonstration, anatomical structures, tools, and techniques all feature as relevant parts of the unfolding treatment; they constitute the endodontic scene, and their sense derives from their place and function in the treatment. The apex locator referred to in excerpt 1, for instance, is not just described or shown for instructional purposes but is introduced and used at a time when it is relevant to determine the working length of the root canal. The equipment is, as it were, being ready to hand.

The aim of this chapter has been to explore how dentists, instructors, and students approach and deal with the mediated nature of the recordings—how relations between what is shown in the recordings and what is seen and done in the dentist's surgery are addressed as practical matters of production, interpretation, and instruction. Even though students and instructors in interviews said that the video recordings "show how it really looks like," the relation between what is seen in the recordings and what the dentists actually see and do were recurrently addressed in the seminar room. Like any recording, the broadcast of endodontic procedures provides a particular view of the event in terms of perspective, framing, depth of field, focus, contrast, colours, and other aspects (cf. excerpts 6 and 7). Additionally, the coordination of the endodontic treatment and the camera operation necessarily involves some compromises: the number of edits in each demonstration was relatively restricted, and the camera that was used did not always provide the best view of the scene (excerpts 1, 2, and 4). Nevertheless, a change from one camera to another was regularly tied to the steps and procedures of the unfolding treatment and the associated orientations of the dentist.

Because the three cameras used in the demonstrations recorded each scene from different positions and with varying focal lengths—from what could be considered a long shot to an extreme close-up shot—the selection of camera view is crucial in the way the treatment is portrayed and understood. The camera fastened to the wall gives an overview of the whole scene, including all the participants and their relative positions and orientations. This view makes it possible to discern whether the dentist is looking at X-rays, preparing instruments, or perhaps has temporarily left the room—activities that the other two cameras are unable to capture. However, although this view is appropriate for displaying what the dentists do, it does not show how things are done; most importantly, it fails to provide enough detail to follow the actual endodontic procedures. It is therefore mainly used at times when the dentist is working outside the patient's mouth. The strengths and limitations of the extreme close-ups produced by the microscope camera have the opposite effect. This camera provides a lot of detail, but the field of view is very restricted, which could make it difficult to follow the relevant actions. When this camera is selected, a lot of potentially relevant things take place outside the frame of the shot. It does not show the actual switch from one tray to another (excerpt 4), and because it shows only the fingers of the dentist and the dental nurse, it might be hard to discern who is doing what (excerpt 5). Despite this, one might still claim that it is not until these close-ups that the field of endodontics enters the scene. In contrast to those of the other cameras, this view enables the students to see the root canals and the tissues surrounding them, as well as how fingers and tools are working inside the tooth.

Of course, it is not just the technology that sets limits to what the students are able to observe. To see anatomical structures in the patient's mouth or formal procedures in and as the embodied actions of the dentist, a certain level of competence is required. Despite their different physical positions, the dentist and the seminar leader can "expect each other to be able to see and categorize the world in ways that are relevant to the work, tools, and artefacts that constitute their profession" (Goodwin, 1994: 615). Although the instructor and the students in one sense have the same visual access to dentist's surgery, they are asymmetrically positioned with regard to endodontic competence. From the seminar leader's position, it is possible to monitor, assess, and instruct the camera use of the dentist as well as the perception of the students. When the broadcast is showing something that is not instructionally useful, she can ask the dentist to move the camera or switch to another (excerpts 1 and 2); alternatively, she can account for the differences between what the students and the dentist see (excerpts 3 and 6). Moreover, similar to the function of the CCTV supervisors in surveillance and control centres, the instructor can use what she sees to comment on what is happening outside the frame of a particular shot (excerpt 4). The seminar leader continually comments on what the dentist sees, does, thinks, knows, and so on, thereby treating the dentist's actions as predictable in relation to generalized and more or less scripted procedures; in this way, the instructor's comments work to connect the particulars of the broadcast with a more conceptual and procedural understanding of endodontics. By producing a witnessing account of the affairs found on the screen for the benefit of the students, practical and professional achievements are rendered as instructions in and through the epistemic orders of endodontics.

Acknowledgement

This work was supported by the Swedish Research Council (Nr: 2010–5225) and conducted within the University of Gothenburg Learning and Media Technology Studio (LETStudio). The project is approved by the Regional Ethical Review Board, and informed consent has been collected from all participants involved in the study. We thank the students and instructors who took part in the study, as well as this volume's editors and two anonymous reviewers for their comments on an earlier draft.

REFERENCES

Andrén, M. (2012). The social world within reach: Intersubjective manifestations of action completion. *Cognitive Semiotics*, 7, 1–36.

Broth, M. (2008). The studio interaction as a contextual resource for TV-production. *Journal of Pragmatics*, 40, 904–926.

Broth, M. (2009). Seeing through screens, hearing through speakers: Managing distant studio space in television control room interaction. *Journal of Pragmatics*, 41, 1998–2016.

Broth, M. (this volume). Pans, tilts, and Zooms: Conventional camera gestures in TV production.

Castellucci, A. (2003). Magnification in endodontics: The use of the operating microscope. *Practical Procedures & Aesthetic Dentistry*, 15(5), 377–384.

Cowie, E. (2011). *Recording Reality, Desiring the Real*. Minneapolis: Minnesota University Press.

Engström, A., Juhlin, O., Perry, M., & Broth, M. (2010). Temporal hybridity: Mixing live video footage with instant replay in real time. In *Proceedings of ACM CHI 2010*. (Atlanta, Georgia), (pp. 1495–1504). New York: ACM.

Genette, G. (1988). *Narrative Discourse Revisited*. Ithaca, NY: Cornell University Press.

Goodwin, C. (1994). Professional vision. *American Anthropologist*, 96, 606–633.

Goodwin, C., & Goodwin, M.H. (1996). Seeing as a situated activity: Formulating planes. In Y. Engeström & D. Middleton (Eds.), *Cognition and Communication at Work* (pp. 61–95). Cambridge: Cambridge University Press.

Heath, C., & Luff, P. (1992). Collaboration and control: Crisis management and multimedia in London Underground line control rooms. *Computer Supported Collaborative Work (CSCW)*, 1(1–2), 69–94.

Heath, C., & Luff, P. (1996). Convergent activities: Line control and passenger information on the London Underground. In Y. Engeström & D. Middleton (Eds.), *Cognition and Communication at Work* (pp. 96–129). Cambridge: Cambridge University Press.

Heath, C., Luff, P., & Sanchez Svensson, M. (2002). Overseeing organizations: Configuring action and its environment. *British Journal of Sociology*, 53(2), 181–201.

Heinemann, T., Lindström, A., & Steensig, J. (2011). Addressing epistemic incongruency in question–answer sequences through the use of epistemic adverbs. In T. Stivers, L. Mondada, & J. Steensig (Eds.), *The Morality of Knowledge in Conversation* (pp. 107–130). Cambridge: Cambridge University Press.

Heritage, J., & Stivers, T. (1999). Online commentary in acute medical visits: A method of shaping patient expectations. *Social Science & Medicine, 49*(11), 1501–1517.

Jefferson, G. (1987). On exposed and embedded correction in conversation. In G. Button & J.R.E. Lee (Eds.), *Talk and Social Organisation* (pp. 86–100). Clevedon, UK: Multilingual Matters.

Koschmann, T., LeBaron, C., Goodwin, C., & Feltovich, P. (2011). "Can you see the cystic artery yet?" A simple matter of trust. *Journal of Pragmatics, 43*(2), 521–541.

Laurier, E., Strebel, I., & Brown, B. (2008). Video analysis: Lessons from professional video editing practice. *Forum: Qualitative Social Research 9.* www.qualitative-research.net/index.php/fqs/article/view/1168/2579

Lindwall, O., & Lymer, G. (2014). Inquiries of the body: Novice questions and the instructable observability of endodontic scenes. *Discourse Studies, 16*(2), 266–289.

Livingston, E. (2000). The availability of mathematics as an inspectable domain of practice through the use of origami. In S. Hester & D. Francis (Eds.), *Local Educational Order: Ethnomethodological Studies of Knowledge in Action* (pp. 245–270). Amsterdam: John Benjamins.

Merleau-Ponty, M. (1962). *Phenomenology of Perception.* London: Routledge.

Mondada, L. (2003). Working with video: How surgeons produce video records of their actions. *Visual studies, 18*(1), 58–73.

Mondada, L. (2006). Video recording as the reflexive preservation and configuration of phenomenal features for analysis. In H. Knoblauch, J. Raab, H.G. Soeffner, & B. Schnettler (Eds.), *Video Analysis: Methodology and Methods* (pp. 51–67). Oxford: Peter Lang.

Mondada, L. (2009). Video recording practices and the reflexive constitution of the interactional order: Some systematic uses of the split-screen technique. *Human Studies, 32,* 67–99.

Mondada, L. (this volume). The surgeon as a camera director: Manoeuvring video in the operating theatre.

Perry, M., Juhlin, O., & Engström, A. (this volume). Dealing with time, just in time: Sense-making and clip allocation in multi-person, multi-stream, live replay TV production.

Raymond, G. (2010). Grammar and social relations: Alternative forms of yes/no initiating actions in health visitor interactions. In A.F. Freed & S. Ehrlich (Eds.), *"Why Do You Ask?": The Function of Questions in Institutional Discourse* (pp. 87–107). Oxford: Oxford University Press.

Reit, C., Bergenholtz, G., & Hørsted-Bindslev, P. (2010). Introduction to endodontology. In G. Bergenholtz, P. Hørsted-Bindslev, & C. Reit (Eds.), *Textbook of Endodontology* (2nd ed.). (pp. 1–7). Western Sussex, UK: Wiley-Blackwell.

Rystedt, H., Reit, C., Johansson, E., & Lindwall, O. (2013). Seeing through the dentist's eyes: Video-based clinical demonstrations in preclinical training. *Journal of Dental Education, 77*(12), 1629–1638.

6 Cameras in Video Games

Comparing Play in *Counter-Strike* and *Doctor Who Adventures*

Eric Laurier (University of Edinburgh)
Stuart Reeves (University of Nottingham)

1. INTRODUCTION

Three-dimensional video games remain a rapidly evolving new medium, bringing together gameplay, narrative, architecture, computing, and cinema. Correspondingly, for a number of existing schools of inquiry, they raise absorbing questions about game theory, storytelling, space, human–computer interaction, and the moving image. In the space of this chapter, our ambitions are necessarily modest; we wish to concentrate on only one of the devices that arises out of the trading between cinema, television, and gameplay that is nevertheless at the heart of the video-ness of video games: the camera. How we play video games is dependent on and generated by the uses of the camera: a game-camera is modelled upon the optical set-ups of mechanical and digital cameras and yet, as we shall see, is distinct from them. For instance, the game-camera is an invisible point without virtual representation. Game-cameras are central to playing 3D video games because they present a mediated view into, and a perspective upon, the "visibility arrangements" of the game (Watson, 1997). They are at the core of analysing, at any moment, what has just happened, what is currently happening in the game, and what might happen next. The interplay between using the game-camera and the visibility arrangements of the game produce not just the experience of 3D spaces but the very play of the game.

Accordingly, the present chapter explores the relationship between game-playing and the carefully crafted movements of visual perspective that players employ in and through the 3D environments that are characteristic of modern video games. Much of the methodical "work" of play engaged in by players involves rendering complex game spaces intelligible through scrutiny of the virtual environment (VE) and linking together sequences of achieved perspectives. We say "achieved" because even the so-called first-person perspectives that are provided by the movement of the camera are not isomorphic with the glances that may be made by the naked eye. Instead, for both first- and third-person perspectives, visual awareness is achieved by looking with and through camera lenses (Macbeth, 1999; Mondada, 2003). Thus, competence in the manipulation of video perspectives becomes an essential acquisition for players as they seek to engage with the game itself and/or with other players. Through instructive comparisons with other settings in which cameras are used to "look around" and render the scene intelligible (e.g. surveillance [Luff et al., 2000] or endoscopic medicine [Mondada, 2003]), the findings of this chapter will help inform a wider understanding of the manner in which environments are made sense of through video technologies.

1.1.   First Person and Third Person

Our analysis is based upon a set of vignettes drawn from a small corpus of video recordings of a first-person shooter (FPS) that, as the name implies, has a first-person perspective and an interactive, narrative game that, by contrast, involves third-person perspectives. A characteristic feature of first-person games is that players experience the 3D environment through the eyes of an avatar (i.e. a virtual embodiment). By virtue of this feature, to move the character is usually to move the camera, and, of game relevance, to move the camera is to move the person. However, within the games, it is sometimes the case that lenses can be attached (e.g. sniper sights, binoculars) to allow zooming in and out. Third-person games show a view from behind (and usually above) the character. The player's avatar and the avatar's relationship to the course of play within the game are made visible via the game-camera, which has an indirect coupling to avatar movements. Thus, for third-person games, the view in and around the game's environment can typically be manipulated by the player to inspect the scene without actually moving the position of the player's avatar within the environment. Because it is coupled to the avatar, the camera cannot move around the game independently of moving the avatar.

1.2.   Cameras-in-Interaction

Early work in praxeological studies of the film camera by Macbeth (1999) made clear the differences between looking with human eyes and looking with a (mechanical) camera. When a camera moves quickly from a first perspective to a second perspective, it both creates a blur and also struggles to find the second perspective. As Macbeth (1999) noted, the quick glance that members of society make from one thing to a second thing and back again, without missing that second thing, are almost impossible with a camera. Glancing is a routine technique for how sighted members of society remain aware of settings and activities within those settings. In all manner of settings, members organize their actions for their glance-availability and make available their monitoring of those settings through the visibility of their glancing (Sudnow, 1972). Glancing's absence from camera operation is specifically significant because managing the visibility of actions of one's own avatar, other players, opponents, or obstacles is central to the skills of playing video games (Reeves, Brown, & Laurier, 2009).

   Macbeth's early work on camera movement has been taken up in other settings where cameras are used (Licoppe & Morel, 2012; Chapter 5 by Lindwall, Johansson, Rystedt, Ivarsson, and Reit, this volume; Chapters 1 and 3 by Mondada, this volume). In endoscopic surgery (Mondada, 2003), surgeons direct camera operators both to perform the surgery but also to show students what they are doing. As part of this role, the surgeon makes explicit and tacit requests to the camera operator. The requests precede the next appropriate actions, so that, when the camera is moved, it then provides the visibility of the thing that the surgeon wishes to work on and/or show to the audience of students. The availability of the image is then an ongoing concern of the surgeon as it is, of course, for video game players. The camera operators themselves track the course of action of the surgeon, and their skills are apprehended in how they will routinely provide the appropriate adjustment of the camera without the need for a request by the surgeon. Although these paired tasks in surgery might seem tangential to gameplay, as we will see later in the chapter, having two people (or more) involved in a game raises similar issues around coordinated action.

   Taking up Mondada's approach, Broth (2004, 2009) explored how multiple camera operators in a live broadcast offer up shots to their editing team. Rather than doing this verbally, camera operators make visible their offers by rapidly panning or zooming the camera and then stabilizing a shot of a speaker. The brisk movements of the camera, in the context of the production room setting, become see-able as actions such as "the operator searching for a shot" In the course of such a search, when the camera settles and has a face in focus in its middle, then at that point this person is being offered for the editor to select for broadcast. What both Mondada and Broth's studies bring to the fore is how the movement, framing, zooming, and focus of the camera make actions visually available to the parties (e.g., as responses, proposals, searches). Framing and zooming perform similar work in the operation of cameras in games.

   Finally, of most obvious relevance to our chapter is Keating and Sunakawa's (2010) work on what they call "machine gaze" (rather than cameras). Expanding upon our brief earlier remark about glancing in video games, they suggest:

> The screen is necessarily a focus of gaze during game play, and the software has powerful gaze-shifting properties. Without moving their heads, eyes, or bodies, players can invoke—not only through symbols of speech but through the machine software—new gaze or sight parameters. They can rapidly switch between a first-person perspective and a third-person perspective, managing the actions of the self in relation to others in multiple ways. Gamers thus have individual and enhanced human-eye points of view on participation space to communicate and coordinate. (Keating & Sunakawa, 2010: 346)

As becomes apparent from their study, there is a form of glancing in video games because players become adept at switching between the multiple camera perspectives that they are offered and then constructing unusual virtual visibility arrangements of the game because it can be seen from multiple perspectival points. Switching between the multiple perspectives provided by game-cameras is distinct from the naked eye presented with a landscape and also different again from the qualities of the physical screen on which game-camera perspectives are graphically rendered. Yet it is common enough to find settings where looking jumps between perspectives (e.g. looking in the rear-view mirror of a car). Keating and Sunakawa's (2010) study also brings to light the importance of the "participation cues" that happen in the space around the computer. In their study, team players were sat together at a LAN party and coordinated their moves by talk, gesture, and handling of the keyboard (see also Sjöblom, 2011). We can begin then to see how gameplay is produced not only from the skilled operation of cameras and the courses of actions that are generated by the game but also in the physical ecology of the computer display and the actions that surround it.

1.3.   Interaction in Virtual Environments

Early studies of VEs, although not focusing on virtual camera perspectives per se, have examined how users look around, with and through these environments, focusing in particular on the relationship between newly emerging collaborative virtual environments (CVEs) and the transformation of preexisting everyday visual practices in them (Hindmarsh, Fraser, Heath, Benford, & Greenhalgh, 1998; Hindmarsh, Heath, & Fraser, 2006). For instance, Hindmarsh and his collaborators (Hindmarsh & Heath, 2000; Hindmarsh, Fraser, Heath, Benford, & Greenhalgh, 1998) explored how CVE users establish (or more usually fail to establish) common points of reference through using the arms of avatars within the environment to point at objects.

Visual practices have been central from the outset both to the ways in which users of CVEs are embodied and to how they engage in talk (Bowers, Pycock, & O'Brien, 1996). Designers of CVEs themselves have supported these emerging visual practices by, for instance, developing interactional models to control visual and aural awareness (Benford & Fahlen, 1993). In early CVEs such as MASSIVE (Greenhalgh & Benford, 1995) and DIVE (Carlsson & Hagsand, 1993), the visual field was all the more pertinent because such environments were limited by simplistic graphical capabilities (e.g. simplistic geometries and low-polygon-count models, limited animation, basic light models, etc.). The fragmentation and disruption caused by the primitive visual displays of rooms, corridors, furniture, and so on provided insights into ordinary visual practices, such as predicting the trajectories of action by others or establishing common points of reference (Hindmarsh & Heath, 2000).

Although multiuser games existed prior to the advent of CVEs and have been the focus of a number of studies (e.g. "Multi-User Dungeons" [Dourish, 1998]), the introduction of ever more complex 3D VEs brings relevance to this prior work on visual practices in CVEs through turning towards learning and knowing the game (Sjöblom, 2008; Bennerstedt & Ivarsson, 2010). The development of online collaborative platforms in the rapidly evolving games sector has introduced new technologies that advance both the possibilities of playing together and the visual features within gameplay. Irani, Hayes, and Dourish (2008) consider how users' self-perception and reciprocity of that perception are reshaped by the software construction of online collaborative VEs. They argue that rather than the ongoing attempt to simulate the properties and practices of "real-world" environments, VEs might instead "create a novel platform for interaction" (Irani, Hayes, & Dourish, 2008: 195).

Moving beyond this literature, we see that game design for VEs, by its very ethos, has established all manner of unconventional and imaginative forms of visual practice. Situated on the border between a number of existing visual fields, game design and by extension gameplay itself bring together the following topics:

> *New game-relevant visibility practices.* For example, in a game a window allows a player to see an opponent inside a building, and opponents will thus also try to avoid being seen through windows by a change of trajectory or some other means.
> *Combination of novel challenges for the player.* Game designer innovation around preexisting formats provides familiar resources for varied arrays of entertainment, skill, reasoning, narration, involvement, tactics, scoring, winning, losing, rules, aesthetics, nerves, and more. The multiple concepts collected by the word "game" always then require further definition.
> *Influence of cinema.* The growing implementation by game designers of cinema's grammars for the display and recognition of characters, actions, events, scenes, and more.

Cutting across all three of these topics are the uses of virtual cameras that both display the environment and create perspectives to play from, within, and with. So our study in this chapter enriches the existing body of research exploring visual practices in VEs by a direct examination of the overlooked relevance of virtual camerawork itself.

1.4. Cameras in Games

The centrality of the camera to 3D video games is marked out in the very title of the ever popular *first-person* shooter genre. In these games, the camera is predominantly positioned as if it were looking through the eyes of the player's avatar, which acts as a surrogate or proxy for their own view on the VE.[1] Nitsche has written the most comprehensive treatment of cameras in video games in his recent book, *Video Game Spaces: Image, Play, and Structure in 3D Worlds* (2009). He begins by drawing upon research in film and media studies on the camera's role in cinema to chart how the positioning and movement of the camera are used to produce a sense of space and perspective in film. However, video games radically change the purposes of cinema camerawork when translated into a video game. Nitsche argues that video games hybridize two spaces: cinema's screen with its static audience and the built spaces of architecture with its mobile inhabitants. Effectively, computer games are built environments within which players can pan, tilt, dolly their cameras, swap cameras, and swap lenses as part of their ongoing courses of action of exploring, chasing, dodging, killing, and so on.

By contrast with cinema, where the choice of camera, its movement, and its lens is tied to narration, emotion, and other concerns of the film-makers, what the camera shows in video gameplay is restricted by its requirement to support the playing of the game (Nitsche, 2009). Consequently game players are not led by the game-camera's movements, as audiences are when they watch films, though interestingly gameplay has hybridized with film-making, as Nitsche also notes (on spectators, see also Taylor & Witkowski, 2010). The game player's handling of game-cameras is then closer to that of the physical camera operator directing the camera than it is to the spectator of a film. In addition, the field of possibilities offered by cameras in cinema versus games is typically very different; while the cinema camera is tied to the physicality of the camera and the set (although this does not hold, say, for some special effects shots), the virtual camera in video games is not.

Having noted these critical differences, Nitsche takes us through the variety of modes in which cameras have been employed within video games since their inception. For 3D games, Nitsche identifies four dominant camera behaviours that are used within gameplay:

> "Following camera." A third-person perspective that lies slightly behind the player looking over their shoulder or above their head.
> "Overhead view." A different third-person perspective, top-down and similar to that from a plane or satellite.
> "First-person point of view." Positioned as if the camera were on a headset in line with the player's eyes.
> "Predefined viewing frames." The camera has pre-scripted behaviours at certain places within games (such as cuts or swapping to the view of your killer when you die. (Nitsche, 2009: 102)

Following cameras position the virtual camera outside of the player's avatar such that the player can see their own avatar and something of the surroundings of the environment they are playing within. Of course, in many games the exact behaviour of third-person cameras may vary. In contrast, first-person cameras are tightly coupled with the player's manipulations of their avatar. At times, these two may be mixed together; for instance in the role-play game *Fallout 3* (2008), a mixture of first-person and third-person camera positions are employed during its step-by-step combat system. Other games, such as the *Resident Evil* series (1996–present) combine following cameras with static cameras set-up in CCTV-like positions. The two games we are concerned with in this chapter fit within the first- and third-person cameras, respectively.

The virtual "lenses" used in video games have further aspects of the properties of real-world cameras. At one level, these properties are used for aesthetic purposes by designers (e.g. lens flare, giving the game a more cinematic feel). At another level, the properties of lenses are offered as instruments to players of first-person shooting games. As we will see later in this chapter, players can select weapons whose telescopic lenses can then augment the player's capacity to investigate distant locations and, of course, aim accurately at remote opponents.

Finally, in various games the optical qualities of mechanical cameras are actively ignored to support novel gameplay. For instance, the first-person shooter *Aliens Versus Predator 2* (2001) provides the player with a number of different alien avatars to select and play with that modify both the game's visual presentation and its play. Differing sizes of avatar offer the player different heights of game-camera perspective, movement abilities (e.g. an alien can run across ceilings, whereas the human cannot, thus corresponding to different camera capabilities). Avatar selection also alters the optical qualities of vision they provide (e.g. the predator has limited colour vision, thus modifying visual acuity). Breaking with conventions of camera height, movement, and colour in these games helps remind us of the use of camera conventions as a resource in the intelligibility of play in the majority of 3D video games. In spite of this, we note that cameras are rarely topicalized in games. An exception is *Warco*[2] (2011), where the player takes control of a virtual video camera, records shots through its virtual viewfinder, and then subsequently assembles them into news footage.

Having provided a brief survey of the variety of game camera possibilities, we would now like to examine in detail how the camera is involved in the playing of two particular games.

2. STUDY ONE: PLAYING IN THE FIRST PERSON WITH A CAMERA FOR LOOKING AND AIMING: *COUNTER-STRIKE*

At the time of writing, *Counter-Strike: Source* ranked as one of the most popular games on Steam,[3] a major games distribution platform. Originally developed in 1999 as a free modification to an existing first-person shooter called *Half-Life*, *Counter Strike* (CS) was subsequently released as a commercial game in its own right. Usually team-based, like many FPS games, CS involves navigating richly detailed 3D VEs with the goal of eliminating other players as well as achieving certain objectives (such as the capture of a particular landmark in the game).

To orient the reader to typical aspects of CS that players engaged with, we offer an outline of the game experience as follows: a player selects a suitable server from a list of active game servers made available at the start of a session. The majority of play is performed online, with remote game servers acting as secure, authoritative hubs. The game itself is played on a particular set of maps, each of which is effectively a self-contained 3D VE. Typically the player joins a server midgame, dropping into the action after they have selected a server (and therefore joining the current map and game type that is being played on that server). Players are then presented initially with a choice of two teams: terrorists and counterterrorists. Players choose one of these sides to play on when they enter, what is for them, the first round of the game. As CS works on a round-based system, the player must wait until the current round has ended before they are "spawned" with the rest of a team at particular points on the map.

As mentioned, the characteristic perspective provided by FPS games is that of seeing through the eyes of the avatar. The graphical rendering of this perspective is then presented on the physical display to the player, who may then attend to relevant parts of that display during play. In CS, like the majority of 3D games, interaction with the avatar is enacted via manipulations of keyboard and mouse. Thus, in CS, the perspectives provided by playing the game are, for the most part, constrained by the player-controlled movements of a humanoid-shaped avatar via the game's keyboard and mouse interface.

The camera is sited on the avatar's "head" and directed by movements of the mouse. Players of CS typically use the keys "w," "a," "s," and "d" for forward, sidestep left, backpedal, and sidestep right movements, respectively. These actions are conducted concurrently with use of the mouse, producing streams of game-camera perspectives, rendered graphically to the screen. In this way, players may peer into the VE through the physical display, used as a porthole. It is through this porthole that they observe and conduct game actions (running, jumping, shooting, etc.). Players' planar movement in the VE is strongly tied to the orientation of the perspective created through this combination of mouse and keyboard—for instance, pressing a key for forward moves the avatar in the direction determined by where the centre point of the head perspective is currently directed, which itself is controlled by the mouse. Beyond this, the movement of the game-camera is constrained by a number of aspects, such as the limitations of the avatar (e.g. it does not fly or pass through walls), and, more generally, by the game's physics (e.g. the player can travel only at a running pace), by the geometry of the spaces travelled through, and by the physical ability of the player to engage in dexterous manipulations of keyboard and mouse (Reeves, Brown, & Laurier, 2009).

2.1. Establishing What Is Happening by Moving the Camera

Intrinsic to many FPS games is the strong coupling between a player's manipulations of their avatar and the game-camera perspectives that are produced by and crafted in those movements. Transcript 1 (panels 1–20[4]) introduces these aspects. The player has his brother sitting to one side (Reeves, who is also video-recording the play). It is a common feature of gameplay, even where there are no dual controls, that peripheral participants in the

Transcript 1 Moving the camera through rooms and doorways. (Player's speech bubbles are from the right, and participant's are from the left.)

game provide game-relevant (and game-irrelevant) talk (Lin & Sun, 2011; Aarsand & Aronsson, 2009). The round has just started, with the players having selected and joined a server and waiting for the current round that they have dropped into to finish.

The player's camera, as they navigate a series of rooms, is continuously and tightly coupled to the position and orientation of what would be their avatar's head, though, as we have noted already, this head shot remains fixed straight ahead. With such tight coupling, players can precisely point their camera around the environment during movement. Glossing this, we can say that throughout the series of rooms, the player maintains camera perspective in a balance between looking for the action ahead and minimizing their visibility to their opponents. Producing a perspective for looking at what is happening has to be weighed against pointing the weapon at potential threats.

To try to both look around but also have their weapons upon likely targets, players become adept at "dollying" the camera. However, the film professional terms of "dolly" and "camera" need to be discarded in order to understand the players' sense-making within the game. To reiterate, for the players there is the ongoing concern of both seeing what is happening in the game and avoiding being seen by their opponents within the limits offered by the game's graphics engine, by their screen, and, just as importantly, by the game's designed environment of exposed spaces, cover, vantage points, traps, and other features.

As we have argued, crucial to playing the game is arranging the camera's perspective to allow for the ongoing surveying of the scene (Luff, Heath, & Jirotka 1999) in order to anticipate what's next. Turning to an episode of actual play, we see how the player approaches and then moves through a door, fires at the opposing side, and then is killed.

Rather than approach the doorway at a right angle to it, the player and the remote player ahead have moved their avatars around to provide a view through the door that is ajar (panels 1–2). Through their adjustment of the camera perspective, they can thus see something of the view into the next room from a distance and can move then onward along this line of sight. As their movement continues (panel 3), we see something of the payoff with the game-camera angle now offering at first a sliver and then a full view of the next doorway. They very edging forward of play is produced by the camera, through carefully approaching openings that allow the player to both see ahead and be seen by distant opponents ahead.

Edging forward is done not only with a concern for visibility, but it is also built with a concern to bring the centre point of the camera to bear upon features of the environment from which enemies are likely emerge. In the fragment, this is achieved by the player crouching down their avatar (panel 7), which thereby cranes the camera downward while also increasing the accuracy of the weapon (shown by a narrowed target point). Near-instant firing upon the opponent when they become visible (and ideally before they see the players and kill them) is a core component to this rapid round-based game. Thus the kind of camerawork being conducted expertly here by the player combines the "exploratory" (i.e. seeing where to go next) and the "preparatory" (i.e. being ready to act).

The visual orientation of other players' avatars is visible to team members and is used as resources by each player. The team member's crouch ahead is recognized as a response to the next room, and, in turn, our player performs a characteristic stop-crouch-zoom (panels 7–8) when they approach the same room. Having established a position that is surveying one perspective at this doorway, our player zooms from a slightly different angle, thus increasing the overall territory ahead that is being surveyed by his team. Both their individual lines of sight are kept narrow enough to maintain minimal visibility for the players and thus making it harder for the opposing team to see them and shoot them. A wider field of scrutiny of the room ahead is thus coproduced and may then give them the advantage over their opponents.

2.2. Establishing What Is Happening by Switching Lenses

By selecting certain weapons with telescopic lenses, players are given further control over the virtual optics of the game. Each choice of perspective comes with a balance of properties that both augments and limits what can be seen. In panels 6–7 transcript 1, the player increases the accuracy of the weapon and the fidelity of what is being looked at, but for all that players gain, they sacrifice other capabilities within the game. Looking through the telescopic sight reduces the player's field of view, and the game automatically reduces the player's maximum speed of travel through the game spaces, modelling the limitations imposed by crouching while moving forward.

While camera operators zoom as part of the practices of recording (Introduction by Broth, Laurier, & Mondada, this volume), the game-relevant practices of zooming via lens selection and game-camera perspective production by the player are meshed; using an in-game weapon like the sniper rifle is like using a lens selection. In transcript 2, we see the player manipulating their perspective by orienting the mouse in tandem with changing the optical qualities of the camera by zooming. Echoing the framing of telescopic lenses, the sniper rifle is enclosed in a circle easily distinguishable from the regular rectangular of the screen. The sniper rifle has two levels of magnification that the player can use.

To pass through to the most powerful level of zooming, the player must initiate a zoom to the first level (this is done simply using right mouse button clicks) and then cycle through "normal"—"zoom level 1"—"zoom level 2"—"normal"—and so on. The optical functions of the weapon here are, of course, intended to support aiming and firing on targets that are some distance away. They allow more than this, though; the different levels of magnification are used to conduct different kinds of visual inquiry that

Transcript 2   Zooming in and sweeping back and forth with the gun scope.

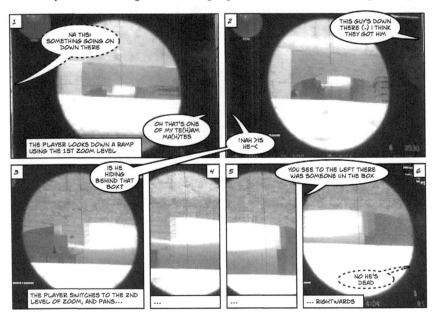

are relevant to producing distinct visibilities for different courses of action (Mondada, 2003). Cycling through the levels of magnification enables the player to briefly peer closely at a narrow territory of interest within a wider perspective.

Before the sequence in transcript 2, the player had been surveying the scene before then zooming in on the underpass. As the transcript begins, the player zooms in and frames the shot so as to make relevant the tunnel and its opposite opening (panel 1) for their closer scrutiny. With the area of scrutiny aligned by the zoom, the onlooker provides the first analysis of what they can see: "ths: something going on down there." There is then an as yet unspecified game action visible to him. The player responds with an oh-prefaced recognition (panel 1), his laughter throughout the recognition accounting for the fact that he had his cross hairs tracking a figure below the bridge that he now recognizes as one of his teammates.

The player then makes further sense of what they can see: "this guy's down there I think they got him" (panel 2). "[T]his guy" refers to one of the enemy whom they had seen earlier below the bridge (which had led to the current inquiry into what was happening ahead). The onlooker responds in disagreement with the conclusion that the enemy had been killed (panels 2–3). In the light of this disagreement over what has happened below the bridge, the player swaps to the higher magnification zoom, which then provides a more detailed view than when the onlooker noticed that there was "something going on." The player's use of magnification allows them both to see both movements and detritus. These are intelligible to the experienced player as the visible evidence of a close combat situation (e.g. when players die, their guns fly out of their hands [panel 3]). Because the greater magnification provides a restricted view of the area of interest, the player combines this level of zoom with a slow paced sweep of the ramp and tunnel area (panels 3–5).

The sweep finished, the player's cross hairs linger on the right side (panels 5–6), making that area relevant as the point where a new enemy player might yet emerge. In response to the right side being established as the player's focus, the onlooker tries to redirect the scope to the left (panel 6). Even though they are trying to redirect the scope, the onlooker also accepts that doing so might no longer be the case by putting it into the past tense ("there was someone behind the box"). This "was" provides some ambiguity over whether the enemy player "was alive" or "was there but has now gone somewhere else." The player responds with a correcting report on that opponent's status (panel 6), supposing the onlooker has not understood what happened, and ascribes the first understanding of an enemy player that was alive.

As noted earlier, Macbeth tells us that "cameras can't glance" (1999: 151) in the way that human eyes can, but he also points out that we treat the camera's limited field as having an "outside." In the player's view of a video game, there is also an outside, and the camera will be adjusted in response to projected everyday courses of action (e.g. an object moves out of shot going rightwards), audio (e.g. indicating enemy approaching), lighting effects, and so on. Irani, Hayes, and Dourish (2008) also note this lack of peripheral vision in the "mediated looking" within VEs. The limited view of the game provided by the player's single first-person camera is supplemented in the game by further camera resources that are unlocked after the player is killed within the game, and it is to those camera resources that we will now turn.

2.3.   Cameras after Death: What Happened and What Others Can See

The penalty for death in *Counter-Strike* is the player losing control of his avatar until the next round while the surviving players continue to fight. In correspondence with being killed, the camera coupling is modified: the camera perspective "leaps out" of the avatar and pans up to present an overhead, now third-person perspective of the player's body. In terms of Nitsche's typology, these are "predefined viewing frames" (2009: 93): first, the camera is moved automatically to provide a brief dramatized view from above the dead body of the avatar. Second, the game briefly offers the player the perspective of the player that killed him. It thus supplements an already available Schützian "reciprocity of perspectives" with a literal swapping of perspective, the instructional character of which is derived from the sequential organization of its presentation to the player (i.e. first-person view of death, third-person view of the player's body, and the view from their killer's perspective). In future rounds of the game, the perspective of their opponent can then be used by players to provide tactical resources, given that the player (now) has a sense of what weapon the enemy team member was using and where they were shooting from.

Once the predefined enemy player view finishes, a new form of control of the game-camera is returned to the player. The game-camera control offered to the dead is intriguing, given our interests in the properties and uses of cameras within games. What is returned to the player is not control of any of the movement of the cameras; instead, the player's relationship to the game shifts to something similar to that of an editor in the studio being able to swap between the cameras of his team members who remain playing. The metaphor ends there, however, because the player is not trying to broadcast or sequence these camera perspectives and usually flicks through them to pass the time while waiting for the next round to begin.

The automated camera provides an occasion for an analysis of what happened to lead to the player being killed. Transcript 3 is the continuation of transcript 2, in which the player and onlooker were closely inspecting the underpass. When the player is killed, we see the camera jumping from the player's body and then providing a number of perspectives in rapid succession. The camera moves into position behind the player's body and looks down a tunnel in the orientation the player was facing when hit (panel 10), spins around to provide a view of where the player just came from (panel 11), and finally spins once again to trace a line of sight between the player lying dead on the ground and the enemy player (panel 12).

Transcript 3   Finding out what happened through the automated camera.

After the player is hit, he expresses his surprise: "oh >what the?<" (panel 11), a response cry that is also raising a question over what happened. Its question format showing that the source of the shots that killed him is pending rather than being immediately reportable. The onlooker is the first to analyse the sequence of camera perspectives automatically provided and says with a questioning intonation, "that was someone (.) down there?" The directional sense of "down there" is provided in relation to the automated panning action of the camera. The onlooker's candidate solution to who killed the player suggests that the attack came from an as yet unseen enemy present in the tunnel itself.

However, the camera algorithm was still unfolding, and the alternate perspective of the camera offers the opportunity for the player to provide a subsequent solution to what happened because it shows a known sniping point: "err no guy up there." The player's "up there" is located by his pointing (panel 12) to a location on the display where a balcony overlooks the tunnel.[5] On the basis of these two examples, we can grasp how the automated camerawork offers resources for resolving puzzles around "what just happened?' and "how did I get killed?"

3.   STUDY TWO: PLAYING IN THE THIRD PERSON WITH A CAMERA FOR LOOKING AROUND: *DOCTOR WHO*

Before we deal with the camera set-up in this next game, we need to say a little bit about the workings of this game, which differs from *CS*. The *Doctor Who Adventure Games* (DW), belonging to the adventure game genre, are built upon the characters of The Doctor and his then current companion Amy from the popular and long-running BBC sci-fi series. In 2010, when the data was collected, there were four games in the series. For each adventure, the players arrive in a new place in a particular time period where one or another alien presence is endangering the locals. Quite what has happened and what the players need to do to complete the adventure are discovered in stages as the game progresses. Unlike *CS*, they are not playing against other players online or locally, though in some of their challenges there are computer-generated monsters that can kill the Doctor or Amy. Also, unlike the routinized familiarity of a small number of virtual environments for the *CS* player, a central task in adventure games (and *DW*) is navigation in an unfamiliar environment that, aside from the villains and monsters, also contains a number of usually fatal hazards. This feature lends itself to our study in that it permits us to describe camerawork where the nature of the environment is uncertain (as opposed to *CS*, where enemy player actions produce uncertainty). During the game, the player is usually moving the Doctor avatar with Amy following. For certain challenges, the avatar is swapped to Amy, and/or the avatar works alone temporarily. If either of the avatars is killed, then the game restarts from their last successfully completed section of the game.

The game can be played alone or with someone else involved. In the data that follow, there are a father (Laurier) and his young son playing together. Their participation in the game is through a more varied set of participation pairs than the onlooker-plus-player pair in the previous section. They shift between player-plus-onlooker, player-plus-planner, and player-plus-player (Aarsand & Aronsson, 2009). It is worth noting that, although siblings and peers playing together is common, play involving parents and children is relatively rare (Aarsand & Aronsson, 2009).

As in CS, players of DW manipulate both keyboard and mouse to make moves within the game. In terms of the camera mechanics, the player's avatar is moved by one control (keyboard), and the camera is moved by the other control (usually the mouse). Characteristic of third-person perspective games, the camera's coupling to the avatar has inertial characteristics like a Steadicam, and its distance from the avatar is also modelled on a "spring" connection. When the character runs forward, the spring stretches, and when the character slows down, the spring automatically pulls the camera closer to the avatar. This form of coupling also means that the camera's position is such that it floats upwards when following the player as they run through the environment. However, in a significant departure from the first-person perspective, the camera can be swung around by the player, out of synch with the body movements of the avatar. It can be panned, tilted, and craned around the avatars, allowing views from the ceiling down to the floors and vice versa, producing views of the characters from the front, sides, and rear, and so on. Such manipulations of the game-camera by the player are, at points, major resources in progressing in the adventure.

Even though the game-camera's operation is not cinematic, it does require the players to organize two kinds of actions: first, camera actions (e.g. panning, tilting, and rolling) that produce appropriate exploratory or preparatory perspectives for looking around or for next actions and, second, the movement of the avatar (and thus the camera) through the VE. These are controlled from separate computer inputs (keyboard and mouse), and the player and coplayer share or swap the controls from time to time according to the ongoing sequence of action.

3.1.   Convergent and Divergent Looking

We join the players in this game where we left off with CS in the midst of a collaborative examination of what is displayed on screen. While much of the time they share a focus in the gameplay, they do not always converge on the same thing. In fact, the possibilities for divergent orientations towards what is being displayed on the screen is all the more apparent in their playing DW because the father is more closely involved than was the case of the player and his brother in CS. What the father takes on for much of the time is the navigational work of establishing where in the complex labyrinth of the game they are and where they need to go to next. In the meantime, the son is devoted to controlling the avatar and, from time to time, operating the game-camera.

We join them as they are in the midst of trying to find their way around a maze of tubular corridors in a seafloor station of some kind. The tunnels have windows allowing them to see the wider undersea neighbourhood of buildings and connecting corridors.

When the camera is simply following the avatar, it provides a straight-ahead, centred perspective. The avatar's arrival at the junction makes relevant an enquiry, and the player asks "so which way" (panel 1), thus also directly requesting help from the father as a coplayer. The directional help being requested makes relevant the paired category in the adventure game of player-plus-navigator.

We also see two behaviours of the camera's automated coupling to the avatar's movements. The camera is initially stretched behind the Doctor as he runs, and then, when he stops at the junction, it slows down to catch up with him (panels 1–3). Secondly, when the player turns the doctor to the right, the inertia delays the camera from swinging immediately behind him (panels 4–5).

Although transcript 4a gives us a sense of the camera set-up within the game, if we swap to a view of the players around the screen, we can see more of the physical-virtual ecology of the father, son, and game-camera.

Transcript 4a   The following camera and turning the avatar. Player's speech is from the right, and coplayer's is from the left throughout the transcripts of DW.

Transcript 4b Pointing over a screen to indicate direction.

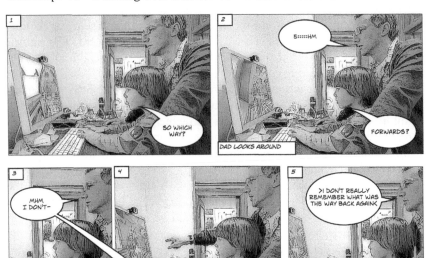

The possibility of gesturing around and over a shared screen is common across a wide variety of gameplay (Keating & Sunakawa, 2010) and, more widely, video screens (Heath & Luff, 2000; Hindmarsh & Heath, 2000). The father and son are in a huddle around the computer, with the son controlling the keyboard and mouse and the dad close behind him, looking over the top of his head. As player and coplayer, they can monitor the screen for what is currently happening. What the coplayer can do, given that his hands are free from the controls, is then to gesture across, at, on, and around various features that emerge in the game's environment by virtue of their graphical rendering on-screen. We thus see the coplayer suggesting "try that way" (transcript 4b, panel 4) while simultaneously pointing towards the right-hand corridor.

In this fragment of the gameplay, the camera is transparent (i.e. it is not topicalized); the coplayer is giving a direction gesture not all that different from one that we might see from a passenger in a car towards what can be seen of the junction ahead through the windscreen. As mentioned earlier, the screen provides a shared porthole into the VE that is ongoingly aligned for the two players. Because the players are already accessing the game through a porthole, much of the time they do not need to establish an alignment of perspectives in the way that pedestrians exploring urban environments do. The latter may be facing in different directions or be differently placed in relation to lines of sight and so on that then require work to align their visual orientation towards the environment (see Mondada, 2009; Laurier & Brown, 2008).

Transcript 5a   Running through the tunnel.

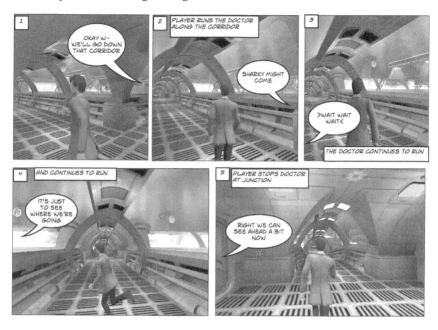

Having said that, the porthole, or windscreen, produces a shared perspective, what we began to see in transcript 4b was the possibility of nonaligned/divergent orientation towards the features of the environment. This becomes clearer in the second data fragment.

In transcript 5a, panel 1, the player accepts an earlier proposal from the coplayer to select a particular corridor. He warns of one of the threats they face when they travel in the windowed corridors (e.g., "sharky," a shark that smashes the glass and drowns them). The player's concern is about being visible to the shark, and so he hurries through the glass corridor. The coplayer, in the face of the avatar rushing through the glass corridor, requests that he wait (panel 3) and then elaborates that why he is instructing the player to wait is navigation relevant (panel 4). The player, ignoring the request to wait and then ignoring the account for the request, continues running his avatar still farther down the corridor (panel 4). When the player does finally halt, it is at a junction out of sight of sharky because there are no immediate windows. The coplayer is trying to do reconnaissance work that is being denied by the player whose course of action is to leave behind the windows as fast as possible to avoid the shark attack.

If we shift towards how this plays out within the game's ecology of screen and controls, we can see that the coplayer is also looking at the peripheral area of the screen (transcript 5b, panels 2–5) where the windows are.

Transcript 5b   Looking at different areas of the screen.

As already noted, the lack of alignment is generated by the player's desire to avoid sharky and by having to drive the avatar, and he is thus attuned to the corridor ahead for upcoming junctions. The corridor ahead is kept centre screen by the following game camera. The coplayer, in the meantime, is inspecting the sides of the screen, examining the buildings and other corridors visible through the windows of the corridor in the hope of working out where they are in the maze of corridors.

In Chuck and Candy Goodwin's work (Goodwin, 1997; Goodwin & Goodwin, 1996) on the distributed work of controlling airports, staff located in the operations rooms distribute the work of monitoring the airport across multiple screens showing various CCTV views. At certain critical junctures, they can draw upon their multiple cameras to find out what is causing a particular problem in the airport. For the game players here, while they can distribute the work, only one screen offers a single rendered graphical game-camera perspective. However, what the player and coplayer can do here is to scrutinize different regions of the screen.

3.2.   Looking Around with the Camera

So far, we have examined elements of how the automatic following camera perspective of the game is used by the players and how the distribution of the visual tasks around the screen is then accomplished. What we will turn to now is the direct manipulation of the camera using the mouse. This sits in useful contrast with the first-person shooter game (*CS*), where we saw how camerawork was effectively one and the same as avatar action. The differences in *DW* allow us to consider what happens when the camera movement can be decoupled from the avatar movement.

In transcript 6, the player is approaching a T-junction at the end of a corridor, and this time, rather than moving his avatar, he switches to moving the camera to look around from a fixed point in the midst of the junction.

When the player engages the mouse, the camera is lifted towards the ceiling (panels 2–3), producing a view from above. Immediately and rapidly after this, the player begins a somewhat inelegant sweeping scan of the environment at the junction by panning, tilting, and craning the camera with the planar movements of the mouse (panels 5–7). The player continues the camera's rapid movement whilst formulating a halting question about direction (panels 10–12). As the coplayer interrupts with an emphatic solution to

Transcript 6   Fast-panning the camera.

the player's troubles, the player himself is already repairing the pan of the camera by lowering it back down and slowing its movement.

As it was with the first-person shooter, handling the camera is not only for exploring the VE but also for preparing and positioning the camera perspective to provide an adequate view for future action. This becomes obvious in sections of the game where, as in *CS*, the players are struggling against an opponent who can kill them (rather than navigating or solving puzzles). In transcript 7, they have to advance through the corridor while remaining in a moving red spotlight because the shadows are fatal. The speed of the spotlight has been designed as a challenge because it does not move at quite the same speed as the avatar and so requires adjustments of pace. The son finds this too difficult and asks his father to take over the controls of the game. They have discovered (having been killed three times in prior attempts) that the traverse requires precise timing in entering into the moving spotlight. Timing their actions to the spotlight is made easier by adjusting the camera perspective to look down the corridor towards the moving spotlight. As we join them, the corridor ahead is not the one they must take, and the avatar has just been turned away from it.

When the avatar is turned on the spot to face the tunnel with the spotlight (panels 1–3), the automatic following camera leaves the players with a perspective from the side of the avatar. This difficult corner movement is part of the design of the game that requires bringing together avatar and camera controls in a more accomplished coordinated move. In a slow and

Transcript 7   Panning camera to prepare for the next action.

steady movement the player pans the camera to provide a view from behind the avatar. The camera pan needs to be even more carefully crafted in that it also requires craning downward for a long view down the corridor with the moving spotlight (panels 4–5). The player accentuates the slow speed in his accompanying account of his camera movement by extending his utterance "aro::und" along the course of this movement. There is perhaps a hint of instruction in this, given his son's repeated rapid pans (as in the previous section). Upon completing both his utterance and the movement, the camera is brought to rest by the player in position behind the avatar. Located behind and relatively low, this preparatory camerawork then provides the longer view of the moving spotlight. It is then perfectly positioned to prepare them for the next action of moving the avatar forward into the spotlight. The coplayer, tracing and projecting the trajectory of the curve of the camera, as well as the movement of the spotlight, warns the player not to make his move yet (panel 5).

Within this second study, we have elaborated and expanded on the points of the first study, examining how the player and coplayer undertake distributed game-playing tasks on a shared single screen; how the camera itself becomes topicalized within the game; and how the camera is operated to prepare for next actions within the game.

4. CONCLUSION

Even though this chapter has explored fragments of play from only two of the myriad video games that are currently played around the world, it has begun to uncover camerawork that is common to many of these games. In the games that we have considered here, the camera's view is also used to analyse the visibility of players to their opponents; our study has revealed how game-cameras mediate the visibility of a virtual environment and what is happening in that environment. Both algorithmic and human action are involved in the production of these camera perspectives, and both provide pertinent resources for play. In bringing this chapter to a close, we summarize key analytic points raised by the two studies and their implications.

In our first study, we examined three features of camera activity in *Counter-Strike* (CS). We began by exploring how perspectival control of the camera is a skill that the player must master: that is, successfully playing the game often relies on successful camerawork. Secondly, we saw how important the role of non-first-person (often quite "cinematic") camera perspectives are for players in terms of resolving normal game troubles such as "how did I get killed?" Finally, we explored how zooming provided optical modifications of regular camera perspectives, offering new ways of scrutinizing the VE, and, relatedly, the ways in which these optical characteristics, in affording different visual acuities, were enmeshed in the routine forms of looking and glancing enacted by the player. Zooming, in particular, may be seen as developing a form of camera glancing that is very unlike unaugmented human vision. (We do not routinely zoom in on distant details, though we could perfectly well carry binoculars with us everywhere.)

In our second study of the *Doctor Who Adventures Game* (*DW*), we saw how the following camera with separate controls is brought to bear in a range of practices. Playing the game together required an ongoing division of labour between player and coplayer in different elements of the gameplay (e.g. moving the avatar, panning the camera, scrutinizing the screen). In exploring the movement of the camera and how it connected to the movement of the avatar, we highlighted convergent and divergent visual inquiries of the game as visible on the screen. Throughout both studies we examined the manipulation of the camera to find and produce perspectives that were relevant to the next move in order to navigate through the labyrinthine environments of both games.

The main contribution of this chapter is in explicating *game-playing in and as* a matter of camerawork. At the same time, our chapter contributes to the growing set of studies of seeing with a camera (see the Introduction to this volume by Broth, Laurier, & Mondada) and is of a particular form where the phenomena seen with the camera can be seen only via a game-camera. Without the virtual camera, there is no playing *Counter-Strike* or *Doctor Who*. It is thus a particular kind of camera whose centrality means that it is easy to overlook the fact that it is a camera at all. Indeed, the moment-by-moment, practical work of operating the game-camera has remained largely ignored as a foundational feature of play within video games studies. From our two case studies in this chapter, we have begun to describe how the panning, dollying, and zooming of cameras are sequentially organized in and draw upon the sequential organization of the playing of video games. If we wish to understand video practices in video games, then we need to move beyond listing their many and varied configurations (e.g. Nitsche, 2009) in order to explore how these technical configurations are drawn upon, assembled, and reconfigured in and through gameplay.

The other side of this contribution is in a deeper understanding of *embodiment* in virtual environments. Despite a significant body of literature exploring the character of embodiment in VEs (e.g. Hindmarsh, Fraser, Heath, Benford, & Greenhalgh, 1998), typically such work neglects or glosses the role of the virtual camera; for instance, in Hindmarsh, Heath, and Fraser (2006), the view or viewpoint is presented yet not examined as a resource or topic for the user.

Finally, in describing game-playing practices in and as virtual camera-work and by deepening understandings of embodiment in VEs, this chapter also helps us expand and reconfigure prior understandings (e.g. Irani, Hayes & Dourish, 2008) about how looking around virtual environments is done practically. The idea of seeing-with-the-camera has become ever more relevant and interesting for game players and for the designers of games (Nitsche, 2009) and is perhaps at odds with the initial idea of the simulation of seeing-with-human-eyes that caught the attention of earlier researchers on VR environments (Hindmarsh, Heath, & Fraser, 2006).

Acknowledgements

Our thanks go to our patient family members: Reuben and Philip. Part of this research was funded by the EPSRC ref. EP/F03038X/1. For allowing us to use their visual images from their games: Steam (www.valvesoftware.com/company/index.html) and BBC Doctor Who Adventure Game (www.bbc.co.uk/doctorwho).

NOTES

1. We note that while first- and third-person perspectives are common and that second-person perspective games are extremely rare, the game Zato being one example in which players see their own embodiments "through the eyes of" an enemy player (www.indiegames.com/2011/04/interviewing_indies_in_japan_s.html).
2. www.wired.com/gamelife/2011/09/warco
3. www.steampowered.com
4. Note that this balcony is hard to see in the relatively low-resolution screenshots.
5. This is something we have only briefly seen in *CS*, for instance transcript 3, panel 12.

REFERENCES

Aarsand, P.A., & Aronsson, K. (2009). Response cries and other gaming moves—Building intersubjectivity in gaming. *Journal of Pragmatics*, *41*(8), 1557–1575.

Benford, S., & Fahlén, L. (1993). A spatial model of interaction in large virtual environments. In *Proceedings of the Third European Conference on Computer-Supported Cooperative Work* (pp. 109–124). Dordrecht: Kluwer.

Bennerstedt, U., & Ivarsson, J. (2010). Knowing the way. Managing epistemic topologies in virtual game worlds. *Computer Supported Cooperative Work (CSCW)*, *19*(2), 201–230.

Bowers, J., Pycock, J., & O'Brien, J. (1996). Talk and embodiment in collaborative virtual environments. In *Proceedings of the SIGCHI Conference on Human Factors in Computing Systems* (pp. 58–65). New York: ACM.

Broth, M. (2004). The production of a live TV-interview through mediated interaction. In C. van Dijkum, J. Blasius, H. Kleijer, & B. van Hilten (Eds.), *Proceedings of the Sixth International Conference on Logic and Methodology*. Amsterdam: SISWO.

Broth, M. (2009). Seeing through screens, hearing through speakers: Managing distant studio space in television control room interaction. *Journal of Pragmatics*, *41*, 1998–2016.

Carlsson, C., & Hagsand, O. (1993). DIVE: A multi-user virtual reality system. In *Virtual Reality Annual International Symposium, IEEE.* (pp. 394–400). New Brunswick, NJ: IEEE.

Dourish, P. (1998). Introduction: The state of play. *Computer Supported Cooperative Work (CSCW)*, 7(1), 1–7.

Goodwin, C. (1997). Transparent vision. In E. Ochs, E. A. Schegloff, & S. A. Thompson (Eds.), *Interaction and Grammar* (pp. 370–404). Cambridge: Cambridge University Press.

Goodwin, C., & Goodwin, M.H. (1996). Seeing as situated activity: Formulating planes. In Y. Engeström & D. Middleton (Eds.), *Cognition and Communication at Work* (pp. 61–95). Cambridge: Cambridge University Press.

Greenhalgh, C., & Benford, S. (1995). MASSIVE: A collaborative virtual environment for teleconferencing. *ACM Transactions on Computer-Human Interaction*, 2(3), 239–261.

Heath, C., & Luff, P. (2000). *Technology in Action*. Cambridge: Cambridge University Press.

Hindmarsh, J., Fraser, M., Heath, C., Benford, S., & Greenhalgh, C. (1998). Fragmented interaction: Establishing mutual orientation in virtual environments. In *Proceedings of the 1998 ACM Conference on Computer Supported Cooperative Work* (pp. 217–226). New York: ACM Press.

Hindmarsh, J., & Heath, C. (2000). Embodied reference: A study of deixis in workplace interaction. *Journal of Pragmatics*, 32, 1855–1878.

Hindmarsh, J., Heath, C., & Fraser, M. (2006). (Im)materiality, virtual reality and interaction: Grounding the "virtual" in studies of technology in action. *Sociological Review*, 54(4), 795–817.

Irani, L. C., Hayes, G. R., & Dourish, P. (2008). Situated practices of looking: Visual practice in an online world. In *Proceedings of the 2008 ACM Conference on Computer Supported Cooperative Work* (pp. 187–196). New York: ACM Press.

Keating, E., & Sunakawa, C. (2010). Participation cues: Coordinating activity and collaboration in complex online gaming worlds. *Language in Society*, 39(3), 331–356.

Laurier, E., & Brown, B. (2008). Rotating maps and readers: praxiological aspects of alignment and orientation. *Transactions of the Institute of British Geographers*, 33(2), 201–216.

Licoppe, C., & Morel, J. (2012). Video-in-Interaction: "Talking Heads" and the Multimodal Organization of Mobile and Skype Video Calls. *Research on Language and Social Interaction*, 45(4), 399–429.

Lin, H., & Sun, C.-T. (2011). The role of onlookers in arcade gaming: Frame analysis of public behaviours. *Convergence: The International Journal of Research into New Media Technologies*, 17(2), 125–137.

Luff, P., Heath, C., & Jirotka, M. (2000). Surveying the scene: Technologies for everyday awareness and monitoring in control rooms. *Interacting with Computers*, 13(2), 193–228.

Macbeth, D. (1999). Glances, trances and their relevance for a visual sociology. In P. L. Jalbert (Ed.), *Media Studies. Ethnomethodological Approaches* (pp. 135–170). Lanham, MD: University Press of America.

Mondada, L. (2003). Working with video: How surgeons produce video records of their actions. *Visual Studies*, 18(1), 58–73.

Mondada, L. (2009). Emergent focused interactions in public places: A systematic analysis of the multimodal achievement of a common interactional space. *Journal of Pragmatics*, 41(10), 1977–1997.

Nitsche, M. (2009). *Video Game Spaces: Image, Play, and Structure in 3D Worlds*. London: MIT Press.

Reeves, S., Brown, B., & Laurier, E. (2009). Experts at play: Understanding skilled expertise. *Games and Culture*, 4, 205–227.

Sjöblom, B. (2008). Gaming as a situated collaborative practice. *Human IT*, 9(3), 128–165.

Sjöblom, B. (2011). *Gaming interaction: Conversations and competencies in Internet cafés.* Linköping, Sweden: Linköping University.

Sudnow, D. (1972). Temporal parameters of interpersonal observation. In D. Sudnow (Ed.), *Studies in Social Interaction* (pp. 259–279). New York: Free Press.

Taylor, T. L., & Witkowski, E. (2010). This is how we play it: What a mega-LAN can teach us about games. In *Proceedings of the Fifth International Conference on the Foundations of Digital Games* (pp. 195–202). New York: ACM Press.

Watson, R. (1997). Some general reflections on 'categorization'and 'sequence'in the analysis of conversation. In S. Hester & P. Eglin (Eds.), *Culture in action* (pp. 49–76). London: University Press of America Washington, DC.

7 The Televisual Accountability of Reality TV

The Visual Morality of Musical Performances in Talent Shows

Alain Bovet (Telecom ParisTech)
Philippe Sormani (University of Vienna)
Cédric Terzi (University of Lille—EHESS)

The spectacle is not a collection of images; it is a social relation among people that is mediated by images.

(Debord, 2006: 7)

1. INTRODUCTION

Nouvelle Star is the French version of *Pop Idol*, the television program that has turned singing contests into reality TV entertainment and that has been developed and commercialized worldwide by the British firm Freemantlemedia.[1] The French version of the program consists of 15 weekly shows designed to select a new star (*Nouvelle Star*) among thousands of candidate singers. Yet the program is quite different, in at least three respects, from the television coverage of a singing competition among talented volunteers. First, the selection process is not only filmed but set up, organized, and financed by the production team. Second, the vocal performances do not simply happen to be filmed but are entirely staged and retrospectively reassembled to produce a recognizable TV spectacle out of "suitable" television sequences. Third, the TV program addresses its audience in such a way as to position it as playing a central role by voting for the new star via SMS (short message service). In fact, SMS charges make up a substantial part of the program's income. *Nouvelle Star*, be it the program or the crowned candidate, can thus be said to exist in the first place through, and essentially in, its television format and in the social relation that it establishes, as suggested in Debord's epigraph.

In what follows, we will address the so-called televisual accountability of the program. We understand accountability in the sense developed by Garfinkel to emphasize the inseparability of social action and its intelligibility-observability-reportability-for-all-practical-purposes (Garfinkel, 1967). "Televisual" is our gloss for a large number of professional and lay practices and for technologies that make this television program accountable as a cultural product of a distinctive kind. We will focus on two aspects of televisual accountability. First, we will offer a preliminary presentation of the essential orientation of various aspects of the program vis-à-vis its televisual format. This will be done through the succinct description of a number of episodes of the trajectory of Soan, the winner of the 2009 season. We will attempt to describe how Soan has been (made) a televisually accountable new star. In other words, it is in and through specifically televisual means that Soan gradually qualified as an acceptable winner. We will be interested in how this occurred, that is, in the "occasioned production" of his successful trajectory on TV (Koschman & Zemel, 2008).

The third section of our contribution will be devoted to what appears as the most crucial component of the televisual accountability of the examined program. As mentioned, viewers are called upon to take on a decisive role in the final part of the season, when they are expected to vote for the *Nouvelle Star* via charged-for SMSs. Following Garfinkel an colleagues' invitation to find out "what about [a jury's] deliberations makes them a jury" (Garfinkel, Lynch, & Livingston, 1981: 133), we propose seeing the task of turning the viewer into a juror as a problem to which the program offers practical solutions. In other words, we suggest examining the program itself as a kind of tutorial for and exercise in the ad hoc assessment of vocal performances. We will analyse two auditioning sequences from the first show of the 2009 season. We will describe how the televised material appears to have been (re)assembled to convince viewers to conceive of themselves as competent "jurors" of vocal performances, that is, the so-called produced occasion of their expected votes.

A concern of the following analyses is to examine how the visual morality of musical performances is reflexively tied to their manifest achievement, as available and made available via the talent show (hence the gloss "visual morality"). In both sections, we shall examine how the television material contributes to defining the practical conditions of a "successful degradation ceremony" (Garfinkel, 1956), as virtually all candidates must be submitted to humiliating trials and assessments for the new star to be selected.[2]

Both analyses focus on video at work, in that they account for how video practices and technologies define and specify talent shows as a social phenomenon and particular kind of reality TV. Yet our analysis is not based on video recordings of television staff at work, which might have been the usual and preferable way of addressing video at work in our setting. This usual preference, however, proved notoriously difficult to satisfy, given the restricted backstage access to the production sites of reality TV and this of talent show in particular. At least, it has proved impossible for us, so far, to gain access to those sites as video ethnographers.[3]

Besides this trivial but hardly remediable access problem, we want to briefly outline a number of methodological considerations on video analysis before proposing our own video analyses of televisual accountability, as encountered and experienced in the case of *Nouvelle Star*.

2.   PRELIMINARY REMARKS ON THE ORDINARY INTELLIGIBILITY OF A TALENT SHOW

In our view there is far too little armchair research in sociology. (Francis & Hester, 2004: 35).

For this chapter, we mostly rely on video clips of the talent show in question, as broadcast on television and thus ordinarily available to its audience. In that sense, we didn't leave our armchair. Yet the armchair analogy also points to the self-reflective stance that we shall adopt for analytic purposes, reflecting upon how our ordinary television experience was possible as such (see Francis & Hester, 2004).

This self-reflective stance may be contrasted with Macbeth's (1999) ethnographic and ethnomethodological interest in the "shot as a continuous course of analysis" in nonfiction filmmaking (cf. Macbeth, 1999: 135). Macbeth, by and large, focuses upon how *filming*, in its very course and conduct, embodies an ongoing visual analysis by the cameraperson, where his or her ordinary operations of, say, focusing or zooming in on manifest that analysis. This "praxeology of seeing with a camera" (151), then, provides the focal concern of (ethno-)methodological discussion.[4] The prioritization of that concern, however, begs a phenomenological question, namely, how was the phenomenon enacted and experienced in the first place, so that it lent itself to being filmed in the way it seemed to? In other words, focusing upon the camera operator's filming operations, on the basis of the distinctive focus and selections exhibited, begs the question of the ordinary intelligibility of the phenomenon filmed because its ordinary intelligibility made possible that focus and those selections to start with, as well as their sometimes debatable character ("Why did you focus on this? Another angle might have shown that . . . ," and so on). Put simply, we might be in risk of putting the cart before the horse, where the analyst's special interest (e.g. the investigated medium) is taken as the point of departure and basis of the descriptive analysis, rather than the other way round—his or her ordinary experience of the filmed phenomenon, i.e. the perceived message.[5]

The presently adopted, self-reflective stance, in contrast, aims at putting the horse in front of the cart by setting out with our ordinary experience of the *watched* program, the television program *Nouvelle Star*, as an analyzable phenomenon. Furthermore, it invites us to distinguish more clearly between the ordinary intelligibility of the encountered phenomenon and its descriptive analysis in technical terms (Lynch, 2000; Quéré, 2004; Widmer, 2006); if we disregard this analytic distinction, the former intelligibility could be denied perhaps but certainly not be made explicit (for further discussion, see Ryle, 1954; Schütz, 1962). Accordingly, as Francis and Hester suggest, we will "start with what is observably the case concerning our sense, experience and understanding, and then subject this to analysis" (Francis & Hester, 2004: 37).

As far as the television program *Nouvelle Star* is concerned, it appeared to us that we could and indeed did watch it as a kind of reality TV, where "real" performances, albeit staged, were observably achieved and ordinarily intelligible as such. These observable achievements, furthermore, afforded seemingly anyone, closely or remotely involved, with a moral economy, inviting judgments to be made on the recorded, yet "real" performances (i.e. as if they weren't staged or reassembled). The program, in other words, seemed to afford both its viewers and participants with a distribution platform for an instantaneous fame-or-shame allocation, with the amount of the latter manifestly increasing as the program went on, whilst being expressed or made imaginable by phrases such as, "I could have sunk through the floor" (cf. Garfinkel, 1956: 421). The watched program, indeed, appeared to us—possibly by professional bias—as a "talent show" implying "degradation ceremon[ies]" (ibid.).[6]

How could our awkward experience be had? The remainder of this chapter answers the question in two steps. First, it describes how the serial production of shows and castings could (and can be) understood as setting up the practical conditions of any "successful (de-)gradation" of performing candidates, thus preparing the "felicity conditions" for any witnessable performance, as well as for our awkward experience (Section 3). Second, we will describe how these conditions are brought to bear whilst they are played out in and through the evaluation of a single candidate, as that evaluation had been filmed, recorded, and partly reedited and is thus rendered amenable to repeated inspection (Section 4). The pervasive concern of our self-reflective analysis, in sum, is to demonstrate not only how the broadcast performances of candidates were filmed (Macbeth's focal interest) but also how the serial ordering of shows and castings display their *recognizable orientation towards being filmed and broadcast*—that is, their "local order and intelligibility as reflexively produced by their display to and for the camera" (Mondada, 2006: 52). Video-at-work can thus be recovered and respecified as an institutionalized feature and embodied orientation, a mundane phenomenon and moral reality, the relations of which are further discussed in the Conclusion to this chapter, also (but not exclusively) with respect to our analytical professional bias. Again, we shall not so much question that bias—or, positively put, professional vision—but rather sum up how it was possible to be had (Section 5).

3.   THE TELEVISUAL ACCOUNTABILITY OF A *NOUVELLE STAR*: THE CASE OF SOAN, WINNER OF THE 2009 SEASON

The program *Nouvelle Star* consists of more or less 15 weekly shows, broadcast on Tuesday nights on the French M6 channel. The general idea is to select the new star from thousands of candidate singers aged between 16 and 34. The first four shows are devoted to the *casting phase*, i.e. the auditioning of thousands of candidates in four cities of France (and sometimes other French-speaking countries) and the designation of 120 candidates for the next phase. The fifth and sixth shows are devoted to the *theatre phase*: out of the 120 candidates, 15 are selected to participate in the final competition. The ten last shows consist of live broadcasts at the end of each of which the candidate who received the lowest number of viewer's votes is excluded. The winner of the final show is crowned the *Nouvelle Star*—the exclusive identification of the successful candidate in terms of the program's name aptly suggesting that he or she has best incarnated what the program calls the "new star."

As mentioned, the program cannot be reduced to the coverage of an autonomous singing contest. It should rather be seen as constantly achieving the televisual accountability of assessable vocal performances and of their actual assessments. This section will present the main features of this phenomenon through the description of some episodes of the winning trajectory of a candidate named Soan during the 2009 season. Except for an initial use of ethnographic observations, the description will be based on the ordinary intelligibility of television sequences of Soan's trajectory. Rather than a dubious retrospective explanation of Soan's victory, the analysis will be focused on the specifically televisual means by which he was made to appear on the screen as at least an acceptable candidate and eventually as an acceptable winner.

As we will see, Soan's first appearance in the program had more to do with his look than with his vocal performance. The casting shows consist of a selection of candidates auditioning before a jury made up of French musical celebrities. The candidates have to queue for hours outside the building before they perform a preaudition. If their audition is successful, they can perform in front of the jury.[7] Ethnographic observation revealed that—and how—the queue outside the building was exploited by the production team to scout interesting candidates. Since they had not yet sung, the selection could be based only on the visible features of the candidates. Some candidates in the queue had obviously anticipated this form of selection because they had come with quite an elaborate and spectacular look. The selected candidates were then briefly interviewed with the queue in the background by a small production unit. The generated sequence could be broadcast if the candidate was selected to be part of the program.

Soan's first appearance in the program suggests that his selection was based on the logic just described. He showed up and was manifestly noticeable, due to what can be described as his "gothic look" (with tattoos, make-up, jewels, and dark clothes), which stood in a strong contrast to the commercial pop music trend of the program. Such an elaborated marginality made Soan so salient among the hundreds of candidates that a queue sequence was devoted to him. It appears then that Soan was first scouted as a marginal candidate and possibly interesting outsider. It should be noted again that this marginality was first and essentially built on visible features. This is confirmed by the fact that the audition itself was not quite successful, Soan being criticized for his poor vocal abilities. He was nevertheless selected for the next step, thanks to his "character"[8] rather than his singing abilities.[9] The theatre phase led to a similar result: far from being seen as a possible winner, Soan was kept because he was thought to bring something peculiar to the program, mostly through his marginal look[10].

Soan's first live appearance proved decisive in terms of the program. He sang "*Le vent l'emportera,*" one the greatest hits of the indie rock band Noir Désir. As removed as it was from the pop entertainment trend of the program, Soan's performance was nevertheless acclaimed by the jury and obtained a very high score from viewers. An important part of Soan's achievement was again visual: make-up, tattoos, jewels, and clothes that clearly distinguished him from the other candidates. When he finished the song, he covered his eyes with his hands, revealing two eyes drawn on each of his palms. The figure[11] thus composed became Soan's visual signature and reappeared in the program every time a sequence was devoted to him.

Yet the praise was tempered by one of the jurors who said that "there is no subtlety, everything is forced." The following week, in an edited sequence prefacing Soan's new performance, that criticism was replayed and followed by a statement by Soan: "Of course if I always come dressed the same way and propose nothing new . . . I mean being at top speed and passionate is surely moving, but it can also be heavy so yes she is right I have to shift into something else."

The editing of the sequence invites viewers to hear Soan's words as a reaction to the juror's assessment.[12] Interestingly, Soan's reaction turned the criticism into a visual issue related to the way he was dressed. It was also the case in the strategy underlying his new live performance, which consisted of singing "*Ma petite enterprise*" ("My little business"), the greatest hit of the then recently deceased French singer Alain Bashung. The song itself did not "go into something else" because, as successful as it was, it remained in the same indie rock register as the song of the previous week. What changed was rather Soan's look: he appeared in a classical suit, though without a tie and with ranger boots. This visual choice was related to the song itself, which tells the story of a businessman. The performance was once again acclaimed by the jury, the previously critical juror being especially laudatory: "you really delivered the song as a master, and for someone singing in the subway, singing 'my little business knows no crisis' I find that very strong really, and still more in a suit, bravo mister, classy, thank you," As for the first live show, the images of Soan singing in a suit systematically reappeared in the sequences of presentation that preceded his subsequent performances.

This example shows that visual aspects of performances are a common concern of jurors and candidates. It is not a backstage affair; it is made explicit when jurors assess performances and when candidates define strategies. Soan showed particular concern for the visual aspect of his performances. It is even how he explained his success in an edited sequence of the final live show:

> I was definitely caught out at my own game because I thought I had to do something so that every live show was a little story, that the whole was coherent too so I was so demanding of myself thinking I was inferior to the others or something like that because I had the impression that if I stopped doing this trick . . . Maybe that is what made me stay actually.

According to this quote, the visual aspects of performances are a concern not only of the jurors and candidates but also of the viewers who are assumed by Soan to vote on this basis.[13] When jurors assess candidates and even when candidates assess themselves, the visual dimension is an integral part of the performance. In the case of Soan, the jury considered that it amply compensated for his limited vocal abilities.

For this reason, the broadcast highlights of Soan's trajectory appear as television scenes rather than vocal performances. While there are many cases of scenes of Soan without the sound of his singing, we found no instance of Soan singing without being shown. This asymmetrical relationship is an illustration of the televisual accountability of reality TV talent shows. Although it shows *that* the candidates are assessed on a visual basis and actively make themselves assessable as such, it remains to be shown *how* this is achieved in the course of the assessment of a vocal performance Our analysis of two particular auditioning sequences will be focused on the detailed orderliness of the television sequence that makes the candidate's singing available to the viewer as a performance to be assessed.

4.　THE VISUAL MORALITY OF VOCAL PERFORMANCES

As we have seen, the viewer's evaluation may be based on television sequences that stage various aspects of the candidate's trajectory and stance. It was more specifically argued in the previous section that this material had provided the viewer with a tutorial to select the candidate Soan as the *Nouvelle Star*. Such a selection implies, as the other side of the same coin, the degradation of thousands of contenders. The emphasis on the degradation of (more or less) "ordinary people" is one of the most remarkable features of reality TV and, as such, has engendered innumerable controversies, for instance on the voyeuristic and sadistic aspects of such sequences (see e.g. Fitzgerald, Housley, & Reynolds, 2011).

We would now like to turn our attention to the detail of the organization of such selection/degradation sequences. We will focus on the audition sequences of the first phase of the season, the castings. Our first analysis will be devoted to the first audition of the first show of the season in order to see what kind of relation to the vocal performances is being proposed to the viewer. In this case, the viewer is provided from the very beginning with a rule, the violation of which serves as a basis for the degradation of the candidate. A second, though shorter analysis will be devoted to another audition sequence of the first show. While in this sequence the candidate is positively assessed rather than degraded, it will allow us to demonstrate that various types of moral judgements are made available through similar specifically televisual means. Whatever the actual treatment of the candidate, the viewer is invited to enjoy the trial.[14]

4.1. Making the Unrecognizability of the Song Visible to the Viewer

As mentioned, the analysed audition is the first of the whole season.[15] Before the audition itself, the program consists of a brief reminder of the previous seasons, which also includes implicit procedural instructions. The viewer is taught in particular that there are two evaluative authorities. The first ones are the viewers, who are directly addressed, in the plural second person, as the ones who, having been "moved" by some of the candidates, "selected" the New Stars of the previous seasons. The other evaluative authority is "a jury of four experts, sharper and more demanding than ever." One of the jurors, Sinclair, a famous funk musician, is described as "sensitive . . . but intractable on the musicality and accuracy of the performances." Obviously relying on the knowledge of its viewers, the program does not make explicit the distribution of authority between the phases of the season, which we described in Section 3.

The other important information is given by the voice-over just before the first audition itself. We will now use transcripts to address this phenomenon in its circumstantial details. The transcription has been adjusted to the specific purposes of the envisaged analysis.[16] The transcript runs in two parallel columns. Each row corresponds to a single shot of the TV program. In the left column is the translated transcription of what is said during the single shot.[17] In the right column is a succinct description of the type of shot and of what happens in it. We will not refer, as is usually done, to the lines of the verbal transcription but to the numbered shots.

For the sake of clarity, we will occasionally complement the transcripts with screen shots.

Here is the beginning of the audition. The sound consists of an edited mix of voice-over and recording from the audition setting.

(1) *Benoît* [shots 1–7]

1	VO	dressed up made-up studious focused the jury already does well	Front shot of the jury, seated in front of a curved table.
2	VO	it is now up to the candidate to do likewise	Horizontal split-screen. Above: general shot of the audition room. Ben enters the audition room. Below: Front shot of the jury.
3	Sin	now come on	Front shot of Sin.
	Man	here we go	Sin raises his right hand.
4	Sin	let's go	Front shot of the jury.
	VO	first rule	
5	VO	sing a famous song and do so recognizably	Back shot of Ben. Ben enters the audition room.
6	Ben	good evening	Front shot of Ben.
	Lio	hi	Ben enters the audition room.
7	Mnk	hi	Front shot of Mnk.
	Sin	hi	
	Mnk	it's here	

After setting the stage (shots 1–2), the voice-over states a "first rule" (shots 4–5): "sing a famous song and do so recognizably." The formulation of this first rule just before the first candidate starts his audition gives a tutorial turn to the program. The audition can then be seen as instantiating the rule or making it relevant in one way or another. For now, it is important to note that the formulation of the rule is made by the voice-over. In other words, it results from the post-production work rather than being a formulation in and of the audition scene itself. The viewer is not invited to wonder whether the candidate had been instructed to sing according to this rule, another one, or any rule at all but rather to watch the vocal performance as instructed by the rule and thus to determine whether the candidate follows or violates the rule and receives positive or negative sanctions from the jury. In short, whether the candidate had been "set up" is not shown or suggested as a relevant concern. The promise, then, is not so much the vocal performance itself as its inescapable assessment as an enjoyable spectacle. This reasoning seems at least available to any viewer. If one adds that this viewer has also been categorized as a juror, the audition to come may appear as a form of assessment tutorial—a tutorial, however, that upon closer inspection seems to be based upon the setting up of the candidate.

Before the vocal performance itself, the candidate enters the studio, where the four jurors[18] are seated in front of a curved table. After an exchange of greetings, A. Manoukian, one of the jurors, apparently takes on the role of the host on behalf of the jury.

(2) *Benoît* [shots 7–11]

7	Mnk Sin Mnk	hi hi it's right here	*Front shot of Mnk.*
8	Mnk Ben	don't be afraid what's your name/ benoît	*Front shot of Ben.* *Ben smiles.*
9	Mnk	and you're going to sing/	*Profile shot of the jury.*
10	Ben	uh stand by me	*Front shot of Ben.*
11	Mnk	ok there you go	*Front shot of Mnk.*
12	Ben	♫if the sky/ that we look upon\ .. ♫	*Front shot of Ben.* *His right hand goes up and* *down in rhythm.*

After possibly attempting to reassure Benoît (7–8), A. Manoukian asks him his name and the title of the song he is going to sing. Once he has obtained the answers to both questions, A. Manoukian gives the floor to Benoît, who starts singing without further ado (12). The editing[19] of the sequence is, perhaps unsurprisingly, articulated as an alternation of shots of both parties to the interaction: Benoît and A. Manoukian (and the rest of the jury), who are mostly shown when they speak. The verbal interaction achieves what appears as the minimal requirement for the assessment to come: the pairing of a named candidate and a famous song, the latter being tacitly ratified by A. Manoukian's invitation to Benoît to start singing (instead of asking him, for example, "What's that song? Who sang that one?"). With the elements introduced prior to the audition itself, the vocal performance about to start is expected to allow both the jury and the viewer to assess Benoît's ability to offer a recognizable version of "Stand by Me." Here are the first four shots of the delivered song itself.

(3) *Benoît* [shots 12–17]

12	Ben	♫if the sky/ that we look upon\ .. ♫	*Front shot of Ben.* *His right hand goes up and down* *in rhythm.*
13	Ben	♫ .. should tum*ble/ and fall .. ♫	*Front shot of Sin.* *Sin keeps his head down to the* *table, apparently reading. *Sin* *raises his head towards Ben and* *raises his eyebrows. Then Sin* *lowers his eyebrows and quickly* *raises them again.*
14	Ben	♫and the mountains/ . should♫	*Front shot of Ben.*
15	Ben	♫crumble . to the sea\ .. ♫	*Front shot of Man and Mnk.* *Man writes. Mnk looks at Ben.*
16	Ben	♫ .. ♫	*Front shot of Lio.* *Lio lowers her head to the* *table.*
17	Ben	♫I won't cry♫	*Front shot of Ben.* *With his eyes shut, Ben waves* *his right hand up and down in* *rhythm.*

The introduction of shot 13 makes rapidly clear that the vocal performance in itself will not be the sole focus and theme of the television sequence. It is confirmed by the quick alternation of shots of the candidate and of the jury (12–17), which indicates that, if there is anything to be seen and understood, then that is simultaneously Benoît's singing and its evaluation by the jury. More precisely, shot 13 shows the juror who was previously qualified as "intractable on the musicality and accuracy of the performances."

Figure 3.1   Sinclair [shot 13].

Although a number of glosses of Sinclair's gesture may be available to the viewer,[20] there is hardly any doubt that he is not enthusiastic about Benoît's performance. In this respect, shots 15 and 16 can be seen as attempts by the production team to (re-)assemble the visibility of a collective disapproval of Benoît. In this perspective, shot 15 is not very informative because it seems to show a temporary suspension of assessment by A. Manoukian and P. Manoeuvre. In contrast, Lio's downward head movement in shot 16 is made visible as aligned with Sinclair's disapproval.

The jurors know that, at any time during the evaluated performance, their bodies may be scrutinized by the candidate in search of an assessment signal. The competence of "jurors of a TV show" consists partly in making nonverbal assessment visible to the camera.[21] The production team thus constantly monitors (and frequently anticipates) the jurors' nonverbal behaviour and, through live editing, turns it into a coherent array of assessment signals that progressively assemble a collective evaluation.

This first part of the assessment sequence shows that at least Sinclair and probably Lio react negatively to Benoît's very first verses. The previous qualification of Sinclair as intractable invites the viewer to cast serious doubts about the accuracy of Benoît's rendition of "Stand by Me," while the formulation of the first rule, to "sing a famous song and do so recognizably," provides that same viewer with a reason to hear the song as unrecognizable.

It should be noticed that this assessment is available to the viewer on the sole basis of a common-sense watching of the television sequence, with or without knowledge of the melody of "Stand by Me." The negative assessment and its focus on unrecognizability are formulated and upgraded in the following shots.

(4)   *Benoît* [shots 17–23]

17	Ben	♫I won't cry♫	Front shot of Ben. With his eyes shut, Ben waves his right hand up and down in rhythm.
18	Ben	♫I/ won't cry no I won't\ . ♫	Front shot of Sin. Sin suddenly turns his head towards the other jurors, then turns again to Ben and slowly raises his head but still staring at him.
19	Ben	♫ .. [shed a tear]♫	Front shot of the jury. Lio waves her left arm as she sings, turning to Man and Mnk. Mnk shakes his head when he replies.
	Lio	♫[I won't cry]♫ isn't it that/	
	Mnk	I don't get the melody at all	
20	Lio	hey [are you sure]&	Front shot of Lio. Ben's shoulder appears on the left of the screen.
	Ben	♫[just]♫	
	Lio	&you are in the melody because I don't know it	
21	Lio	at all ♫I [won't cry/] .. ♫&	Front shot of Ben. Ben looks at Lio, nodding, then looks at Man.
	Man	♫[won't cry/]♫	
22	Lio	♫&no I [won't cry/] .. ♫	Front shot of the jury. Lio and Man wave their left arm as they sing.
	Man	♫[won't cry/]♫	
	Lio	♫mhm mhm\♫	
23	Lio	[you]	Front shot of Ben. Ben looks at the jury.
	Ben	♫[I-] hum I won't cry .. I/ won't♫	

Shots 17 and 18 are critical in that they correspond to the beginning of the second verse. Once repeated, the incorrect singing[22] appears as intended by Benoît or at least not accidental. This intentional aspect is congruent with Benoît's attitude as displayed in shot 17, which shows him fully and seriously engaged in the song, as opposed to, for example, trying to remember the melody. In shot 18, the intractable juror's sudden head movement towards the other jurors suggests a quest for intersubjective confirmation, which could be glossed as a question, such as, "Do you hear what I hear?" and at the same time signals an apparent problem or concern, both to the jurors and to the candidate, through turning back to him. For the viewer, shot 18 is a visual invitation to inspect the ongoing song in search of singing troubles. This truly audiovisual combination invites even a viewer who would not know the song "Stand by Me" to identify troubles in Benoît's rendition of it.

There is an upgrading in the strength of negative assessment between shots 18 and 19–22. Whereas in shot 18, Sinclair's gesture may constitute a correction-invitation device, Lio's taking of a turn at singing/talking in shot 19 operates as an interrupting heterocorrection. Lio intervenes with a candidate singing repair, followed by a request for confirmation to the other jurors. Though it does not confirm Lio's candidate repair, A. Manoukian's turn does confirm Lio's so far implicit diagnosis. After that confirmation, Lio overtly interrupts Benoît in shots 20–22 with an almost rhetorical question, "Are you sure you are in the melody?" This is followed by an explicit evaluation of unrecognizability, "because I don't know it at all," and again a candidate singing repair, "?I won't cry/ .. ?." This correction is confirmed and strengthened by P. Manoeuvre who joins Lio's singing in shots 21–22.

Lio makes explicit what was largely anticipated: the first candidate sang a famous but unrecognizable song and thus has failed to follow the first rule (whether he had been instructed on the rule's jurisdictional relevance for his performance remains an open question). Yet Lio's formulation is what retrospectively invited viewers to watch the entire sequence as organized from the beginning under the auspices of the rule "sing a famous song and do so recognizably." In this case, the production work seems to have exploited the local and occasioned relevance of that rule. The rule in question appears to be reified in that it is presented as governing the action from the beginning. This interesting feature has been observed in numerous other sequences of the program, which are retrospectively made visible as ordered in a way that was not available in the endogenously developing course of action. This can be taken as a telling case of "professional vision" (Goodwin, 1994) in reality TV, grounded in a specific multimodal analysis by the production team itself.

From this point on, Benoît has to take the correction into account and attempt to sing recognizably. As the following shots indicate, his attempts are met with the jury's growing hilarity.

(5)   *Benoît* [shots 23–36]

23	Lio	[you]	*Front shot of Ben.*
	Ben	♫[I-] hum <u>I</u> won't cry .. I/ won't.♫	*Ben looks at the jury.*
24	Ben	♫cry no I won't\ .. ♫	*Front shot of Man and Mnk. Man and Mnk look at Ben. Mnk smiles slightly.*
25	Sin	♫be af-♫	*Front shot of Lio.*
	Ben	♫shed a tear\ .. ♫	*Lio smiles.*
	Mnk	((laughter))	
	Sin	♫be af-♫ mhm tss	
26	Ben	°♫just as long♫°	*Front shot of Ben. Ben smiles slightly.*
27	Sin	what a crook	*Front shot of the jury.*
	Lio	[((laughing)) yes what a crook]	*Sin turns towards the other jurors.*
	Mnk	[((bursts into laughter))]	
28	Lio	((laughing)) you are conning us benoît	*Front shot of Man and Mnk. Mnk laughs and turns towards Man.*

29	Lio	you're not singing the song ((laughing))	*Front shot of the jury.* *Lio raises her left index finger.*
30	Lio	[that you said you'd sing to us]&	*Front shot of Lio.* *Lio keeps her index finger raised.*
	Mnk	[((laughter))]	
31	Lio	and [and we were a little shy] last year&	*Front shot of Ben.* *Ben smiles and rubs his hands.*
	Sin	[he's a hell of a crook]	
32	Sin	[bastard xxxx]	*Front shot of the jury.* *Lio extends her hands, her eyes wide open.*
	Lio	&[we said mhm] but this year	
33	Lio	we rebel against crooks of your kind	*Front shot of Lio.* *Lio looks at the other jurors and then at Ben.*
34	Lio	[my dear benoît]	*Front shot of Ben.* *Ben smiles and spreads his hands.*
	Sin	[you won't have] ben e. king	
35	Sin	on the phone will you	*Front shot of the jury.* *Sin looks at Ben.*
	Mnk	((laughter))	
36	Lio	come on benoît let's go	*Front shot of Ben.* *Ben stops singing and smiles when Mnk bursts into laughter.*
	Ben	♪if the sky/ [that we look upon\]♪	
	Mnk	[((bursts into laughter))]	

Benoît's manifest degradation culminates with Sinclair's characterization of him as a crook and its expansion by Lio. It can be noted that the crook category implies a deceptive intention. Benoît is not just out of tune but intentionally attempting to deceive the jury and the viewer, in turn justifying the jury's anger or at least strong irony. The rest of the audition consists mainly of variations on the crook theme. It results in an undoubtedly good sequence, even though it does not indicate the next *Nouvelle Star*.

This first analysis of an assessment sequence shows that, as Garfinkel (1956: 420) suggested, successful degradation ceremonies imply communicative work designed to modify the definition of the situation. We emphasized the orientation of this communicative work to the viewer of the program, who, through simply watching the show, is provided with the moral means that may ground his or her assessment of the candidate. In the case observed, Benoît was made accountably watchable as having violated the first rule. If Benoît could be seen that way, however, then this seemed to have relied upon a particular articulation of visual assessment in situ, as made recognizable and filmable by the jurors' behaviour and by the post-production reassembly of the filmed assessments. In other words, the scenic intelligibility of the assessment sequence is the common-sense material that the production team exploits in order to build up a tutorial sequence through in situ and post-production work.[23]

What holds for degradation also holds for selection. We will now briefly turn to a selection sequence, the interest of which also lies in making visible the presupposed relationship to the viewer.[24]

4.2.   Making a "Great Singer" Visible to the Viewer

The second part of the same show includes a selection of the auditions that took place in Lille in Northern France. After a few unsuccessful candidates, Melissa is introduced by the voice-over as being an "exception." A brief sequence, shot in the waiting room, is devoted to her and to her mother who came to support her. She then enters the audition room and is asked her age, name, and the title of the song that she is going to sing. She is then invited to start singing.

(6)   *Melissa* [shots 7–11]

7	Man	when you wish\	*Front shot of Man and Mnk.*
	Mel	♪I/ lo::ve♪	*Mnk raises his eyes towards*
			Mel as she starts to sing.
8	Mel	((snaps her fingers in	*Front shot of Mel.*
		rhythm(#)))♪you/. # . #	*At the bottom of the screen:*
		but I:: #gotta stay	*MELISSA 17 ANS –*
		#true/ . # . #♪	*MAUBEUGE.(MELISSA 17 YEARS*
			OLD – FROM MAUBEUGE)
9	Mel	♪my moral's #got me on	*General shot of the audition*
		my #knee::s/♪	*room. Man shakes his head in*
			rhythm.
10	Mel	♪I'm #begging please\#	*Front shot of Man.*
		stop #playing #ga: #:#♪	*Man looks at Mel, smiles and*
			shakes his head in rhythm.
11	Mel	♪:#:mes . I don't know#	*General shot of the audition*
		what this . #i::s/♪	*room.*
			Man turns his head towards
			the other jurors then again
			towards Mel.

The first shot of the singing itself (7) immediately shows that Melissa at least catches the interest of one of the jurors who raises his eyes towards her. Shot 8 allows the production team to show the singer and to insert her name, age, and origin at the bottom of the screen. Shot 8 also shows that, while singing, Melissa snaps her fingers, which marks the rhythm visibly as well as audibly. The introduction of shot 9 demonstrates again that the purpose and logic of the audition sequence is to show not the performance and then its assessment but rather the performance as being constantly assessed. In shot 9, the rhythmic "affordance" offered by Melissa's finger snapping is being grasped by at least one of the jurors. As a consequence, shot 10 is devoted to this juror, Man, and reveals that his smile is connected with witnessably competent singing, and it thereby clearly indicates a positive assessment of the performance. Shot 11 is identical to shot 9 but shows in addition that Man turns towards the other jurors, apparently in search of confirmation of his positive uptake of the performance. Though formally equivalent to shot 18 of the previous analysis, which we glossed as "Do you hear what I hear?," what shot 11 signals here is a remarkably good performance rather than a problem in the rendition of the song.[25] Another similarity with the sequence previously analysed is an upgrade in the ongoing assessment that is made visible in the succession of shots (the difference being that no rule seems to have been formulated and shown to viewers at home prior to the singing performance).

(7)   *Melissa* [shots 12–15]

12	Mel	♫cause you #got me good #just like you #knew♫	*Front shot of Mel.*
13	Mel	♫you #wou:::ld . # .#♫	*Horizontal split screen.* *Above: front shot of the host and Mel's mother, both seated.* *The host shakes her torso and head in rhythm.* *Below: front shot of Mnk.* *Zoom up to a close-up of Mnk smiling.*
14	Mel	♫I don't know #what you #do/♫	*Horizontal split screen.* *Above: front shot of the host and Mel's mother, both seated.* *The host shakes her torso and head in rhythm.* *Below: profile shot of Mel.*
15	Mel	♫but you #do it well\ # I'm un#der your #spe: ♫	*Front shot of Mel.*

A new visual device, the split screen, is introduced in shots 13 and 14. In shot 13, it allows the viewer to see two remote scenes at the same time (see also Mondada, 2009). The upper part of the screen shows the host of the show and Melissa's mother in what appears to be a viewing studio, where they are seated in front of screens, as made visible in shot 21. While the mother is focused on watching the screens, the host moves to the rhythm of the song. The shot of the studio may be used when relatives or friends of the candidate are available. It allows the program to produce good sequences, for example of parents witnessing the gradation or degradation of their children. A recurrent and sadistic use of the device consists in turning off the screen in the middle of the performance before its explicit assessment, in order to augment the parent's anxiety and to film it. Significantly, the mother and the host have access to the audition via TV screens rather than from the backstage of the audition room. The lower part of the screen shows a close-up of one of the jurors, whose large smile undoubtedly indicates a positive assessment of the performance. The split screen may be taken to suggest that the viewer's attention is as focused on the assessment as it is on the vocal performance. We will see this even more clearly in a subsequent split screen shot.

The following shots exhibit a continuation of the upgrading of the positive assessment by the jury.

(8)   *Melissa* [shots 16–19]

16	Mel	♪-#:ll: #:#: I said relea#:#:♪	*Front close-up shot of Sin,* *silently snapping his fingers.* *A panoramic to close-up shot of* *Lio, staring at Mel, leaning* *forward, with half-closed eyes.* *Lio shakes her torso and head* *in rhythm.*
17	Mel	♪#:se♪	*Front shot of Lio and Sin, same* *behaviour as shot 16.*
18	Mel	♪yea #:#:#:se h now you think that♪	*Front shot of Mel*
	Lio	((laughs))	
19	Mel	♪I # #:#♪	*Front shot of the jury.*
	Lio	((laughs))	*Pronounced gestures by Lio. Mnk*
	Mel	♪will be some thing#♪	*and Sin, smiling, turn towards* *Lio, then towards Mel.*

Shots 16–19 display a number of features of the jurors' behaviour (rhythmic movements of various parts of the body, smiles, exchange of glances, etc.), which reflexively assemble an unambiguously positive assessment. It is particularly the case for juror Lio, who almost mimetically embodies the most dramatic phase of the song, the long expansion of "release" in shots 16–18. When it is finished, her audible laughs can be heard as an enthusiastic positive evaluation. The obvious character of the ongoing assessment is in its turn made visible in and through the following shots.

(9)   *Melissa* [shots 20–21]

| 20 | Mel | ♪on the side#: #♪ | *Front shot of Mel, who seems to* *hide her smile by lowering her* *head.* |
| 21 | Mel | ♪cause you got# to understand that# I nee::d a man♪ | *Horizontal split screen* *Above: front shot of the host* *and Mel's mother, both seated.* *The mother begins to cry and* *covers her mouth with her hand.* *Shaken by sobs, she turns* *towards the host. The host* *smiles at her, lays her hand on* *her arm and rubs her shoulder.* *Below: back shot of the host* *and Melissa's mother, in front* *of two TV screens, with Lio on* *the left screen and Mel on the* *right screen.* |

Figure 9.1   Melissa's mother and the host in the viewing studio [shot 21].

In shot 20, Melissa's attempts to hide her smile, obviously caused by the jury's enthusiasm, show not only that the candidate is the first witness of the ongoing assessment but also that she can be used by the program to make the ongoing assessment visible.[26]

This reflexive configuration culminates at shot 21, which again exploits, though distinctly, the split screen device. As in shots 13–14, the upper part of the split screen is a front shot of the host and the mother in the viewing studio. Yet their behaviour has changed significantly: the mother begins to cry, and the host, no longer moving in rhythm, displays affectionate support. The lower part of the split screen is a back shot of the same scene. Far from being redundant, the lower part shows that what moves the mother so much are two screens in front of her, the left one showing juror Lio enthusiastically smiling and moving in rhythm and the right one showing Melissa not only singing but exhibiting the joyful uptake of her ongoing positive assessment.

In the economy of the program, the mother can be said here to be and to personify the intended viewer, in that she is moved to tears[27] by the candidate's assessment as broadcast.[28] It is such moved, progressively trained, and possibly exhausted viewers who are liable to respond via charged-for SMSs to the tireless summons to which they are subjected again and again during the live shows. Conversely, the explicit statement of the setting up of candidates, as tentatively described in this chapter, would possibly have viewers turn off their television sets and go elsewhere, say, to the movies.

5.   CONCLUSION

Reality TV talent shows may constitute a perspicuous setting for the analysis of video at work. In Section 3, we showed that it is mostly on the basis of (re-)assembled television scenes, rather than strictly vocal performances, that a candidate gradually appears as a possible *Nouvelle Star*. In Section 4, we attempted to examine further the video work by which the candidates are made available for their assessment by the viewer of the program. It is not simply because the viewers are repeatedly instructed to send charged-for SMSs that they will do so. Voting this way presupposes that they have been able to assess the candidates who appear on their television screens. This assessment ability is highly specific. It is provided by and for the program, in and as its course. In the cases we have examined, it is presupposed that viewers be able to recognize a great singer and to detect a crook. Watching the program includes experiencing the availability of the assessment accomplished by the jurors. Far from being an expert and esoteric practice, the assessment of candidates is immediately available to any viewer, where that immediacy, in turn, seems to hinge upon the partial disappearance of the setting-up procedure of the candidates. The described "scenic availability" (Jayyusi, 1988) is essential for the working of the program, which both logically and financially requires the participation of the viewer. It is achieved through an array of video practices, some of which have been examined in this study.

The televisual accountability of the morality of vocal performances results from the professionally competent practices of the various members of the production team. As such, they could and should be documented by the kind of ethnographic video-supported workplace study that we were not allowed to do. Yet such a study would still have to account for the immediate and mundane availability of the product of such situated and distributed work—in the present case, the ordinary intelligibility of a talent show. What we proposed in this study is the analysis of some of its main features. In our view, such an investigation can be seen as a respecification of reality TV, which has to be grasped as a specific modality of television rather than as a distinct genre. In this respect, reality TV appears as a privileged topic for the study of video at work.

NOTES

1. This paper is based on a joint French and German research project (ANR-DFG) on evaluation processes in reality-TV casting shows. The project was coordinated by Olivier Voirol and directed by Axel Honneth at the Institut für Sozialforschung in Frankfurt and Louis Quéré at the Institut Marcel Mauss-CEMS, EHESS, Paris. We thank the members of the German team, Cornelia Schendzielorz and Olivier Voirol, for the fruitful discussions we had with them on various points of this paper. We also thank the anonymous reviewer whose fine remarks helped make the text clearer.
2. As we shall see, "communicative work [is] directed to transforming an individual's total identity into an identity lower in the group's scheme of social types. . . . [This] is called a 'status degradation ceremony'" (Garfinkel, 1956: 420).
3. What we did have access to were the queues of candidates waiting to be auditioned because they line up on public urban space. Some initial descriptions in Section 2 will be based on this in situ observation.
4. A similar interest is pursued by Relieu (1999).

5. Pursuing this special interest may have questionable consequences because the indirectly approached practices, described via the filming operations that make them visible, risk being cast as *analytic* concerns from the outset, rather than as mundane matters, as directly pursued and expressed by participants in the setting (including those of a production team distinguishing between different types of "shots"). For instance, Mondada, in a paper that draws upon Macbeth's discussion, sketches a "multi-modal analysis of next speaker selection" (our summary) by showing, via different camera views, how different modalities (speech, gesture, and gaze) appear to be articulated for timely speaker selection to occur in and as part of the filmed interaction (2006: 56–58). Yet the relationship between that analytic description and its vernacular presentation, as a "work session between agronomists and computer scientists" (ibid.: 56), is not made explicit analytically. The same criticism applies more generally to the "institutional talk" program (see Hester & Francis, 2000, 2001).

6. For a related experience and descriptive analysis, consider Fitzgerald, Housley, and Reynolds (2011). For an analysis inspired by Foucault's notion of discipline, see McIlvenny (2009).

7. The preaudition step does not appear at all in the TV program, suggesting that the jury directly auditions thousands of queuing candidates.

8. An important aspect of Soan's character is to have been a busker in the Parisian subway.

9. As one of the jurors ironically told Soan, "We finally thought that with your closed voice and your bad articulation, you were quite indispensable to the program. We'll keep you."

10. Soan's look was more noticed than praised. One of the jurors even called him Quasimodo, after the ugly hunchback character of Victor Hugo's novel *Notre Dame de Paris*.

11. The figure was a visual allusion to the cover picture of a record of Les Têtes Raides, another French indie rock band.

12. It may not have been really the case. What matters to us, though, is not what really happened but what the program really and accountably invites the viewer to see and understand. More generally, Soan should not be made personally responsible for his televisual appearances, which were obviously elaborated on or imposed by the production team. On at least two occasions, Soan clearly stated on-air that he was not allowed to choose the songs he had to sing and that, for the choice of which, he was also assessed.

13. In the next section, we will specify how the viewer is trained to assess the vocal performance visually.

14. Recall Debord's quotation used as epigraph of this text: "The spectacle is not a collection of images; it is a social relation among people that is mediated by images."

15. Here and in the rest of the text, the description adopts the perspective of the TV viewer, to whom the audition was presented as the first of the season. Whether or not it was really the case is the kind of issue that was debated at length in the innumerable critical forums devoted to the show, notably but not only on the website of the program.

16. See Bovet (2007) for a similar analysis of the live editing of political debates.

17. The verbal transcription adopts most of the usual CA conventions, except for the following: the singing parts are delimited with ♫ symbols. / and \ indicates raising and descending intonations. & indicates that the delivery of the same turn continues without interruption at another line of the transcript (also started with &). See the Appendix at the end of this chapter for

the identification of the speakers and complete transcripts in their original language.

18. The four jurors are French celebrities. André Manoukian (Mnk in the transcript) is a jazz musician and producer. Philippe Manœuvre (Man) is a rock journalist. Sinclair (Sin) is a funk musician. Lio (Lio) is a pop singer. Their celebrity is partly or entirely due to their appearance on the TV program.

19. At least four cameras are in the audition room. There is an on-the-spot selection of cameras. The sequence is slightly edited in post-production, as shown by some clearly discernible cuts.

20. In a data session, Lorenza Mondada invited us to notice a "sulky" lip movement at the very beginning of shot 13, that could be seen as a prefiguration of the following (and upgraded) head and eyebrows gesture. It suggests that one can always go further in the description of the material that is exploited by the production team in order to (re-)assemble meaningful television sequences. It also reminds us that a transcript is never completed but deemed sufficient (or not) for analytical purposes.

21. On common-sense manipulations of various "parameters of interpersonal observation," see Sudnow's classical study (Sudnow, 1972), as a respecification of Goffman's pioneering work (Goffman, 1959, 1963, 1971).

22. The television sequence manages to make Benoît's singing appear incorrect according to the rule instead of, for example, alternative or idiosyncratic.

23. In that sense, it seems relevant to distinguish between Garfinkel's and the program's degradation ceremonies: whereas the former seem to fulfil the functional role of restoring the social order, the latter have a distinctive pedagogical intent.

24. If the productive reassembly made possible the negative assessment and patent degradation of the candidate (e.g. as a crook rather than a singer), it seems to have made the setting up of the candidate disappear as a constitutive part of the assessment situation.

25. In this respect, the comparison suggests that when a juror turns his/her head towards the other jurors, he/she theatrically signals something special, which the course of action reflexively establishes as good, bad, funny, or so on.

26. This observation is inspired by Goffman's remark that the faces of pedestrians passing each other can be used as a rearview mirror (Goffman, 1971).

27. Of course, various kinds of emotion can do the trick. It may also be out of indignation caused by a particularly obnoxious juror that the viewer wants to support a candidate. Interestingly, this is what happens in the explicit assessment part of the same audition. Juror A. Manoukian tells Melissa that she "looks like a seventies prostitute out of a Melville film," which causes her to burst into tears. This became a famous sequence in the 2009 season and led to various replays and staging involving the juror, the mother, Melissa, and the clothes she was wearing during this audition.

28. Though, as a mother, she has a specific entitlement to cry over her daughter's performance, it is (literally) from the position of a(ny) television viewer that she is moved to tears.

REFERENCES

Bovet, A. (2007). Donner à voir le débat politique. Le montage en direct d'un débat télévisé. *Bulletin suisse de linguistique appliqué*, 85, 181–202.

Debord, G. (2006). *The Society of the Spectacle*. London: Rebel Press.

Fitzgerald. R., Housley, W., & Reynolds, E. (2011). Degradation and redemption as an interactional spectacle on the Jeremy Kyle Show. Paper presented at the 12th IPRA Conference, July 3–8, 2011, Manchester, UK.

Francis, D., & Hester, S. (2004). *An Invitation to Ethnomethodology: Language, Society and Interaction.* London: Sage.

Garfinkel, H. (1956). Conditions of successful degradation ceremonies. *American Journal of Sociology 61*, 420–424.

Garfinkel, H. (1967). *Studies in Ethnomethodology.* Englewood Cliffs, NJ: Prentice Hall.

Garfinkel, H., Lynch, M., & Livingston, E. (1981). The work of a discovering science construed with materials from the optically discovered pulsar. *Philosophy of the Social Sciences, 11*, 131–58.

Goffman, E. (1959). *The Presentation of Self in Everyday Life.* New York: Doubleday Anchor.

Goffman, E. (1963). *Behavior in Public Places. Notes on the Social Organization of Gatherings.* New York: Free Press.

Goffman, E. (1971). *Relations in Public: Microstudies of the Public Order.* New York: Basic Books.

Goodwin, C. (1994), Professional vision. *American Anthropologist, 96*, 606–633.

Jayyusi, L. (1988). Towards a socio-logic of the film text. *Semiotica, 68*, 271–296.

Koschmann, T., & Zemel, A. (2009). Optical pulsars and black arrows: Discoveries as occasioned productions. *The Journal of the Learning Sciences, 18*, 200–246.

Lynch, M. (2000). Against reflexivity as an academic virtue and source of privileged knowledge. *Theory, Culture, and Society, 17*, 27–53.

McIlvenny, P. (2009). Communicating a "time-out" in parent–child conflict: Embodied interaction, domestic space and discipline in a reality TV parenting programme. *Journal of Pragmatics, 41*(10), 2017–2032.

Macbeth, D. (1999). Glances, trances, and their relevance for a visual sociology. In P. L. Jalbert (Ed.), *Media Studies: Ethnomethodological Approaches* (pp. 135–170). Lanham, MD: University Press of America.

Mondada, L. (2006). Video recording as the reflexive preservation-configuration of phenomenal features for analysis. In H. Knoblauch, B, Schnettler, J. Raab, & H.-G. Soeffner (Eds.), *Video Analysis. Methodology and Methods. Qualitative Audiovisual Data Analysis* (pp. 51–68). Bern: Lang.

Mondada, L. (2009). Video recording practices and the reflexive constitution of the interactional order: Some systematic uses of the split-screen technique. *Human Studies, 32*, 67–99.

Quéré, L. (2004). Pour une sociologie qui "sauve les phénomènes"? *Revue du MAUSS, 24*, 127–145.

Relieu, M. (1999). La réalisation et la réception du produit télévisuel comme accomplissements. In J.-P. Desgoutte (Ed.), *La mise en scène du discours audiovisuel* (pp. 35–65). Paris: L'Harmattan.

Ryle, G. (1954). Technical and untechnical concepts. In *Dilemmas. The Tarner Lectures 1953* (pp. 82–92). Cambridge: Cambridge University Press.

Schütz, A. (1962). *Collected Papers I: The Problem of Social Reality.* The Hague: Nijhoff.

Sudnow, D. (1972). Temporal parameters of interpersonal observation. In D. Sudnow (Ed.), *Studies in Social Interaction* (pp. 259–279). New York: Free Press.

Widmer, J. (2010). La sociologie comme science rigoureuse. In *Discours et cognition sociale. Une approche sociologique* (pp. 283–290). Paris: Editions des archives contemporaines.

APPENDIX

Transcripts 1 and 2

VO	Voice-over
Sin	Sinclair, juror
Man	Philippe Manoeuvre, juror
Ben	Benoît, candidate
Lio	Lio, juror
Mnk	André Manoukian, juror
Mel	Melissa, candidate

Transcript 1 *Benoît* [shots 1–36]

1	VO	habillé maquillé studieux concentré le jury fait déjà bonne figure	*Front shot of the jury, seated in front of a curved table.*
2	VO	c'est maintenant au premier candidat d'en faire de même	*Horizontal split-screen.* *Above: general shot of the audition room.* *Ben enters the audition room.* *Below: Front shot of the jury.*
3	Sin Man	allez hop c'est parti	*Front shot of Sin.* *Sin raises his right hand.*
4	Sin VO	on y va on envoie première règle	*Front shot of the jury.*
5	VO	interpréter une chanson connue mais reconnaissable	*Back shot of Ben.* *Ben enters the audition room.*
6	Ben Lio	bonsoir bonjour	*Front shot of Ben.* *Ben enters the audition room.*
7	Mnk Sin Mnk	bonjour bonjour c'est ici	*Front shot of Mnk.*
8	Mnk Ben	n'ayez pas peur vous vous appelez comment/ benoît	*Front shot of Ben.* *Ben smiles.*
9	Mnk	et vous allez nous chanter	*Profile shot of the jury.*
10	Ben	euh stand by me	*Front shot of Ben.*
11	Mnk	allez c'est parti	*Front shot of Mnk.*
12	Ben	♫if the sky/ that we look upon\ .. ♫	*Front shot of Ben.* *His right hand goes up and down in rhythm.*
13	Ben	♫ .. should tum*ble/ and fall .. ♫	*Front shot of Sin.* *Sin keeps his head down to the table, apparently reading. *Sin raises his head towards Ben and raises his eyebrows. Then Sin lowers his eyebrows and quickly raises them again.*
14	Ben	♫and the mountains/ . should♫	*Front shot of Ben.*

15	Ben	♫crumble . to the sea\ .. ♫	*Front shot of Man and Mnk.* *Man writes. Mnk looks at Ben.*
16	Ben	♫ .. ♫	*Front shot of Lio.* *Lio lowers her head to the* *table.*
17	Ben	♫I̲ won't cry♫	*Front shot of Ben.* *With his eyes shut, Ben waves* *his right hand up and down in* *rhythm.*
18	Ben	♫I̲/ won't cry no I won't\ . ♫	*Front shot of Sin.* *Sin suddenly turns his head* *towards the other jurors, then* *turns again to Ben and slowly* *raises his head but still* *staring at him.*
19	Ben Lio Mnk	♫ .. [shed a tear]♫ ♫[I won't cry]♫ c'est pas ça/ je comprends rien à la mélodie	*Front shot of the jury.* *Lio waves her left arm as she* *sings, turning to Man and Mnk.* *Mnk shakes his head when he* *replies.*
20	Lio Ben Lio	dis donc t'as [t'es sûr]& ♫[just]♫ &que t'es dans la mélodie parce que moi je la connais pas	*Front shot of Lio.* ***Ben's shoulder appears on the*** *left of the screen.*
21	Lio Man	du tout ♫I [won't cry/] .. ♫& ♫[won't cry/]♫	*Front shot of Ben.* *Ben looks at Lio, nodding, then* *looks at Man.*
22	Lio Man Lio	♫&no I [won't cry/] .. ♫ ♫[won't cry/]♫ ♫mhm mhm\♫	*Front shot of the jury.* *Lio and Man wave their left arm* *as they sing.*
23	Lio Ben	[you] ♫[I-] hum I̲ won't cry .. I/ won't♫	*Front shot of Ben.* *Ben looks at the jury.*
24	Ben	♫cry no I won't\ .. ♫	*Front shot of Man and Mnk.* *Man and Mnk look at Ben. Mnk* *smiles slightly.*
25	Sin Ben Mnk Sin	♫be af-♫ ♫shed a tear\ .. ♫ ((laughter)) ♫be af-♫ mhm tss	*Front shot of Lio.* *Lio smiles.*
26	Ben	°♫just as long♫°	*Front shot of Ben.* *Ben smiles slightly.*
27	Sin Lio Mnk	quel escroc [((laughing)) quel escroc oui] [((bursts into laughter))]	*Front shot of the jury.* *Sin turns towards the other* *jurors.*
28	Lio	((laughing)) là tu nous escroques **benoît**	*Front shot of Man and Mnk.* *Mnk laughs and turns towards* *Man.*
29	Lio	tu ne nous chantes pas la chanson ((laughing))	*Front shot of the jury.* *Lio raises her left index* *finger.*
30	Lio Mnk	[que tu nous as dit que tu nous chanterais]& [((laughter))]	*Front shot of Lio.* *Lio keeps her index finger* *raised.*

31	Lio	et [et nous étions un peu timides] l'an dernier&	Front shot of Ben. Ben smiles and rubs his hands.
	Sin	[c'est un escroc de l'enfer]	
32	Sin	[fumier de la xxxx]	Front shot of the jury. Lio extends her hands, her eyes wide open.
	Lio	&[on faisait mhm] mais cette année	
33	Lio	nous nous rebellons contre les escrocs de ton espèce	Front shot of Lio. Lio looks at the other jurors and then at Ben.
34	Lio	[mon petit benoît]	Front shot of Ben. Ben smiles and spreads his hands.
	Sin	[c'est pas toi qui va avoir] ben e. king	
35	Sin	au téléphone après hein	Front shot of the jury. Sin looks at Ben.
	Mnk	((laughter))	
36	Lio	allez benoît vas-y	Front shot of Ben. Ben stops singing and smiles when Mnk bursts into laughter.
	Ben	♫if the sky/ [that we look upon\]♫	
	Mnk	[((bursts into laughter))]	

Transcript 2 *Melissa* [shots 1–21]

1	Man	bonjour mademoiselle/	General shot of the audition room. Mel comes from the right and stands in front of the jury, seated in front of a curved table.
	Mel	bonjour\	
2	Man	comment vous appelez-[vous/]	Front shot of Mel.
	Mel	[mel]issa	
3	Man	melissa vous avez quel âge/	Front shot of Man and Mnk. Mnk raises his eyes towards Mel. Man writes.
4	Mel	j'ai dix-sept ans et demi\ je vais avoir dix-huit ans dans six jours\	Front shot of Mel.
5	Man	qu'est-ce que vous allez nous inter-	Front shot of Man and Mnk. Man looks at Mel.
6	Man	-préter [ce s-]	Front shot of Mel.
	Mel	[alors] mercy de duffy/	
	Man	o:k/	
7	Man	quand vous voulez\	Front shot of Man and Mnk. Mnk raises his eyes towards Mel as she starts to sing.
	Mel	♫I/ lo::ve♫	
8	Mel	((snaps her fingers in rhythm(#))) ♫you/. # . # but I:: #gotta stay #true/ . # . #♫	Front shot of Mel. At the bottom of the screen: MELISSA 17 ANS – MAUBEUGE.(MELISSA 17 YEARS OLD – FROM MAUBEUGE)
9	Mel	♫my moral's #got me on my #knee::s/♫	General shot of the audition room. Man shakes his head in rhythm.

10	Mel	♫I'm #begging please\# stop #playing #ga: #:#♫	*Front shot of Man.* *Man looks at Mel, smiles and shakes his head in rhythm.*
11	Mel	♫:#:mes . I don't know# what this . #i::s/♫	*General shot of the audition room.* *Man turns his head towards the other jurors then again towards Mel.*
12	Mel	♫cause you #got me good #just like you #knew♫	*Front shot of Mel.*
13	Mel	♫you #wou:::ld . # . #♫	*Horizontal split screen.* *Above: front shot of the host and Mel's mother, both seated. The host shakes her torso and head in rhythm.* *Below: front shot of Mnk. Zoom up to a close-up of Mnk smiling.*
14	Mel	♫I don't know #what you #do/♫	*Horizontal split screen.* *Above: front shot of the host and Mel's mother, both seated. The host shakes her torso and head in rhythm.* *Below: profile shot of Mel.*
15	Mel	♫but you #do it well\ # I'm un#der your #spe: ♫	*Front shot of Mel.*
16	Mel	♫: : #11 # . #I said #relea/:::#:::#:♫	*Front close-up shot of Sin, silently snapping his fingers. A panoramic to close-up shot of Lio, staring at Mel and leaning forward, with half-closed eyes. Lio shakes her torso and head in rhythm.*
17	Mel	♫#:::#se♫	*Front shot of Lio and Sin, same behaviour as shot 16.*
18	Mel	♫yeah::: now you think I:# . #♫	*Front shot of Mel.*
	Lio	((laughs))	
19	Mel	♫will be some #thing♫	*Front shot of the jury. Pronounced gestures by Lio. Mnk and Sin, smiling, turn towards Lio, then towards Mel.*
	Lio	((laughs))	
20	Mel	♫on the #side . # . #♫	*Front shot of Mel, who seems to hide her smile by lowering her head.*
21	Mel	♫cause you got# to under#stand that I #nee:d a man#♫	*Horizontal split screen.* *Above: front shot of the host and Melissa's mother, both seated.* *The mother begins to cry and covers her mouth with her hand. Shaken by sobs, she turns towards the host. The host smiles at her, lays her hand on her arm and rubs her shoulder.* *Below: back shot of the host and Melissa's mother, in front of two TV screens, with Lio on the left screen and Mel on the right screen.*

Part III
Assembling

8 The Mediated Work of Imagination in Film Editing
Proposals, Suggestions, Reiterations, Directions, and Other Ways of Producing Possible Sequences

Eric Laurier (School of GeoSciences, University of Edinburgh)
Barry Brown (Mobile Life, University of Stockholm)

There are hosts of widely divergent sorts of behaviour in the conduct of which we should ordinarily and correctly be described as imaginative. The mendacious witness in the witness-box, the inventor thinking out a new machine, the constructor of a romance, the child playing bears, and Henry Irving are all exercising their imaginations; but so, too, are the judge listening to the lies of the witness, the colleague giving his opinion on the new invention, the novel reader, the nurse who refrains from admonishing the "bears" for their subhuman noises, the dramatic critic and the theatre-goers. Nor do we say that they are all exercising their imaginations because we think that, embedded in a variety of often widely different operations, there is one common nuclear operation which all alike are performing, any more than we think that what makes two men both farmers is some nuclear operation which both do in exactly the same way. (Ryle, 2009: 233)

1. INTRODUCTION

1.1. Exercising Our Imagination

Gilbert Ryle (2009) warned against the mistake of treating imagination as if it were formed out of a gallery of mental images seen inside the head. Ryle's attack on the "ghost in the machine" was a necessarily destructive ground-clearing exercise for philosophical work on imagination. Our ambition in this chapter is more positive, building upon Ryle's redescription of imagination in worldly terms. We pursue the exercise of imagination in the editing of a feature-length documentary film. The editing of a documentary is concerned with the analysis of video, and, in common with the other contributors to this collection, we are trying to teach ourselves more about the analysis of video from other groups whose routine business is to analyse video. Where a number of those authors have been interested in optical and movement actions of cameras (e.g. switching between camera lenses, zooming, and panning) we pursue here the play actions of video players (e.g. winding, rewinding, pausing, etc.). These video practices are part of the skilled handling of images and audio that allow the editing team to see and also edit towards the film-yet-to-come.

Although central to the creation of films, the editing process has been a cause for complaint by some directors, compared by the French director Renoir to washing the dishes after the feast that was shooting the footage (Orpen, 2003). Editing is slow, repetitious, fiddly labour in stuffy rooms, often lacking any windows. Yet close collaboration in the editing suite has been central to the success and originality of many prominent films (e.g. Walter Murch and Anthony Mingella's *The English Patient*, discussed in Ondaatje, 2002) During the weeks, months, or years that a feature film is in the edit, there is a repeated cycling through and over of the audiovisual sequences that comprise the emerging film. The editorial cycle is not simply the repetitive work of French-polishing a chair; it is a profoundly reasoned process of drawing the plans, cutting the wood, and joining the parts (Livingston 2008). It is then taking the chair apart and building it in a different style; then throwing the original legs away and turning a new set; then, after a miserable week of arguing, deciding that it has to be a table. In each editorial cycle, there are more or less complex progressions of planning, assembling, assessing, proposing, formulating, and more. In circling through these interlinked and dependent practices, the current assembly of the film is related to in terms of what more it might need. In making sense of a proposal for how any part of the film could be, its recipient will be required to imagine what this newly proposed cut or sequence or scene might be like in order to be able to accept or reject it. For film editing to begin and to continue, then, there have to be existing filmic materials and a film-yet-to-come. The existing edit is there to be worked upon, to be seen for its relationship with that final filmic object, where that object is itself constantly changing by dint of the edit's progressive establishment of what it is.

1.2. From the Editorial Moment to Editorial Cycles

Though central to the final appearance of a film, editing is an overlooked element of film production (Ondaatje, 2002; Vaughan, 1983). The invisibility of editing is all the more curious given that it is the only aspect of film production that is distinctive to film when compared to other performance arts. Unsurprisingly, there have also been relatively few studies of editing work by the social sciences (Thornton Caldwell, 2008). Recent work has begun to reveal what is involved in the live-editing of talk and sports shows on television (Broth, 2008, 2009; Engström, Juhlin, Perry, & Broth, 2010; Chapter 9 by Perry, Engström, & Juhlin, this volume). The exercise of creative imagination in these time-limited settings is perhaps less obvious than it is in the struggles to produce original works in post-production. We can compare the length of time spent in the edit suite: hours for live broadcasts compared to weeks or months for the feature documentary. Indeed, live-editing in some ways departs from other forms of post-production because it lacks the repetitions of the editorial cycle that we will examine in more detail in this chapter. Even when selecting amongst action replays, live-editing is completed in an amazingly rapid editorial cycle (see Chapter 9 by Perry, Engström, & Juhlin, this volume).

Howard Becker was one of the first sociologists to touch on the nature of editing in his study of the social worlds of artists. He explored the "editorial moment" (Becker, 1982: 198) that involves artists making choices, amongst the tools and materials they have at hand, in order to add, remove, amend, revise, and transform what they have created so far. Using mimeos of T. S. Eliot's poems and Becker's own contact sheets from his photography practice, Becker treated the editorial moment as an internal dialogue with absent others from the art world—one that can be recovered, to some extent, from the traces left on Eliot's mimeo and the annotations on Becker's contact sheets. He points out that artists' assessments and formulations (e.g. "it swings" for jazz music) are frustratingly vague for the sociologist and yet felicitous for the artists involved. This is because, firstly, it is competence in the practice that provides for the reliable, appropriate, and meaningful use of the assessments (which sociologists often lack). Although their assessments remain open to disagreement from other practitioners, their application to this or that element of the artistic medium is almost always understood. Secondly, what Becker alludes to, and what we will return to later, is that the part or feature of the medium made relevant by the assessment being produced at that particular juncture resolves the ambiguity of the assessment that is being provided of it.

What Becker called the "editorial moment" is extended into the "editorial cycle" by Clayman and Reisner (1998) in their study of newspaper editorial meetings. Where Becker's description of the editorial moment remained one of the individual in the studio, the newspaper editorial meetings studied by Clayman and Reisner bear a close resemblance, in their routine structure, to the editing of feature films. No longer an internal silent debate between the artist and the absent others of his art world, the editorial meeting is a talkative, institutional, and potentially lengthy series of practices for establishing what will go into the newspaper, on what page, and on which particular part of the page each story will appear. On the basis of observing a number of such meetings in different newspaper offices, Clayman and Reisner break the cycle into four stages:

1. preliminaries
2. story review
3. story selection
4. aftermath

Where the film editing workflow departs from newspaper editing is around how long and how many times each sequence of the film is put through the cycle. For the newspaper, it is once, but for a film, it is potentially tens or hundreds of times. Film, of course, also departs from newspaper editing through the medium and the practices in which its meaning is realized. In the editing suite, there is only infrequently a "story" to be dealt with. As we shall see, editors are usually reviewing and selecting amongst a wider array of features of the medium (e.g. scenes, sequences, quotes, clips, colour, transitions, etc.) The media that come together in the film editing suite shape not only the final film itself but, even as they are being reshaped, the very making of that final film. It is a process that overlaps with the newspaper journalist's writing and editing of particular stories, the picture editing, the layout, and so on. This is not to say that questions over images and layouts and so on do not arise at all in the newspaper editorial meeting; they are missing from Clayman and Reisner's study because, as they note with some dismay in their article, only having recorded the audio they miss, amongst other things, "the photos, graphics, written story lists and other materials commonly introduced in such meetings" (1998: 180).

1.3. Media for Assessment and Imagination

Even though photos, graphics, and the other media required for editing were missing from Clayman and Reisner's work, they have been studied by a number of researchers in architectural practice. Murphy (2004, 2005) examined a routine problem for architects and their clients posed by the materiality of the plan of a building: it is flat. It thus requires the exercise of imagination to visualise the project-relevant elements of the three-dimensional building-that-is-to-come, such as corridors, doors, and stairs. In an educational setting, Lymer (2009, 2010) again focused on plans but in his case on how plans are assessed by tutors and lecturers during crits (i.e. presentation, review, and criticism). Both Murphy and Lymer help us to understand the centrality of the media to the work. Similarly, Monika Büscher's (2001) doctoral research on landscape architecture captures how multiple media, including plans and samples of building materials, are brought into the exercise of imagination in visualizing the landscape-to-come. Büscher points out that the language and gestures around materials are vague and that it is the materials that provide details of texture, colour, dimensions within the gestalt of the speech situation. Quite how the building materials are to be assessed is accomplished through not only what is said about them but also how they are "picked up, turned, held or placed to be compared with others or with pictures in the product information catalogues" (2001: 123). From Murphy's, Lymer's, and Büscher's work, we can then begin to draw out how imagination is required to find the building-yet-to-come in the current media of plans and samples, as well as the role of media as both requiring imagination for their assessment but also providing resources central to the joint exercise of imagination. They document the work that needs to be done with the plans to make intelligible what might be wrong with the current plan for the building, and to imagine alternatives for what the building might become (Lymer, 2010).

Having introduced three studies of architectural practice to help underline the centrality of media, it is worth reminding ourselves briefly of what differentiates the medium of film from that of the architectural plan. The first is a flat paper plan over which meetings are held, and the second is an animate and "sounded" medium that is played during editing. In other simpler and more familiar words, video is audiovisual. Editing video involves assembling multiple media: camera shots, text, graphics, animations, CGI, foley, voice-over, music, and more. Those multimedia aspects of video are of less relevance to our purposes here than the fact that video is, for lack of a better phrase, playable. As a playable medium, video provides for a variety of actions; it can be cued, played, replayed, paused, looped, interrupted, scrubbed, rewound, moved frame by frame and repaired (Greiffenhagen & Watson (2009).

In and through its playing, the characteristics of video are made available to its viewers—its duration, its sequencing, and its lamination of multiple media. The centrality of montage to understanding editing that dominates the work of Deleuze (1992, 2005) and others emerges from the study of finished (for all practical editorial purposes) films. The focus on the cut in the theory of montage has eclipsed our understanding of the practice of editing as it happens. During the edit, the montage is still in process; quite what will be cut in relation to what will be cut is still being tried out. The piecing together of the film requires the manipulation, configuration, assembly, disassembly, and reassembly of multiple playable media (Greiffenhagen & Watson 2009). In editing-as-it-happens, the film is not produced in the way that film theorists would watch the final product by playing through the film and only perhaps replaying a few key scenes.

Three buttons are central to video actions that produce the film during editing: <<, >, and >> (on a keyboard, they are usually "j," "k," and "l"), and beyond these keys, editors have quite a few more keyboard shortcuts at hand. These three buttons allow video to be played forward, backward, speeded up, or slowed and stopped. Video actions produce the appearances of the section of emerging film that is being edited, and these appearances are part of the imaginative work of the editorial team in their proposals, assessments, and decisions about the film-yet-to-come. Perhaps because, even in the age of video recording and playback devices (from VHS to VLC), videos still tend to be viewed after one touch of the play button, the close examination of video actions beyond "play" has been more apparent in studies of video data sessions (Tutt & Hindmarsh, 2011; Tutt, Hindmarsh, Shaukat, & Fraser, 2007), which also require playing, pausing, replaying, rewinding, and so on.

In the edit, because the film is still in construction and still being formulated, clips, sequences, and sounds need to be viewed and reviewed in skilful ways by and through playing sequences that may not only be unfinished but also have parts missing. Continuing the work of assembling the film and identifying what it lacks are accomplished also in the talking and gesturing in, around, and over the playing, replaying, winding, and rewinding. For the field of conversation analysis, there are intriguing parallels between how talk and video are both constructed sequentially and the fact that video editing utilizes the sequential properties generated by cutting from one clip to another and from one scene to another. For the assembled filmic object that we will observe being edited later in this chapter, it has already been built up through earlier editing, creating sequences: this goes after that, this is before that. When these two things (clip plus clip) are paired, a relation of adjacency pairs is created for the viewer/hearer (Jayyusi, 1988). Moreover, the assembling that is done in editing puts audio to picture, laminating one to the other (see McCloud, 1993, for a similar relationship in comics between panel and speech bubble). Later, the clips and the audio will be watched and heard as a gestalt; however, while in the making, the gestalt is constantly disassembled and reassembled into its parts to consider other possible assemblies.

1.4.   Imagining the Film-to-Come through Proposals and Assessments

Early work on invitations, requests, and proposals (Davidson, 1984; Houtkoop-Steenstra, 1987, 1990), when it has been taken up in institutional settings, has tended to be in medical settings (Heritage & Sefi, 1992; Stivers, 2002). There are a number of differences in the institutional setting of film editing, not least the project and objects involved. However, the pertinent distinction is in the standardized relation pair of patient and health professional, which are oriented towards and produced in medical encounters. The editor and director are on a much more equal footing as members of the film-making profession, and each may well have done the other's job at points in their career. Maynard's recent study of real estate agents and misdemeanour court trials (Maynard, 2010) provides us with comparable negotiation on proposals between peers. He delineates a set of responses (the snappily titled "defer, demur, deter") arising in negotiation. His work provides us with a sense of how proposals can be met not only with deferring, demurring, and deterring but also with counterproposals. The counterproposal connects with Büscher's (2001) studies of imagination-in-action, although with the crucial difference that in Maynard's research negotiations are between opposed parties from different teams. For Büscher's landscape architects and, in this chapter, for the editor and director as part of the same production team with a shared project, they are not trying "to develop the most advantageous positions they can relative to each other" (Maynard, 2010: 140).

Of most direct relevance to this chapter in terms of media, Broth (2004, 2008) examines the proposal-acceptance sequence in live editing in television production. He shows how camera operators propose shots by swinging their camera, zooming, and then bringing into stable focus a particular person during a live TV debate. These are inescapably visual proposals because the camera operators remain silent throughout the broadcast, using only the movements of the cameras to offer shots to the director. In terms of the previous section, these are particular camera actions that are being used to propose shots, and, in fact, the camera can be used to produce a wider array of actions such as acknowledging, confirming, and agreeing (Chapter 2 by Broth, this volume). In the case of this chapter, video actions are intertwined with talk and bodily gestures because the editor and director have no need to remain silent or hidden during the playback of edited sequences. The connection between assessments of the current edit and the offering of proposals brings the interests of this chapter into connection with Mondada's (Chapter 3, this volume) examination of the relationship between surgeon's directives and their assessment of the shots produced by camera operators.

Although live editing and surgical camerawork bring us close to the organization of film editing, the crucial difference is that the sequencing of the cameras draws upon either the organization of the live event as its fundamental resource (see also Mondada, 2009) or the workplace tasks of surgery and instruction (see also Chapter 5 by Lindwall, Johansson, Rystedt, Ivarsson, & Reit, this volume). The feature film has no such primary tasks; it can sequence itself as it pleases, drawing upon the grammars of story, scenes, and montage and on the conventions of genre or indeed on the organization of everyday or institutional conversations. As already noted, it is the very exercise of imagination in editing that results in the many months that film-makers spend in the editing suite. Whereas the editing of a TV debate takes roughly the time that the debate itself takes as an event, the editing of the documentary that we will present next took nine months. That is the time that it takes to map out a broad structure; to review and assess clips, sequences, scenes, and transitions; and to revisit and transform that broad structure many times over. It is the time that it takes for the careful consideration of alternative clips, sequences, transitions, soundtracks, animations, and more elements that might yet become the finished film. It is in these editorial cycles over nine months that we reconnect with Clayman and Reisner's newspaper editorial cycle (though even that cycle seems like the flight of a mayfly compared to the complexities of movie editing).

1.5.   A Brief Apology for the Difficulty of the Data

For the editing practices that we will turn to in a moment, the media have grown ever more familiar to the editor and director. Relatedly, the cyclical nature of cutting means that there is a shared and evolving awareness of where we are now in the process of making the documentary. For the ethnographer (Laurier) studying the production, this insider knowledge of the film as project and object presented a number of challenges in following the work. Although a basic training in film editing helped Laurier in terms of understanding what was happening, following the making required an ethnography in itself that involved joining the edit for a couple of days at a time, from the outset of editing until its final fortnight. For the reader of this chapter coming to this nine-month project from the outside, it is hard, then, not only to follow the action with an unfamiliar object and project but also to appreciate the film-makers' intimacy with the footage, structure, argument, tone, and more of the film-to-come.

A related difficulty in analysing and presenting this material is in following two courses of action: (1) those being assembled in the documentary and (2) the editing team's courses of action for which the documentary provides both a resource and their object (Luck 2010). For example, we have to understand the transition between scenes that the director and editor are reviewing and understand the reviewing of that transition as it unfolds. To help make following the action simpler, we will work through a single five-minute revolution of the editorial cycle from the review of a recently completed sequence to the agreement on what to do to this sequence next. This will then provide a more easily understandable description of editing practices while offering a detailed description of how imagination is exercised in the editing suite. In terms of our focus upon the proposal sequences and the uses of media, it shows features that are routine in all parts of the edit. However, by the nature of the edit as a project unfolding over several months, the relationship of the part to the whole changes: at the beginning, the whole can change dramatically, but by the end it is locked in. The working relationship between director and editor evolves over nine months. Of perhaps greatest significance for our concern with imagination, we are in the midst of the editing process, so the film-that-is-yet-to-be is yet to be. By the final weeks (which we also studied), the film is almost finalized, though the editor and director still exercise their imagination to see what even the final film lacks and to add what else it might need.

2.   VIDEO AS THE OBJECT AND RESOURCE FOR REVIEWING AND ASSESSING

First, a general remark about the workplace organization of the edit: the majority of proposals of how any sequence should be cut were made by the director and almost all of the actual cuts are made by the editor. Yet while such a broad description matches with the institutional account given during interviews with film producers for our research project[1] of who makes initial proposals and who then transforms them into edited media, it misses the actual organization of how edited sections of the film are jointly reviewed and assessed and how new proposals emerge from the current sequence (that is in itself a form of proposal) for further revisions, additions, deletions, and so on. These are activities that both examine the existing sequences and their constituent clips closely in order to grasp what they are and also edge the film forward towards the film-yet-to-be. This is the work that calls upon and constitutes the intersubjective editorial imagination.

As we join them in their editing suite, the editor and director have been working for about six months editing the documentary. The documentary is on the dangers of celebrity culture to the individuals who become celebrities, to journalism, to charitable work, and to other members of society. The director and editor have collected and assembled most of the material for the film, although several more months of editing are still ahead. During the morning of this particular day, they have already had a preliminary discussion about their day's work. After working for an hour or so separately, the director suggests they review a recently re-edited transition that takes the film into a section of the documentary where experts on the history of journalism discuss the rise of celebrity stories.

Once he has begun playing the sequence, the editor waits for the director to provide an assessment or to intervene in some way. This is an abiding organization of their editorial roles: the editor assembles, and the director assesses those assemblies. Although abiding, it is more complex in its accountability, as noted, because the sequence as it stands is one made on the basis of changes proposed by the director and editor during their last review of the two sequences and their transition. The editor and director watch only 24 seconds of the footage before stopping to begin their assessment and review. This brief viewing takes us from the close of the previous section (which is of a member of the paparazzi sitting in a van) to the opening of the new section where an expert on journalism is showing the director newspapers in his shed. The transition continues with the same expert sitting at his desk in his study, standing by the study door and talking over a newspaper headline, at which point the director interrupts with an "eh" (10). (In the following transcript, the panels are numbered in the upper left.)

In this first part of our examination, we come upon the complexity of making sense of what editors and directors are referring to in playable media: when the video is paused, all that is visible is the frame where the playhead currently lies (and the audio is silenced). To try to understand the problem of reference, a comparison with paintings is useful. If this were a painting, when the one interrupts the other's viewing, then interrupter need only point with his finger to locate the part of the painting he is assessing (Heath & vom Lehn, 2004). In video and film, it as if, when the author and editor stop viewing together, the painting disappears, leaving only the last

Transcript 1 Interrupting playback and replaying. The editor's speech bubbles are from left and director's from the right. Audio from video is in square bubbles. Where bubbles overlap, the speech is overlapping.

tiny section that they pointed at visible. It is thus not surprising that the editor has to seek clarification "see what, what news" (3) when the clip the director's commenting on has been several shots and the "eh" happened when a newspaper image was on screen (1).

Moreover, the editor's initial response to the director's "eh" was not to pause the video immediately but to look away from the playback and towards him to try to locate the reason for the interruption. The director continued to orient towards the monitor in response to the editor turning towards him, thereby reorienting the editor towards the monitor. A common way for viewers of TV to assess broadcast media is simply to talk over the ongoing TV programme (Gerhardt, 2008), although, with the growth of pause and rewind functions on live TV, this may change. However, as we have already noted, the director cannot talk over the footage because the newspapers are now off-screen and we have cut to a close-up of the expert in a room (2). By the editor's confusion over what newspapers are being referred to, we can begin to see that assessments are made sense of in relation to what is currently playing or what has immediately preceded them as providing the object for their assessment. The assessment by the director is complicated by the fact that at last three candidate newspaper clips have been in the last few clips, so he has then to expand the formulation of the object ("newspapers") by adding ("newspapers in the shed").

Having identified the clip in question, the editor then brings it up. They rewatch it, but the editor also prefigures and instructs their viewing (Goodwin & Goodwin, 1997) by providing a capability question with a tag question pursuing it: "you can see lots of boxes can't you" (4). The question does more than inquire into the capabilities of the director, of course; it is a response to the director's negative assessment of the clip of the shed that fails to show newspapers. It accepts the absence of newspapers but brings in the relevance of the boxes as nevertheless making visible an abundance of newspapers. Having replayed the clip that he is asking the director to reassess, the editor gets only a noncommittal wave of the head. It is neither the full disagreement of a shake of the head nor an agreeing nod. In response to this half-hearted acceptance, the editor continues with a second attempt to secure the acceptability of this clip as successfully setting the scene for the newspaper expert. This time he turns the director's attention to how the dialogue will establish what can be seen in the clip: "he says they're newspapers." The director then provides a second, if also mitigated, negative assessment ("a bit muffled") of what can be heard. In fact, bringing up the muffled quality of the audio does double duty because it is also accounting for the director not having heard what might have redeemed the clip (hence the "sorry") and "muffled" begins a shift towards technical problems with the sound.

From examining the reviewing work that is done on the clip, we begin to gain a sense of the ongoing problem of reference to media that require playing. One method is to analyse talk's timing in relation to which part of the video was currently playing. We also examined how the editor's work is to quickly find the section that is being referred to so that it can then be played again in order to be assessed. With the director's concerns established in his negative assessments, we then followed through on how the editor sought to reshape the director's reception of the opening sequence through technical solutions and emphasizing qualities of the media that the director might have missed. The media of picture and sound provide a resource for the director's negative assessment but are also configured by that assessment. Moreover, the editor's combined defence and video actions (e.g. playing, rewinding, and stopping) rely upon being able to reinspect the sections being negatively assessed by replaying them.

3.   PLAYING TO DEFEND THE "INTRO"

We have worked through the problem of assessing media that require playing and the skill of the editor in bringing up the media while also beginning
to defend both its visual appearance and its sound. In the next transcript,
we rejoin them just where we left off, the director having assessed the audio
as "muffled" and the editor continuing his defence.

In panel 11, the editor discounts the director's earlier negative assessment of the audio (the previous transcript 1, 9) with an "oh"-prefaced
solution and a professionally meaningful action (Phillabaum, 2005). "Lift"
means being able to "lift" the speech out of the surrounding background
noise, thus making it less "muffled," and whether such a thing is possible

Transcript 2   Pausing and proposing.

turns on an editor's knowledge of the technical problem that leads to the audio problem. The "oh" also serves to "involve the second speaker's epistemic priority in the matter being assessed, [where] these turns also involve some qualification or disagreement" (Heritage, 2001: 204). The priority is secured by the "lift," which indexes the editor–director standardized-relational-pair (Watson, 1997). The editor has epistemic priority (Heritage & Raymond, 2005) in relation to production jobs such as sound and colour correction. By stating that the sound can be corrected, the editor then also provides an agreement with the immediate problem of poor sound even as it forms part of the ongoing disagreement and defence of the boxes in the shed clip.

In replaying the clip (10–18), the editor resets and equates their access to the sequence of the clips. His replay thus equalizes their authority to judge by sharing their access to the section of the medium under assessment. Looking in more detail at the video actions, we see that the editor shapes how the video is to be received by the director. He pauses the video just after starting it (10) in order to defend the audio, so that their reassessment of the video can then continue with the audio problem set aside. The editor then continues the video of the newspapers in the shed but again pauses, leaving its tail end still unplayed but thereby visible and relevant on-screen. He pauses to provide his positive assessment of the video sequence so far, which is greeted with a neutral "okay" from the director. The editor then provides further grounding for his positive assessment of the clip by underlining, through reporting, the expert's remark "just a few" (15) before then playing the tail end of that clip, which then cuts to the expert's desk that is visibly heaped with newspapers (17), and the expert also now says, "I've got stacks of stories." Then comes a cut from "few" to "stacks," which the editor emphasizes by gesturing over the screen in time with the cut to the heaped newspapers. It is an impressive defence of the clip that he has produced by crafting together playing, pausing, and quoting the clip itself.

Having defended the relational pairing of clips between the shed shot and the desk shot, the editor turns his attention away from the screen to the director. From the director he receives a nod (18). With that minimal gesture (which might be a limited acceptance and/or a go-ahead), the editor then tracks backward to the clip of the paparazzo that precedes the shed clip. He does not play it, however, but instead talks over the image. Whereas before he remarked only that the audio can be corrected, here he calls upon the director to imagine the music associated with the paparazzo that will come to an end, preceding the newspaper shed clip (19–20). In response to this, he receives an agreeing "yeah yeah yeah" (20) (Waring 2007). The editor then again employs his technique of quoting to underline the paparazzo's words and, immediately thereafter, artfully plays that same quote. Building then on the director's already being engaged in imagining the film-to-come from the music to be added, the editor is extending the work of imagining by asking the director to hear how well that quote, made in the clear (e.g.

without background music or noise), will then form a paired relationship with the clip of the newspaper expert approaching the shed. This work of helping the director notice what he might otherwise have missed: what value there is in the current edits, what might be added through analysing what is currently lacking, and what alternatives there could be is all part of the intersubjective editorial imagination at work.

4. PROPOSING CHANGES WITH AND TO THE AUDIOVISUAL MEDIA

In the previous two sections, we briefly mapped out the assessments and defence of a newly edited "intro" section of the documentary and how playing, pausing, and continuing featured in that work What the review establishes is what in this part of the documentary-yet-to-be can be drawn upon for providing the suggestions, instructions, and proposals that the editor will then follow in the next cut of this sequence. It is in the suggestions, instructions, and proposals that the editorial imagination becomes more visible because in this stage the director and editor supply new possibilities for what the film could become. In delivering what the current edit lacks, proposals have acceptance or rejection as their relevant response, whereas assessment have agreement/disagreement as their relevant responses (Davidson, 1984). This does not rule out agreement or disagreement occurring on the way to accepting or rejecting proposals, and, as we have seen already, the editor and director are not in a straightforward agreement about the current edit. When invitations are not immediately accepted, subsequent versions are then provided (Davidson, 1984). In the editing suite, the current edit itself forms the medium for proposing how the opening sequence should be. As in classic conversation analysis studies of subsequent versions, the proposer may add further ingredients, incentives, reasons for coming, and so on.

After the review, the other party proposes how the current edit could be re-edited and then becomes the one who searches for acceptance from the other, and the other is expected to provide acceptance or rejection (though, as Maynard showed, there are other possibilities such as deferring, demurring, or deflecting). Direct proposals are seldom fashioned as directives (despite one of the agents in the edit being called a "director") but are more likely and appropriately done as "suggestions," "requests," "musings" (Wasson, 2000) or, as is common in creative settings, as formulations (Büscher, 2001). To return to Davidson's (1984) studies of proposals, when they are not immediately accepted, the initial proposal or suggestion is usually treated either as the source of some as yet to be revealed trouble for its recipient or as insufficient to be accepted by the other. What offering second or third versions of proposals provides is a place for either belated acceptances or actual rejections. In editorial work (as with other creative studio practices), this elegant and economic method that Davidson documented for dealing with one proposal is built upon in order to generate further proposals that may undo, delete, revise, supplement, or accept the current proposal (i.e. edit).

Reviewing the existing assembly of each section of the film is then not neatly divided from working out what the editor should do with that assembly next because, firstly, suggestions and ideas can and do emerge in the midst of assessing and, secondly, because they are inferentially rich, suggestions can be treated as assessments and assessments as suggestions. In our case, we can see how neatly a switch between the two occurs with a go-ahead nod from the director; the editor had added the final sequential qualities by talking through and playing through the opening sequence (12–16). This skilled interweaving of video play and talk then accounts for the editor's completion and upgrade of his first incomplete formulation (e.g. "I think it's quite a nice . . .") to "I think it'll be a really nice little intro" (16), which had the director nodding in agreement. What the editor also did was to switch tense from the present to the future. The future tense presages a shift from reviewing to proposing that the clip remain part of the documentary-yet-to-be. However, the director has not yet provided either a strong agreement or indeed acceptance of what is now more clearly becoming a proposal to take forward.

In the previous section, we left the editor in the midst of building his proposal by examining the closing clip of the previous scene with the paparazzo. We will return to his presentation of that section. In the next transcript, the editor now slips in some further proposals about this part of the documentary-to-come even though they were not initially reviewing the closing of the preceding scene. He makes relevant the structure by gesturing towards the timeline. The timeline standing for the structure of the documentary in contrast to the monitor (displaying the image). His division of the screens becomes still more apparent for us when he then follows up by gesturing towards the monitor to provide a third recommendation for his proposal:

At 24, where we switch to a view of the editor and director sitting at the two screens, there are already hints of a lack of acceptance by the director. He leans back and away from the editorial huddle around the monitor, a bodily gesture that also indicates a shift in his stance on the edit (see Goodwin, 2007, on embodied shifts of stance). Meanwhile the editor furnishes his own tentative acceptance of the sequence as it stands (e.g. "I- I think that'll work," 24). The criteria are also somewhat cautious—the sequence will "work" (versus won't work) rather than whether it is good or not. He follows this up by turning away from the screen towards the director. This move marks a potential closure of the editor's proposal and assessment, which then waits on the director's reaction. The director remains leaning backward, and when the editor then begins to produce a further account for the edit (25), he is interrupted by the director. The director targets the original clip that all of the editor's discussion has notionally been about with a conditional "if-then" acceptance on the basis of the earliest suggested technical fix. The editor accepts the condition and then attempts to bring their

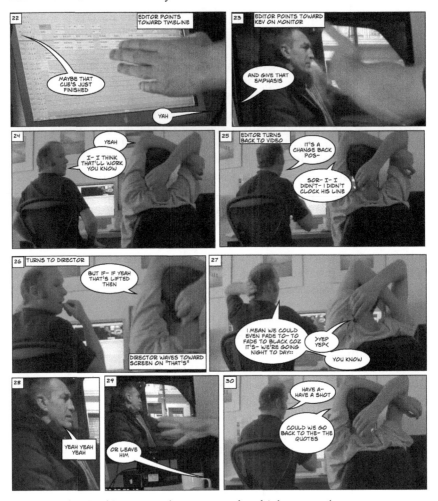

Transcript 3   Working across the screens and multiple proposals.

attention back towards the uncompleted proposals he is now making about the transition out of the previous scene (Transcript 3, 27–30). In the ongoing environment of only mild local agreements, the editor holds onto his position of the proposer by firstly going for the controls and secondly by replaying the a tiny part of the section that closes the paparazzo (28), where the fade-to-black would actually be, once again drawing on their imagination to see that part of the clip with the fade-to–black added.

Playing the final section of that final clip leaves it, then, as relevant for a further alternative proposal, which is to "leave him" and "have a shot" (29 and 30). These brief bursts of playing of those sections make relevant the ending of this sequence, with the editor's finely timed gestures across the two screens animating this section and helping visualize his proposal. "Leave him" he says, gesturing towards the timeline and thus towards the overall structure of the film and then, on the very next word, gesturing towards the monitor to orient them both to the visual. If we recall his earlier proposal, we can see that the gestures here have the same pattern, though this time there is no musical aspect to how the clip will end. The editor, then, is calling upon the director to see both the value in the current edit and to use his imagination to see what it lacks and what might be added to deal with that lack.

The director now finally responds with what then makes what seems to be a request ("could we go back to the quotes" (30) but might also be a counterproposal. If we add a little more of the hearable emphasis ("Could we *go-* could we go *back* to the- the quotes"), this request seems to be requesting that the editor locate and bring up a known-in-common part of their assembly (see similar work between a surgeon and camera operator in Mondada, 2003). In hearing this phrase, the editor does indeed search and then display "the quotes" and in doing so takes us out his work of defending the current sequence through his finely crafted playing and pausing of the video. We turn, in the next section, to consider the director's counterproposals and how they are accomplished.

5. DIRECTOR'S PROPOSALS, EDITOR'S COLLABORATION, AND ANIMATING TEXT

Throughout editing the film, various newspaper stories, photographs, and headlines are relevant to the film, but, as a medium within the film, they also consistently pose a problem. They are by the editor's criteria "dull." The motion of the film stalls when a paragraph of text appears because viewers are transformed into readers and enough time has to be given, with the text either static or scrolling, for it to be read (in films like *Star Wars*, they appear before the film proper begins). Newspaper pages, when simply scanned into an image file, are one of the media within a multimedia film that do not need to be played. For the editor and the director, they need do nothing to make the text available because it is all already there on-screen. Yet if they do too much to the scanned image to make it into a motion image or animation, it becomes unreadable.

Before the quotes appear on–screen, the director provides a first account of his proposal—"to give it extra emphasis" (31). Once the text is visible to them both, he quotes the paparazzo in the van as saying "an onlooker said" (32), and then he goes on to gesture and talk over the text that also has phrase the "an onlooker said." The director helps visualize for them both how the text might be animated by describing the animation's movements while providing a further sense of their character by motioning with his hands across the screen. He possibly anticipates the editor's responding to his hand movements by pulling the zoom slider on the software system when he adds "not now" to the end—"we could do something" (33).

Transcript 4   Animating the text.

This seems all the more likely given what happens next. In response to the orchestra-conductor-like raising of the hands by the director, the editor then tries to manually create the cut the director is proposing by dragging the playhead from the newspaper clip to Kev's quote, allowing them both to see something of what that cut would look like (36).

The director's unfinished formulation "as though that's our" (37), which deals again with the abiding problem of how to close the previous scene, is left uncompleted by the editor. Instead, the editor rubs his chin (doing "thinking," Streeck, 2009), while this time playing through the short section of the newspaper text, which we means they see it now with the audio playing over it (38). Playing it now changes how the newspaper text is to be assessed because it is seen this time as a medium with duration. The director again talks over the text with an unfinished and vague assessment (to which the editor does not provide an agreeing assessment). Meantime, the editor is reinspecting the newspaper text while it plays. Having considered the newspaper text for another time, he provides a definite and potentially disagreeing negative assessment of the visual qualities of the newspaper text as a filmic object.

Visual qualities are one of the abiding concerns of both the editing process, and, in the workplace distribution of film production responsibilities; these qualities are primarily the concern of the editor (Laurier & Brown 2011; Murch, 2001; Reisz & Millar, 1968). However, the director's proposal does not receive a straightforward rejection because the editor moves on to question how it might be improved (39). What this seems to miss is that the director had previously provided the solution in his manual enactment of animating the text. However, the editor repairs the object of his assessment by dragging the playhead back to two cuts earlier in the sequence where there is another newspaper scan (40). They then have another newspaper that requires their imagination to avoid the problem of dullness (in fact, a third newspaper text ["Freddie Starr at My Hamster"] is close by in the next scene when the newspaper expert is speaking at his desk). In this case, we see the director run up against the limits of his imagination at this point with his again vague "something eh visually" (40).

In shifting from the editorial work of reviewing the existing edit to proposing changes, we have seen how, echoing Büscher's (2001) studies of architects, a flurry of proposals and assessments arise as the film-makers compare amongst alternative possibilities for what the documentary could become in the next editorial cycle (and beyond)—the current opening clip of the shed, preceded by a fade-to-black or by a long shot of the paparazzo's van or by an animation of newspaper text. These do not sit as three completely separate options in that various aspects of what might be done may be shared, such as ending the music as one scene ends. However, a different action achieves the sequencing and overlaying of the media. The editor is suggesting they say goodbye to their current character, while the director wishes to underline the idea of "an onlooker said" and made-up quotes in newspapers. Throughout examining the editorial work, we have continued to describe how the editor and director use the media, configure it, and imagine how it could be in presenting their proposals. The editor throughout had direct access to the playhead and to the play, pause, and rewind buttons and artfully used them in presenting his proposal. For his part, the director, with only indirect access to the media via the editor, again voiced for the paparazzo and then used gesture to animate a static image. This asymmetry in who has the play button is typical of the editing suite, yet we see how the proposing work is nevertheless accomplished with this asymmetrical access and the editor's ongoing work in making the relevant clips available for their assessment and imagination.

6. USING THE PUSH OF THE PLAY-THROUGH TO MAKE RELEVANT ACCEPTANCE OR REJECTION

To complete the editorial cycle, we would like to move to the final stage where one or the other of the proposals is then accepted. Houtkoop-Streenstra (1987) breaks acceptance into two sequential elements, firstly confirmation of the proposal and secondly what will, or can, be done to accomplish the proposal. As we have argued, the proposal-acceptance conditions in the editing suite are distinct from earlier proposal-acceptances studies of personal relationships (e.g. between friend–friend, mother–daughter, etc.) but also of professional–client (e.g. advice-giving, medical treatments). We have a professional–professional pair in the relationship, and, as we have seen,

Transcript 5   Play-through, proposal acceptance, and detailing.

both of them make proposals and assessments in relation to the current edit. In the long project of editing a feature film together, the sequences will be revisited, removed, adapted, and built upon through further rounds of assessments and proposals. In the workplace relationship of director–editor, it is the editor who will then act upon the proposal that is accepted, but the director has the last word. What we will examine now is how the last word is produced.

From the extended series of proposals offered by the editor and then by the director, an environment for rejection and acceptance has emerged and thus a selection is required from amongst the current alternative proposals. What the editor does next appears not only to recognize this but also to make it a relevant response to his video action. He plays the whole sequence through.

By doing this play action, the editor re-establishes the sequential context of this section of the documentary and is also soliciting their joint examination of the entire transition. The earlier proposals can now be imagined in relation to the longer sequence of the transition. In other words, the editor is using the uninterrupted play to make an acceptance of one of the proposals relevant. It is not only uninterrupted play of the transition; on this playing of the video, there is an absence of either assessment or proposals from either party. As the sequence reaches the newspaper shed clip that initiated the negative assessment from the director and their analysis of the current edit, this then is also a relevant point for a potentially final selection from the director. At this point, he does indeed interrupt the playback again ("no no no," 42).

The director's interruption at just that point might then be taken as referring once again to the newspaper in the shed with a rejection of it (compared to saying "yes" as it is on-screen), so the director is then required to clarify what his repairing "no" refers to by summarizing the alternate proposals he is deciding between. Interestingly, the newspaper shed appears to have slipped out of focus for the next edit, and instead the director is revisiting the transition through either the newspaper text or the shot of the van driver. He rejects his proposal and selects "saying goodbye to Kev" (43). At the end of each part of the director's acceptances of the "fade-to-black" proposal, the editor provides "yeah" agreement tokens. In fact, the director's acceptance of "saying goodbye to Kev" allows for two editing techniques to achieve the proposal: fade-to-black or a long-shot of the van. It is the latter possibility that the editor raises as an alternative technique (44). Concerning how it's done, the director continues to accept that alternative editorial solution and in an upgraded, closing assessment, "absolutely." Although the director has the last word, the editor is being left with discretion as to how he will fulfil that decision. As we leave them, then, we now have a richer picture of their collaboration and yet also an insight into how the director has the last word—though a last word that has been made relevant by the editor's video action pressing for it.

7. CONCLUSIONS

Although we have followed only one editorial cycle, it is a typical one—a cycle that shifts from viewing to assessing, to proposing, to accumulating multiple proposals, to decision making, and then, finally, to detailing how the proposal can be achieved. A central part of our examination has been the series of media actions born out of video. It is not that these are pre-existing actions that then find themselves materialized in a new (or old medium); these actions arise out of this medium and make this medium available. As noted at the outset of the chapter, these video actions are then similar to the camera actions documented by Broth (Chapter 2, this volume) and Mondada (Chapters 1 and 3, this volume). Whereas the camera can be used to produce zooms, pans, nods, and shakes, video can be used to produce plays, pauses, restarts, rewinds, forward winds, and stops. At the heart of the manipulation and configuration of video is playing it. In the edit, playing video has the referential utility and indexical richness of pointing with a finger in picking out photographs. We saw the referential power of playing video throughout the previous sections: for example, when the editor played through a section in response to the director's assessment, skilfully pausing and restarting while both editor and director talked it over and, in the final section, in using an uncommented-upon and uninterrupted play-through to push for a decision from the director.

In the courses of action, we found that the media actions were assessments and proposals, courses of action familiar to ethnomethodology and conversation analysis (Davidson, 1984). They are not quite the competing proposals that we find in newspaper editorials (Clayman & Reisner, 1998) or in real estate deals (Maynard, 2010). The editor and director are not offering competing proposals in a strong sense; they are imagining the film-to-come from the details of the media made available and relevant through their playing, interrupting, pausing, freeze-framing, and taking other action. Being skilled and creative professionals. the director and editor look for what is missing from the current edit and provide an array of alternatives (Raffel, 2004). We have come a long way from imagination as a mental process that is only indirectly accessible and that is some process nested in each individual creative brain. We have instead examined the editing suite as a place for its intersubjective exercise. In exercising their imaginations, the director and editor might be taking one thing away in an early edit and then later bringing it back (Laurier & Brown, 2011). They are ongoingly assessing, proposing, and reassessing the visuals, audio, dialogue, sequences, and other elements of the existing film in working towards the film-to-come. Through all of this, we come upon the centrality of the media, and Gustav Lymer provides a valuable phrasing for this: film-makers in their editing suite have "an attunement to certain material arrangements" (Lymer, 2010: 121–122).

ACKNOWLEDGEMENTS

Our thanks go to Ignaz Strebel, Nick Fenton, and Chris Atkins for their infinite patience with the ethnographer in their editing suite.

NOTE

1. ESRC Funded Project—Assembling the Line—RES-062-23-0564.

REFERENCES

Becker, H. S. (1982). *Art Worlds*. London: University of California Press.
Broth, M. (2004). The production of a live TV-interview through mediated interaction. Paper presented at the Sixth International Conference on Social Science Methodology, August, Amsterdam. www2.fmg.uva.nl/emca/RC33Broth.pdf
Broth, M. (2008). The "listening shot" as a collaborative practice for categorizing studio participants in a live TV-production. *Ethnographic Studies*, 10, 69–88.
Broth, M. (2009). Seeing through screens, hearing through speakers: Managing distant studio space in television control room interaction. *Journal of Pragmatics*, 41, 1998–2016.
Broth, M. (this volume). Pans, tilts, and zooms: Conventional camera practices in TV production.
Büscher, M. (2001). "Ideas in the Making: Talk, Vision, Objects and Embodied Action in Multi-Media Art and Landscape Architecture." Unpublished PhD, University of Lancaster, Lancaster, UK.
Clayman, S. E., & Reisner, A. (1998). Gatekeeping in action: Editorial conferences and assessments of newsworthiness. *American Sociological Review*, 62(2), 178–199.
Davidson, J. (1984). Subsequent versions of invitations, offers, requests, and proposals dealing with potential or actual rejection. In J. M. Atkinson & J. Heritage (Eds.), *Structures of Social Action* (pp. 102–128). Cambridge: Cambridge University Press.
Deleuze, G. (1992). *Cinema 1: The Movement-Image*. London: Athlone Press.
Deleuze, G. (2005). *Cinema 2: The Time-Image*. London: Continuum.
Engström, A., Juhlin, O., Perry, M., & Broth, M. (2010). Temporal hybridity: Footage with instant replay in real time. In *Proceedings of the SIGCHI Conference on Human Factors in Computing Systems* (pp. 1495–1504). New York: ACM.
Gerhardt, C. (2008). "Talk by Television Viewers Watching Live Football Matches: Coherence Through Interactionality, Intertextuality, and Multimodality." PhD thesis, University of Saarbrücken.
Goodwin, C. (2007). Participation, stance and affect in the organization of activities. *Discourse & Society*, 18(1), 53–73.
Goodwin, C., & Goodwin, M. H. (1997). Contested vision: The discursive constitution of Rodney King. In B.-L. Gunnarsson, P. Linell, & B. Nordberg (Eds.), *The Construction of Professional Discourse* (pp. 292–316). New York: Longman.
Greiffenhagen, C., & Watson, R. (2009). Visual repairables: Analysing the work of repair in human–computer interaction. *Visual Communication*, 8(1), 65–90.
Heath, C., & vom Lehn, D. (2004). Configuring reception: (Dis)regarding the "spectator" in museums and galleries. *Theory, Culture & Society*, 21(6), 45–63.

Heritage, J. (2001). Oh-prefaced responses to assessments: A method of modifying agreement/disagreement. In C.E. Ford, B.A. Fox, & S.A. Thompson (Eds.), *The Language of Turn and Sequence* (pp. 196–224). Oxford: Oxford University Press.

Heritage, J., & Raymond, G. (2005). The terms of agreement: Indexing epistemic authority and subordination in talk-in-interaction. *Social Psychology Quarterly*, 68(1), 15–38.

Heritage, J., & Sefi, S. (1992). Dilemmas of advice: Aspects of the delivery and reception of advice in interactions between health visitors and first-time mothers. In P. Drew & J. Heritage (Eds.), *Talk at Work* (pp. 359–417). Cambridge: Cambridge University Press.

Houtkoop-Steenstra, H. (1987). *Establishing Agreement: An Analysis of Proposal-Acceptance Sequences*. Dordrecht, Netherlands: Foris Publications.

Houtkoop-Steenstra, H. (1990). Accounting for proposals. *Journal of Pragmatics*, 11(1–24).

Jayyusi, L. (1988). Towards a socio-logic of the film text. *Semiotica*, 68, 271–296.

Laurier, E., & Brown, B. (2011). The reservations of the editor: The routine work of showing and knowing the film in the edit suite. *Social Semiotics*, 21(2), 239–257.

Lindwall, O., Johansson, E., Ivarsson, J., Rystedt, H. & Reit, C. (this volume). The use of video in dental education: Clinical reality addressed as practical matters of production, interpretation, and instruction.

Livingston, E. (2008). Ethnographies of Reason (Directions in Ethnomethodology and Conversation Analysis). Aldershot: Ashgate.

Luck, R. (2010). Using objects to coordinate design activity in interaction. *Construction Management and Economics*, 28(6), 641–655.

Lymer, G. (2009). Demonstrating professional vision: The work of critique in architectural education. *Mind, Culture & Activity*, 16(2), 145–171.

Lymer, G. (2010). *The Work of Critique in Architectural Education*. Göteborg: Gothenburg Studies in Educational Sciences.

Maynard, D.W. (2010). Demur, defer, and deter: Concrete, actual practices for negotiation in interaction. *Negotiation Journal*, 26(2), 125–143.

McCloud, S. (1993). *Understanding Comics*. New York: Kitchen Sink.

Mondada, L. (2003). Working with video: How surgeons produce video records of their actions. *Visual Studies*, 18(1), 58–73.

Mondada, L. (2009). Video recording practices and the reflexive constitution of the interactional order: Some systematic uses of the split-screen technique. *Human Studies*, 32(1), 67–99.

Murch, W. (2001). *In the Blink of an Eye, A Perspective on Film Editing* (2nd ed.). Los Angeles: Silman-James Press.

Murphy, K. (2004). Imagination as joint activity: The case of architectural interaction. *Mind, Culture & Activity*, 11, 267–278.

Murphy, K.M. (2005). Collaborative imagining: The interactive use of gestures, talk, and graphic representation in architectural practice. *Semiotica*, 156(1), 111–145.

Ondaatje, M. (2002). *The Conversations, Walter Murch and the Art of Editing Film*. London: Bloomsbury.

Orpen, V. (2003). *Film Editing: The Art of the Expressive*. London: Wallflower.

Perry, M., Engström, A., & Juhlin, O. (this volume). Dealing with time, just in time: Sense-making and clip allocation in multiperson, multistream, live replay TV production.

Phillabaum, S. (2005). Calibrating photographic vision through multiple semiotic resources. *Semiotica*, 147–175.

Raffel, S. (2004). Imagination. *Human Studies*, 27, 207–220.

Reisz, K., & Millar, G. (1968). *The Technique of Film Editing*. London: Focal Press.

Ryle, G. (2009). *The Concept of Mind: 60th Anniversary Edition*. London: Routledge.

Stivers, T. (2002). Participating in decisions about treatment: Overt parent pressure for antibiotic medication in pediatric encounters. *Social Science & Medicine, 54*, 1111–1130.

Streeck, J. (2009). *Gesturecraft: The Manu-Facture of Meaning*. Amsterdam: John Benjamins.

Thornton Caldwell, J. (2008). *Production Culture: Industrial Reflexivity and Critical Practice in Film and Television*. London: Duke University Press.

Tutt, D., & Hindmarsh, J. (2011). Reenactments at work: Demonstrating conduct in data sessions. *Research on Language and Social Interaction, 44*(3), 211–236.

Tutt, D., Hindmarsh, J., Shaukat, M., & Fraser, M. (2007). The distributed work of local action: Interaction amongst virtually collocated research teams. Paper presented at the ECSCW 2007. In *Proceedings of the 10th European Conference on Computer Supported Cooperative Work*, September 24–28, Limerick, Ireland. Berlin: Springer.

Vaughan, D. (1983). *Portrait of an Invisible Man, The Working Life of Stewart McAllister, Film Editor*. London: BFI Books.

Waring, H. (2007). Complex advice acceptance as a resource for managing asymmetries. *Text & Talk, 27*(1), 107–137.

Wasson, C. (2000). Caution and consensus in American business meetings. *Pragmatics, 10*(4), 457–481.

Watson, R. (1997). Some general reflections on "categorization" and "sequence" in the analysis of conversation. In S. Hester & P. Eglin (Eds.), *Culture in Action* (pp. 49–76). London/Washington, DC: University Press of America.

9 Dealing with Time, Just in Time
Sense-Making and Clip Allocation in Multiperson, Multistream, Live Replay TV Production

Mark Perry (Brunel University, UK)
Oskar Juhlin and Arvid Engström
(MobileLife @ Stockholm University)

1. INTRODUCTION

Multicamera television production teams face a number of major difficulties when working to broadcast live video. One of these is how TV production teams work with and across time or, at least, how they integrate historic and real-time visual content in their broadcasts. This historic material may be older information from previous games, but more often in live sports TV, it is recorded material that may have been recorded minutes or just seconds prior to its insertion into the live video feed broadcast. Teams need to do a great deal of sense-making in selecting visual feeds from multiple cameras, made all the more complex when multiple streams of recently recorded content (instant replay footage) is able to be edited and available for use within seconds of the original action taking place. When multiple instant replay operators are all working simultaneously to generate interesting and relevant content that is competing with content from the (also potentially relevant and interesting) real-time camera streams, the problem of selection becomes all the more complex. This is the case confronting live broadcast teams in contemporary sports TV.

Why are multiple visual streams so important for sports TV producers? After all, aren't they just attempting to "show" the game? Well, certainly they need to show what is happening. However, any but the most naïve sports viewer will recognize that sports TV is more than simply a factual account of events as they happen. Multiple cameras are deployed around stadia to show gameplay from different angles to create variations in tempo and emotional atmosphere that enliven the visual imagery, to spin a compelling narrative of the enfolding events, and to provide an enthralling viewer experience. Yet even well produced multicamera productions usually cannot visually explain what *is* happening in the light of what *has* happened, and instant replay is often used for this purpose, drawing from camera angles and footage that themselves may not have been shown in the broadcast. As with the multicamera broadcasts, recent developments in broadcast technology have meant that a very large quantity of content is becoming available for use, and those developments allow multiple instant replay operators to edit this content in nearly real-time conditions.

In this, the focus of our interest lies in the coordination of live televisual broadcasts that involve significant technological support in the form of multiscreen displays, searchable hard drives, customized video editing hardware and control systems, and voice communication systems. The term "live" is used in a variety of ways when talking about broadcast, and to clarify its meaning, we utilize the terms "real time" and "live" to distinguish between their meanings and to limit any possible confusion. By "real time," we refer to the ongoing sequential actions as they actually occur, and by "live," we refer to the broadcast stream as it goes out, which may include both images that are broadcast as they occur in real time and historically recorded images that are produced and broadcast alongside the real-time material. This is a subtle but important distinction in that what is commonly described as "live TV" may include much content that is not real-time.[1] This chapter is therefore an attempt to understand better how and why live broadcasts are made in the ways that they are, as well as how live and nonlive video footage from multiple participants is produced and segued together to create meaningful imagery within a coherent narrative structure.

The chapter also draws on our previous studies on replay production that took place in a somewhat less complex collaborative video production (Engström, Juhlin, Perry, & Broth, 2010). In this paper, we studied how a single EVS (instant replay terminal[2]) operator performed the replay production. This study revealed how searching for a particular activity in the recorded material was conducted, during these constrained and time-critical conditions, through collaboration among the EVS operator, the Vision Mixer, other participants in the production studio, and the remote camera team. This was achieved by the collaborative actions of the team, such as camera operators and producers, who acted on and cross-referenced different temporal trajectories of the various media that they were working on to make sense of the ongoing action and to locate appropriate recorded media for broadcast. This chapter differs from the former analysis in that it is based on fieldwork in which the EVS production was conducted by a number of people working in different teams of collaborating operators. The focus of this paper involves much more talk, and our analysis is therefore more oriented to the complex verbal interactions between operators than our previous work, necessitating a stronger orientation to the concerns of conversation analysis than these earlier studies have merited.

As a large team, replay operators are able to specialize more than a single operator on individual camera footage, in addition to attending to more focused aspects of gameplay. As we see here, multimember instant replay production is based on the functional separation of various tasks or responsibilities. In practice, and as we show, the EVS editing, selection, and organization of work in this scenario takes a very different form from that of the single EVS operator examined in our earlier work. Importantly, the set-up of replay production discussed here depends on many more people working together, and the role of talking becomes more important. This is one of the distinguishing features that differentiate this chapter from these earlier studies, in that it is highly engaged with talk and with how this talk is used in organizing visual content. The following analysis therefore provides an account and analysis of decision making in visual media production; it is its orientation to the visual media that connects it to the other chapters in the book, but the very large size of the team involved, the number of media streams, and the challenges of real-time production differentiate this kind of video work from these studies. Compared against our previous publication, this provides a methodological approach intended to further unpack both the motivations and the actions taken to produce replays and to study more elaborate forms of the use of replays in live TV production; it also extends these studies on the organization of video-based interaction to focus in on the role of talk-in-interaction in this most visual of contexts.

2. BACKGROUND

Our analytic framing is derived from conversation analysis (CA, Sacks, 1992) and may be best described as a form of interaction analysis (Jordan & Henderson, 1995), drawing on literature in CA, ethnomethodology (EM), and workplace studies. Following Mondada (2011: 542), we have attempted to perform a "sequential and temporal approach to understanding," focusing on the unfolding of actions and on showing how understanding is performed "as a collective achievement, publicly displayed and interactively oriented to within the production and the monitoring of action" (ibid.). In this case, we are interested in turn-taking organization—not just conversational turns in talk but, drawing inspiration from Schegloff's term of "talk-in-interaction," foregrounding the interaction and artefacts involved. This dual interest, in the two tethered phenomena of the organization of the coordination within the team and the organization of the broadcast images, is, we believe, a novel concern. In this case, we focus on interaction with and through the video materials that members are engaged in using. With reference to Sacks (1984), we are attempting to locate the "technology" of interaction in video work in order "to take singular sequences of interaction and tear them apart ... to find rules, techniques, procedures, methods, maxims that can be used to generate orderly features in it" (1984: 413). Our use of CA is not specifically intended to identify turn-taking components but to identify how team members' practices, organization, settings, and technologies come together in support of their collaboration and in their production of visual content for broadcast. This has much common ground with ethnomethodology and workplace studies, and our special interest here lies in members' collaborative interactions with and through the visual content and technologies available to them as they unfold temporally and sequentially.

So what we are attempting to examine follows CA's concern with the "organisation of interaction" (e.g. see Schegloff, 2007) and the ways in which interaction is informed by language, embodied action, and the visual content that video production work involves. Schegloff (2007) provides an interesting list of features of interaction (his "generic orders of talk-in-interaction," 2007: xiv), which we reinterpret in the light of our interest in how live and nonlive video footage from multiple participants is produced and segued together. He frames these as problems without which interaction cannot proceed in an orderly way; given our topic of interest, we have repurposed this list to accommodate and foreground the video streams and the visual resources used in video production, in addition to the role of talk that Schegloff identifies, and we have changed his wording accordingly. We have retained Schegloff's titles in these problems to highlight common features that we draw from, although here we have framed these in the particular light of our analytic context:

1. *The turn-taking problem:* multiple operators offer many potential video streams for broadcast. Whose should be broadcast next, and when should they expect to do so? How does this affect the construction and understanding of the members' turns at talk? This is not just a problem for those making the selections, and the EVS team should be seen not simply as computational "resources" for functionally enabling the broadcast but as actors who have real agency in managing these turns in the visual media selected for broadcast.

2. *The action-formation problem:* how the resources of language, the body, the environment of the interaction (including visual media), and the position *in* the interaction are fashioned into conformations designed to be particular actions and to be recognizable by recipients in the production team as such—actions like requesting, inviting, granting, complaining, agreeing, telling, noticing, rejecting, and so on. In other words, in the context of video production, how members' actions are artfully created to be purposefully accountable to others in their team about what they are trying to achieve.

3. *The sequence-organizational problem:* how successive visual streams of content are formed to be coherent with the visual content (i.e. a clip) that had been broadcast prior (or even some earlier clips that had been broadcast) and what the nature of that coherence is. In dealing with this problem, members must work together to organize the sequential presentation of visual material to allow viewers to make sense of what is broadcast—as it is being broadcast. For the team, the practical consequences of the sequence-organizational problem

therefore involves identifying prior/next actions and making projections and expectations possible.

4. *The trouble problem:* how members deal with trouble in speaking, hearing, and/or understanding the talk around them or in seeing or understanding visual content so that the interaction does not freeze in place when trouble arises, that intersubjectivity is maintained or restored, and that the turn and sequence of production activities can progress to possible completion. This is particularly a problem in the production studio, in which not all of the visual content or verbal interaction is available to all of the members because of the technical resource configurations and highly constrained physical layout that they work in.

5. *The word-selection problem:* how the visual and audio components that are selected as the elements of a clip (or a sequence of clips) get selected by the EVS operators as a proposal for broadcast, and how that selection informs and shapes the understanding achieved by the rest of the production team.

6. *The overall structural organization problem:* how the overall composition of an occasion of interaction (i.e. a video production) gets structured, what those structures are, and how placement in the overall structure informs the construction and understanding of the visual and verbal components of interaction (as turns, as sequences, etc.). In the light of video production, this problem is one in which the members shape and make sense of the ways in which TV production is to be done in the context that it occurs within, how they fit the micro interactional elements that they face into the macro scale structures of the production system, and how they might reshape the production system in the light of changes that occur in the doing of all that.

It is with this set of features in mind that we begin our examination of live video replay. We take these, however, not as a programmatic set of questions to be sequentially addressed but as a broad set of concerns that frame the problems that video production teams need to practically address. In doing so, we orient to these features as heuristics, returning to examine these features explicitly only in the final discussion. In this project, we extend Macbeth's (1999) exhortation to examine the "praxeology of seeing with a camera" from an individual perspective to that of a collective of individuals, each with their own specialized roles, in how teams do seeing with many cameras. Recognizing that the TV production process depends on many more modalities than talk, our study belongs to the body of work focusing on the transmodality of interaction (Murphy, 2010) and on the identification of eye gaze, gesture, and body position. The attendance to the visual presentations of activities on the abundant screens and the identification of visually recognizable member categories is of importance in the production of live TV broadcasts (Perry, Juhlin, Esbjörnsson, & Engström, 2009), as the physical movement of cameras is another feature of the interaction (Broth, 2004), as well as the talk mediated through the radio communication system and the body movements made visible in the tight space of the production studio.

We have no theoretical interest at this stage in how the final broadcast is watched by their remote viewers, and, indeed, the corpus of data that we present here is not intended to offer insights into this. However, we have an interest in how the producers orient to the viewers and in the way the production is organized to convey a particular story, in line with recent work by Mondada (2003, 2009). Her analysis (2009) of the making of a debate, through the use of split screen broadcasts as a visualization of grammatical orders in a debate and the production of ways of seeing the work, shares a common concern with ours on how the interaction resonates with the broadcast. She unpacks not just how the team is broadcasting from a studio but also how they are producing a TV debate. The editors and camera operators collaborate to construct a particular way of telling what is going on by being attentive to the talk between participants, which includes anticipation of turns at talk and the identification of potential addressees to emerging questions. Split screens are, for example, used when a question is posed to the audience, which might include more than one person. Mondada (2003) has also shown in her studies of video production in surgical work how the producers can orient to multiple purposes that smoothly run together, such as their deployment in supporting surgeons' need to see for themselves as part of an activity, at the same time producing a view to demonstrate to an audience what they are doing. Talk and gestures are fine-tuned to collaboratively accomplish these multiple ways of using video. Specifically, we show how talk supports them in "looking together" at a large amount of possible views of the same event. Talk and collaboration are used to handle and make use of an asymmetry of access to visual content, as well as providing each other insights into upcoming events.

In all, recent detailed empirical studies are beginning to unpack how interactional features, beyond just conversation, have been applied to enable the production of accounts of activities in broadcast television and video production. These studies are important influences in the continuant study of the making of live visual media, and they give some useful insights into how such an analysis might be applied to our own research context. Our own contribution here is to extend this work on the production of video, in which members construct a view into the live game that they anticipate. We examine how the production team attempt to meet multiple audience concerns, as well as how they achieve and make sense of this in a complex technical, spatial, visual, and auditory setting, drawing from multiple streams of potentially broadcastable material, some of which is temporally out of sequence.

3. SETTING

Data collection[3] took place during early 2010 in an outside broadcast studio (also known as a "scanner") located in a vehicle parked a short distance away from a large, international sports stadium, in which the rugby match that forms the televised event in our analysis took place. The production vehicle can be transported quickly from site to site and opens, concertina-fashion, to provide an enormous working area. This highly expensive custom-built mobile studio is kitted out with an extraordinary array of state-of-the-art live broadcast production and communications equipment (Figures 1 and 2). The layout of this vehicle can be seen in Figure 3, with our analytic focus annotated and highlighted in the two shaded areas: (1) on the instant replay team (highlight shows camera position) and (2) the Director (highlight shows his visual orientation). In the particular match that we present here, visual footage from 20 cameras fed into the scanner, alongside audio links, satellite feeds, and other communication feeds (Figure 4). This set of visual data feeds presents a hugely complex technical exercise (see Figure 5) that must be designed and tested in situ. The number of working cameras and other equipment is usually not possible to determine exactly due to contingencies at the site, with the consequence that all productions are likely to be unique because teams will be working with some personnel and technological configurations that they have not encountered before.

Figure 1   Left to right: Production Assistant, Director, and Vision Mixer.

Figure 2   Gallery wall (part).

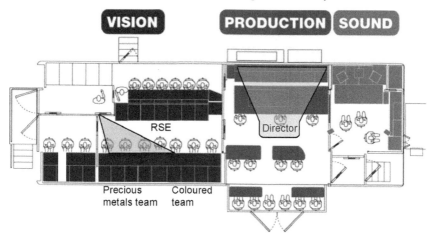

Figure 3   Configuration of the scanner (adapted from SISLive, 2011).

Figure 4   Outside broadcast vehicle in situ.

Two key parts of the scanner are used in image production, the gallery and the instant replay suite. The gallery is composed of a wall of video monitors that display all of the visual feeds and other relevant visual information (such as time displays and match graphics) that are available for broadcast or that may be used for monitoring purposes. It also consists of a desk with control panels that allow users to switch broadcast feeds or

Figure 5 Associated side panel wiring

to create image transitions (wipes, fades, overlays, etc.). Several operators are situated in front of it. The most notable operator in the instance that we observed was the Director, sitting in the centre of the gallery directly in front of the displays (Figures 1 and 3). The instant replay suite is a thin corridor that leads off from the production area, separated from this by a soundproof door. Here, along one wall, is another wide bank of display monitors, lining the external wall for several metres, with seats for seven operators (Figure 3). Underneath these displays sits a desk with several devices, each equipped with a number of switches, dials, and lights. Although the roles of the individuals involved and their work tasks are understandably very technically complex, we will try to present a simplified overview of this.

The role of the Director is to mix various streams of available content for live broadcast. He does this by selecting one of the visual streams on the monitors in the gallery by directly pressing the button associated with that visual feed on his control panel.

Organizationally, he is able to request changes in the camerawork and ask for particular forms of replay material (where this is possible) and is assisted by a production assistant (monitoring time, communicating with the Commentators, etc.), sitting to his left, and a Vision Mixer (assisting with technical aspects of the visual presentation), to his right. He is connected by audio to the camera operators and instant replay operators (as well as other relevant production units) via an intercom.

The instant replay team is organized into two groups, who are coordinated by a replay subeditor (RSE) sitting at the centre of the desk (Figure 3). The two groups (known as EVS operators) consist of six individuals, labelled as primary colours (operators coded as Red, Green, Blue) and precious metals (Gold, Silver, Bronze). Each EVS operator has a nearly identical set of instant replay control units (known as EVS machines) and similar configurations on their monitors (see Figure 6). The replay subeditor's position is unique in that his part of the desk has a different set of equipment on it as well as a different set of display configurations (Figure 7). He is also unique, in that whilst all of the operators can hear the Director's talk from his intercom over a public address system, only the RSE can use the intercom system to speak back to the Director by pressing a button on his desk and speaking into a microphone. As will become apparent in the data that follow, several members of the EVS team recorded in the study were themselves Welsh and keen followers of the Welsh rugby team that they were filming in a major championship match.

Figure 6   EVS team. Left to right: Gold, Silver, and Bronze.

Figure 7   Replay subeditor (on left).

4. ANALYSIS

The focus of our analysis lies on the interaction among the members involved, showing how they organize their activities around the production of visual material for the live broadcast. These include copresent interactions among the precious metals team of operators and their interaction with the RSE and, remotely, the audio interaction between the EVS studio and the Director, as well as the Director's interactions with the camera operators. Together, the work of the instant replay operators is to select recorded footage that is relevant to the camera footage so that replays can be meaningfully cut into real-time camera footage. More specifically, the contribution of this chapter—in line with the aim of this volume—is that we show how selecting a replay segment is a local achievement, with a focus on the clip as the product of a collective action of looking and clip editing. In addition to their orientation to each others' work and actions, these actors have access to other contextual information that may have an impact on their situational awareness to help them make better informed decisions about their own work.

The production team's interaction sits within an institutional context, and we must recognize that their actions and talk are framed by this institutionality, as well as being bounded by the unique spatial and technical setting that their interaction takes place within. This is not mundane interaction or conversation, in the way that much early ethnomethodological conversation analysis (EMCA) work has examined, and this organizational context and set of professional practices are likely to have a substantial role in how utterances and actions are shaped and understood (e.g. Drew & Heritage, 1992; Heritage, 2004). This is relevant in that the forms of interaction will be shaped by the nature of the hierarchical structure of the production unit and the organisational demands of the visual work that they are undertaking, and social interaction within this context is necessarily specifically shaped by and within this particular setting through these institutional concerns. Thus, for example, the Director made the cuts for broadcast, and all of the visuals and commentary regarding the relevance of visual information therefore needed to be structured in a way that would allow him to make selection decisions. Because of the technical configuration in the scanner, he was unable to edit replays or even to scroll through them; he could only request that these be "rolled" by the replay operators themselves. The asymmetrical arrangement of communications between the Director to the replay team also meant that the organizational structure was embedded in the technological apparatus. Moreover, these technological arrangements were not simply a result of technological limitations but, given that they were reconfigurable, must have reflected institutional choices in their configuration. The forms of talk in use were also shaped by professional practices and institutional concerns, with, for example, the Director selecting and announcing coded camera and replay footage without negotiation or a need for making his selections locally accountable to his team members (e.g. cf. Goodwin & Goodwin, 1996).

In terms of the following transcript, a simplified form of Jeffersonian transcription is used, with speaker abbreviations for Director, Commentator, and Bronze recorded below as Dir, Com, and Brz, respectively, and the primary colour team members (off-screen and not available for identification) labelled as CT1, CT2, or as CT? (the latter when they cannot be individually identified). To accommodate the broadcast footage and to give some context to the verbal interaction, the broadcast video is added between double vertical bars with a numeric value indicating the sequential video cuts (i.e. || n ||); the associated footage is also shown in Figures 8–22, taken on the initiation of the cut. These images are oblique because they are taken from screenshots inside the scanner, and the camera was not angled straight at the screen. In its totality, the single sequence examined lasts 1 minute 15 seconds. It is not obviously a particularly unusual data segment, and several other instances from our data set offer a similar set of interactional elements. What we observe in this sequence that makes it interactionally interesting is how the production team collaboratively watch and make sense of gameplay, simultaneously producing topically relevant actions and verbalizations in coassembling image sequences. The episode is separated into several brief excerpts, each of which is analyzed in turn. These episodes are not discrete units and are interconnected in their topical concerns, but this segmentation allows both a pragmatic solution in providing a simple explanation to be interwoven alongside the data, as well as to segment loosely related sets of interactions. The first excerpt begins with the broadcast following camera cuts of a set of passes on the pitch; a problem in gameplay is that collaboratively identified and instant replay footage is very quickly assembled on the back of this identification:

(1)   Forward pass observed (3:20)

```
                || 8 ||
01 Com:   Thomas || 9, 10 || (0.4) to Jones.
02        ((untranscribed commentator commentary continues))
03        ((loud groans/noises from EVS team))
04 Brz:   || 11 || ohhh, he's forward
          ((raises left hand outstretched twd her screen))
05 ?RSE:  blerrr, ... ((refs whistle blows))
06 Dir:   couple of turns
07 Brz:   f|| 12 ||orward.
08 Brz:   forward [pass. yeah. on me
09 Com:          [forward pass
10 Brz:   ON BRO::NZE, (.) ON BRO::NZE
```

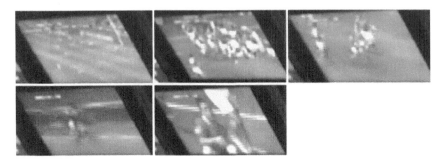

Figures 8–12   Read left to right, top to bottom.

What the footage shows in this sequence is the development of a tussle for the ball (Figure 9) that results in the ball being passed to a red player. The ball is passed on to another player, who catches it and makes a dash for the blue end of the pitch (Figures 10 and 11), culminating in an apparently scoring touchdown (Figure 12). Yet the EVS operators' and subsequently the Commentator's talk around these images demonstrates that all is not as it would visually appear. After the Commentator (Com) begins with a description of passing between players (lines 01, 02) and ongoing play, some of the team members' begin to make audibly recognizable sounds of despair, mimicking, as it were, their broadcast audience. This is followed by Bronze (04), who notes a particular comment on the game: "ohhh, he's forward," again followed by someone saying "Blerrr!" in what approximates to a sound of disappointment just prior to the whistle being blown. These are clearly comments on gameplay and, given the way that they are temporally aligned to poor Welsh play (most of the EVS team being Welsh nationals), are partisan.

All of the broadcast footage here is live camerawork (Figures 8–12), showing different angles and levels of zoom, yet these camera angles are poorly framed to show whether the pass is forward because it is hard to ascertain the action in relation to the pitch (see Figures 9–12). However, at the same time as this, the EVS operators are also watching the cameras that they are responsible for in real time and are able to rely on their insider knowledge of the orientation of these cameras in relation to the pitch. Here, what we can unmistakeably see in the talk at this time is that the team are making sense of what is happening on the field and drawing the attention to others of their own observations as they develop a stronger sense of certainty about them. This can be observed in the initial "forward pass" comments (07–09), followed immediately by confirmation of this as the EVS operators begin to review their recorded footage (notably by Bronze beginning to replay her footage immediately before line 07). At this point, our analysis has now established the form of professional vision held by the team, illustrating how they do *looking together* in making relevant clip selections, but it also identifies their orientation to an audience-like vision in looking with some of the same concerns as their TV viewers.

A forward pass is an important and illegal feature in the game, and it is important to the production team because of its consequences for filming gameplay. However, it is important for them not just because it will result in a game stoppage if this is recognized by the referees. It also means that other things will need to be brought into play in the production. They need to recognize that the referee may (or may not) see the foul and that it will need to be returned to for analysis in a moment of stoppage (which will invariably require instant replay footage). Indeed, because they recognized this before the referee blew his whistle and stopped play, the EVS team were able to make predictions of the next possible turns that the game might take. More than the use of this knowledge later on in the game, they have to attend to some immediate consequences now. Gameplay-relevant graphics may need to be overlaid on the live broadcast for the audience. In case of a longer stoppage, footage needs to be available to fill in for time in which little of interest happens and to add narrative to explain the reasons for stoppage. But there is another reason for the calls made by the EVS operators and team beyond the simple reuse of footage, and this is in allowing the Director insight into what is happening *ahead* of the foul being called by the referee. This allows the Director and RSE to begin to set up a sequence of actions in advance of their being required or at least as early as possible. Attending to the vast number of screens in the gallery composed of the 20 available cameras, the six EVS streams, graphics, and telestration capabilities (see Figure 1) and directing their work to interesting opportunities obviously require a huge and extremely demanding feat of mental agility, even for an experienced professional. Knowing ahead of time what to attend to and what to ask the various operators of the component parts of the system to do has an obvious advantage, and, as we see, this produces a situated practice that is enacted by the other members of the team in searching for what has preceded the foul. So by announcing the foul ahead of its call by the referee, the members are acting to reduce the number of options that the Director and RSE have to attend to. In effect, this allows them to plan ahead in what is a largely uncertain and unpredictable terrain. The sequence then continues, with the analysis showing how this information is made use of in subsequent verbal interactions and image selections.

(2)   Making proposals for broadcast (3:32)

```
11 Dir:     tel[estrate,
12 ?RSE:       ['nything else?
13 Dir:     TELESTRATE
14 ?:       err
15 ?RSE:    gold
16 ?Gold:   ye- yeah gold
17 Dir:     gold
18          (0.5) || 13 || (0.5)
19 ?RSE:    gold (.) then bronze (.) || 14 ||
```

Figure 13   Figure 14

What begins in the live broadcast footage with a close-up of a player (Figure 12) following a disallowed point score (called a "try" in rugby) is followed here with a cut to the linesman (Figure 13) who identified the forward pass and with a cut back to the disallowed try scorer (Figure 14). These could be considered normal patterns of video cutting because they demonstrate first the rationale for the referee's decision, followed by a close-up on the disappointed player. That these sequences are normally anticipated means that the EVS team could be reasonably expected to have some time before their replays are due to finalize their edits and to simultaneously announce their readiness to show pertinent replay material. So at the start of this second excerpt, the EVS team are prepared for an extended period of stopped play, and the Bronze EVS operator has a prepared replay segment ready to roll for the Director. This has now been announced multiple times, both as Bronze spots what she thinks is a forward pass (04, 07) and gains confirmation from her team (09), and this is announced loudly over the intercom to the Director (19). Bronze EVS has also announced that it is visible in her own footage ("on me," 08) and, having the only woman's voice on the team, this is easily recognizable as her, and she reinforces this by loudly announcing "on Bronze. On Bronze" (line 10, from the first excerpt). Notably over this period, the fact that Bronze has picked up the replay footage is not recognized explicitly by the Director. However, he does now make a request that shows he has recognized that something has occurred in the gameplay, as he calls out over the intercom: "Telestrate" (cueing this on 11, then announcing the cut to telestration in 13). This is not a call for Bronze, though: telestration requires instant replay footage from an overview camera (such as Gold) so that the Commentator can annotate it using a stylus, and this is broadcast in real time (i.e. televisual illustration). Thus we can see that he recognizes an important event and that it is likely that a reasonably long game pause will occur in which this telestration can be slipped into the broadcast. Such a call could be reasonably expected by Bronze: it would be unusual to cut directly to the close-up action. Instead, an overview replay would be shown in which the Commentators could show that, how, and when the foul occurred (the forward pass). Only then would this be followed up with a close-up shot from the side (by Bronze), from which it would be hard to determine who was in front of whom were it to be shown on its own without prior overview footage to add this context. This kind of so-called topic orientation is common, and we have observed it in previous studies of ice hockey TV productions (Engström, Juhlin, Perry, & Broth, 2010; Perry, Juhlin, Esbjörnsson, & Engström, 2009). This discussion continues in the next excerpt, in which we show how this observing, along with the clip production and proposal, is followed by new visual content from the live cameras and replays that offer to displace Bronze's apparently increasingly less relevant replay:

(3)   Running Gold and "bumping" Bronze (3:38)

```
20 RSE:    go on. run that (.) I can't see it (.) run
21 ?:      gold
22 Dir:    stand by vt gold
23 ?Gold:  gold
24 ?RSE:   || 15 || stand by vt gold
25 Dir:    run gold
```

```
26 RSE:    run it || 16, 17 ||
27 ?CT1:   reaction on green
28 RSE:    one on bronze as well. one on bronze
29 CT1:    another good reaction! ((off-camera))
30 CT2:    yeah ((off-[camera))
31 multiple voices:   [reaction (.) REACTION on gree:n, ((off-camera))
32 Dir:    °absolutely°
```

Figures 15–17

Here we see Gold's replay cued up and selected, as expected. This is the first replay we have seen broadcast so far. This is preceded by a swipe (i.e. a static image is briefly broadcast; see Figure 16), used as a common indicator to audiences that the broadcast is no longer "live." What we then observe is that during Gold's selection, a new and unexpected turn starts to arise with a call for Green to be shown for its suitable display of visual "reaction" by the players (line 27). It provides a detailed shot in which it is possible to see the facial expressions of a player. This appears to displace the "promised" ("Gold then Bronze") upcoming use of Bronze's replay material, and Bronze produces an immediate verbal response ("one on Bronze as well. One on Bronze"). As we can see, what is announced is not always what is implemented, showing that the sequencing of image selection is not deterministically tied to talk and that these offerings are not so much promises as more advisory in nature. Bronze evidently recognizes the clip competition from Green, as we can observe from her demarcated "as well" (28), which is in direct reference to the alternative clip. The close sequential placement of this turn is clearly produced as a response to the new and competing proposal for showing Green; given that they are competing for limited broadcast time, the likelihood of using both replays is low. What follows is something of a verbal scramble for attention from those representing Green's replay offering. Several loud voices call for Green's footage to be used (31). However, it is unclear to everyone how the Director reacts to this: we are presented with a quietly intonated response ("absolutely," 32) that appears to pair with this call for Green's selection, yet he does not select another replay, remaining on the still rolling overview replay from Gold (still seen in Figure 17). This excerpt makes visible the importance of verbally negotiating for individual camera selections. It is important here to understand that there is an asymmetry of access to visual content among the production team members. The Director can only see the first frame of their selections in his gallery, not the full replay sequences: he cannot know what the replay is or what it will later show, just from what he can see on his monitors in the gallery. Thus we see a distribution of labour as multiple persons do the work of selecting cameras for EVS, and this comes to depend more on the ways in which the replay operators can argue for their case than on the static and uncertain visual information available to the Director. The negotiation then continues.

(4)   A call for replay "reaction" (3:53)

```
33 RSE:    another one on bronze
34 Dir:    going back to 3 (.5) || 16 ||
35 Dir:    w||18||e'll do another one, give me ||19|| another one, number 2
           ((refers to camera 2))
36 RSE:    on bronze
37 Dir:    ok stand (0.5) and reaction
           ((cameras directed to spectators))
38 RSE:    hold it there
39         ((long pause))
40 Dir:    so come back for the penalty
41         ((long pause))
```

Although the RSE makes a call for Bronze to be selected (line 33), the Director gives a forewarning that camera 3 will soon be selected (34) immediately after this. Here, following the deselection of Gold's replay (32) to a live camera, only live footage is used in this part of the broadcast, shifting from cameras 3 to 2. In the EVS studio, the replay search continues, although as can be seen in the audio transcript, nothing interesting appears to be found. This can be observed as the EVS operators keep scanning through replay material without stopping to pick out any selections or verbally commenting on their search, although the RSE vocalizes (also available over the intercom) that Bronze is still ready to present content (36). The Director then makes a request to the EVS team to propose another reaction shot (37); notably, he does not select an existing replay that has been proposed but makes visible a division of labour in the production team. Through this request, the EVS team know that they will be able to select a single reaction replay clip based on a judgement of the content available to them and propose it to the Director (most likely by RSE via a verbal proposal over the intercom). The RSE then notices something interesting in the scrolling footage of one of the EVS operators (38) and (as we later see more obviously in the excerpts that follow) ties his conversation with one of the coloured team's activities on his screens, matching his talk to the timing of the images playing out on the screens in front of them.

(5)   Bronze is selected (4:07)

```
           ((ref is seen to play penalty card in real-time footage))
42 ?:      OEU::AGH!!
43 Dir:    y:ep
44 RSE:    show that again (0.6) that angle (0.4) run it from there (.)
           run it from there
45 Dir:    [come on in 5 ((calling camera 5 to zoom in)) || 20 ||
46 RSE:    [stop stop stop
```

```
47 Dir:    what is it? (0.4) bronze?
48 Brz:    yeahh
49 RSE:    go back (0.7) go back
50 Dir:    stand by bronze? (0.4) and run bronze || 16, 21 ||
```

Figures 18–20

This section begins as one of the players is penalized, and this is followed by what appears to be a groan of disappointment (line 42). This is known to be a topic of concern for the production team because this is anticipated as being topically relevant to their viewers. Penalties typically result in a discussion by the Commentators and may (depending on the length of time available before play resumes) offer an opportunity for replays of the event leading up to the penalty awarded to examine the visual details of the contested event on the pitch. The RSE, who had been commenting on one of the coloured team's replay edits, now takes a much more active role, requesting to see the footage again and suggesting edit points ("run it from there," in 44). As he says this, his speech is coordinated with the rewinding actions of coloured team EVS material (which can be seen in a "tile" on his own display), so that the coloured team's material on-screen actions are temporally tied to his talk; this continues in 46, as he calls on them to "stop stop stop" and again at 49 (and in excerpt 6, in 52). Bronze then finally gets to play her material (50). This is an astonishingly long period to have retained replay footage on-screen, given the normally fast pace of search and video editing activities seen in the room up until this sequence and indeed by the pace of the other EVS operators during the time: her screen remains with the same edited image static onscreen from 15.5 seconds into our video sequence until exactly 1 minute in (clip timing at 4:40). She does this without any direct instruction to keep this active, and we can only surmise that this is done for two reasons: (1) the repeated calls for Bronze by her, the RSE, and Director are not met with its subsequent broadcast; nor, though, are they dismissed because they are continuously referred to by members; (2) this replay is continuously assessed and deemed to be useful and highly relevant to the unfolding game, despite the time elapsed and other game-related activities that follow on.

The excerpt also shows how the actual work of looking at the material and deciding on the editing becomes a collaborative effort. The RSE then gets additional visual resources to suggest what should come next. However, such re-editing of the EVS operators' selections would have taken additional time, which, in this case, was available. In the final excerpt, we see a clear reference to the collaborative nature of attending to temporal concerns by the RSE, as well as to the relevancies of the game dynamic of fitting the replay into the ongoing broadcast without disrupting the viewers' experience of real-time action as the rugby game plays on.

(6) Planning replays for a possible future outcome (4:20)

```
51 ?CT?:  and its reaction's on silver Gav ((man's name))
52 RSE:   go back again
53 ?CT?:  reaction on green
54 RSE:   we'll telestrate that for next time, if, if there's a
          stoppp || 22 || :age, OK?
55        ((with the cut to fig. 22, the broadcast fades into
          a second replay))
56 RSE:   just keep that up there. OK?
57 RSE:   OK
58 RSE:   if they score (.) if they score we'll do it
          ((broadcast cuts to live camera))
```

Figures 21–22

Here, we can observe another feature of broadcast in the conversation, as the team do work to find replay footage that fits into the time available for replay. We see this less explicitly in the fact that Bronze failed to get selected earlier for a long time despite being relevant, ready, and waiting, but the RSE's references to a stoppage (line 54) and then more precisely to a goal (58) are clear verbalizations that new footage is to be kept available to be fitted in. They explicitly do this when (1) there is a natural break of play of a suitable length available to insert prerecorded content and (2) returning to recorded footage as a resource to explain the effect of past events on present ones (i.e. as we see in 58, "if they score") is relevant to the game narrative.

The data sequence examined, we now turn to pull out aspects of the interaction at a more abstract level.

5. DISCUSSION AND CONCLUSION

The analytic focus of this chapter lies in examining the alignment of visual content and talk in organizing members' interaction around video clip allocation to generate a coherent image-based narrative and in showing how they make themselves accountable for their selection of video clip proposals for broadcast. It is worth returning to Schegloff's (2007) "problems" at this point because these pose the core issues that the production team face. Taking these in turn, we have shown, in the instance of this perspicuous case, how the participants achieve this.

From the mass of real-time camera footage and recorded content—only a part of which is visible to all of the members involved—the team manage to agree very rapidly whose content will be broadcast in visual turn-taking (while recognizing that verbal turn-taking is important, we focus here on the video material). It appears that this is tightly tied to the sequence-organizational aspects of action, as successive visual streams of content are made coherent. The participants do so by orienting to some apparently simple interactional features. Narrative features of the game dominate here: certain image selections are visibly understood as normal practice, most likely because they are commonly recognized as actions that will make sense to the viewer. Showing activities that have sequential relevance or typical patterns (e.g. cutting from penalty to referee, to the players involved, to a replay long shot, to a replay close-up) clearly fall into this category, so that the Director and EVS operators both have an idea of what types of footage is likely to be called for. Here, we also see the word-selection problem addressed. As new visual elements are layered into the live broadcast, these delimit the sequential relevance of items that might reasonably follow them, as does the expected time available for them to be played within (e.g. "we'll telestrate that for next time, if, if there's a stoppage," 54). Judgements are being made about the reasonableness of potential visual turns (i.e. visual content made available for broadcast) in the context of the ongoing broadcast footage and their relevance to the game (as can be seen in Bronze's continued holding of her footage).

Nevertheless, other non-narrative concerns also guide these orientations to content for selection. There is an expectation that footage has to be available for use "in time," but this is not always practically possible, and the broadcast needs fill-in footage until the relevant replay material is ready. Similarly, multiple camera angles from different EVS operators may be available, and decisions need to be made on which replay operator to select from. When the Director cannot attend to these directly (as in this case), the RSE makes selection suggestions, and, as we show in the data, this is handled conversationally in combination with the visual resources by the EVS operators and RSE. To do so, EVS operators have to identify and communicate that they have a relevant sequence (and what it is) very quickly so that it can be fitted into the real-time camera footage. The Director verbalizes what he is about to try to do. This allows the replay team to know who is likely to be selected next and gives them an indication of whether to edit, sit on existing footage, or move on to new material. Here, we begin to see the action-formation problem being addressed: shot proposals, requests, agreements, and noticings being presented as recipient-designed recognizable actions. In the case of the Director, these interactions largely occur through the intercom and are necessarily verbal, but on the EVS team, these are more indexical, and talk is clearly tied to the visual imagery present or not present. As we can see, because of this collaboration, the team can review more video material by functionally separating their activities than if they all have access to the same visual resources. However, this division of labour and subsequent selection of an individual operator's material depends on what they are able to make sense of through their talk. This talk is not always sufficient for this purpose, causing them to revisit and re-edit the visual material in a reflexive cycle of live video watching and recorded video editing.

A great deal of organizational work has been deployed to ensure that trouble in the interaction does not occur. The organization of the material resources (intercom, gallery, EVS screens and their layout, RSE screens, scanner floor plan), the team's clear divisions of labour, and their prematch planning are all designed to ensure that problems are minimized. The data present few obvious or terminal troubles that interfere with the production, perhaps as testimony to the skilled professional practices and configured material environment that they work in. As we see, the overall structural organization of the unit is rather different from the emergent structure of talk and interaction in noninstitutional settings, and this environment provides a setting that constrains and scaffolds patterns of communication and delimits possible interpretations that can be layered onto their interaction. We see this, in a very simple example, in the Director's call to the EVS operator to "run gold" (line 25). No conversational niceties are present in this talk, no narrative explanation to make this action accountable or addressing the immediately previous talk, no explanation of what "run" means or when it should be enacted or of its closure in an offering of thanks for its presentation. The Director's words are instructive and do not open an opportunity to extend more talk in a following turn. This talk is brief, utilitarian, and formed to meet the specifically situated demands of the task at hand, as well as reflecting their "differential access to resources and power" (Heritage, 2004: 114). During this kind of talk, members are orienting to their institutional identities, although we also see some slippage between their institutional and ordinary identities (e.g. lines 32, 42; see also Heritage, 2004).

So, in conclusion, the analysis presented here allows a number of features of the setting to be drawn out and examined. We show how team members share video selections, both in copresence and remotely, so that their image selections are made observable and negotiable. We also show how they compare multiple video streams that appear to have timely relevance and examine how they interrogate these competing selections to determine which, in which order, and when they are suitable for segueing into the live broadcast. Such decisions on image selections may be accounted for with reference to their apparent intelligibility, narrative relevance, timeliness, and temporal length, as well as their aesthetic qualities, although these factors are *not* always visible to those making the selection decisions. This may be either because too many parallel video streams are visible for the RSE to attend to and they are too long to fully review in the time available or, in the case of the Director, because these streams are simply not visually available. The members arguing for their own selections are therefore accountable for the relevance of their footage (after the event), and, as we have seen, multiple members may also call for selections to be made, making the proposal appear more warranted. This analysis of the work of instant replay shows how the members of a large and distributed team are able to produce, from a number of real-time camera streams, meaningful and topically relevant material that is suitable for interpolating into a live television broadcast. To achieve this, the team must attend to multiple streams of both live and recently recorded visual content and to use talk and their produced visual resources to make sense of and coordinate their actions. A close analysis of their work shows how this is achieved, referencing an adapted version of Schegloff's generic orders of talk-in-interaction that integrates the visual and verbal resources that they have to hand.

NOTES

1. Due to technical and legal reasons, at the receiver end, it is rare that video content can truly be described as live because of the short delay introduced into the broadcast.
2. EVS is the brand name for the most commonly used device allowing replay operators to perform video editing in live outside broadcasts, and has become the professional term used to refer to instant replay, and by extension, to instant replay operators.
3. Permission was received from both the broadcaster and the participants to undertake this research.

REFERENCES

Broth, M. (2004). The production of a live TV-interview through mediated interaction. In *Proc. Int. Conference on Logic and Methodology*. Amsterdam: SISWO.

Drew, P., & Heritage, J. (1992). Analyzing talk at work: An introduction. In P. Drew and J. Heritage (Eds.), *Talk at Work* (pp. 3–65.). Cambridge: Cambridge University Press.

Engström, A., Juhlin, O., Perry, M., & Broth, M. (2010). Temporal hybridity: Mixing live video footage with instant replay in real time. In *Proceedings of ACM CHI 2010* (Atlanta, Georgia) (pp. 1495–1504). New York: ACM.

Goodwin, C., & Goodwin, M. H. (1996). Seeing as a situated activity: Formulating planes. In Y. Engeström and D. Middleton (Eds.), *Cognition and Communication at Work* (pp. 61–95). Cambridge: Cambridge University Press.

Heritage, J. (2004). Conversation analysis and institutional talk. In K. L. Fitch and R. E. Sanders (Eds.), *Handbook of Language and Social Interaction* (pp. 103–146.). Mahwah, NJ: Erlbaum.

Jordan, B., & Henderson, A. (1995). Interaction analysis: Foundations and practice. *The Journal of Learning Sciences, 4*(1), 39–103.

Macbeth, D. (1999). Glances, trances, and their relevance for a visual sociology. In P. L. Jalbert (Ed.), *Media Studies: Ethnomethodological Approaches* (pp. 135–170). Lanham, MD: University Press of America.

Mondada, L. (2003). Working with video: How surgeons produce video records of their actions, *Visual Studies*, *18*(1), 58–73.

Mondada, L. (2009). Video recording practices and the reflexive constitution of the interactional order: Some systematic uses of the split screen technique. In *Human Studies*, *32*, 67–99.

Mondada, L. (2011). Understanding as an embodied, situated and sequential achievement in interaction. *Journal of Pragmatics*, *43*, 542–552

Murphy, K. M. (2010). Shaping things to come: Temporality and transmodality in design. Paper presented at ICCA10, July 4–8, Mannheim. University of California, Irvine.

Perry, M., Juhlin, O., Esbjörnsson, M., & Engström, A. (2009). Lean collaboration through video gestures: Co-ordinating the production of live televised sport. In *Proceedings of ACM CHI* (Boston) (pp. 2279–2288). New York: ACM.

Sacks, H. (1984) On doing "being ordinary". In J.M. Atkinson and J.C. Heritage (Eds.), *Structures of Social Action: Studies in Conversation Analysis* (pp. 413–429). Cambridge: Cambridge University Press.

Sacks, H. (1992). Jefferson, G. (Ed.) & Schegloff, E. A. (Intro.). *Lectures on Conversation*, Vols. I and II. Oxford: Blackwell.

Schegloff, E. A. (2007). *Sequence Organization in Interaction: A Primer in Conversation Analysis*, Vol. 1. Cambridge: Cambridge University Press.

SISLive (2011). OB 3 HD Production units—Outside broadcast. www.sislive.tv/outside-broadcasts-ob3.php

Contributors

Alain Bovet is Visiting Scholar at Telecom Paristech in Sophia Antipolis. He has taught and published on a variety of communication practices, from everyday interaction to democratic public spheres.

Mathias Broth is Associate Professor in Language and Culture at Linköping University, Sweden. He has published extensively on the work of TV production, as well as on topics related to interaction, language, and mobility more broadly. Broth has previously coedited two special issues of *Journal of Pragmatics* and *Space & Culture*.

Barry Brown is a Professor of Human Computer Interaction at the University of Stockholm and Research Director of the Mobile Life VINN Excellence centre. His research interests include the application of video analysis to technology design and the study of naturally occurring activity.

Arvid Engström is a researcher at Mobile Life VINN Excellence Centre, Sweden. He is an interdisciplinary researcher in the field of Human–Computer Interaction. He does ethnographically informed research and designs live video applications on mobile platforms. He studies situated action for the design of the Instant Broadcasting System, a next-generation production tool for editing mobile live video.

Jonas Ivarsson is Professor and Research Dean at the Faculty of Education, University of Gothenburg. His general research interests concern practices of instruction and technology use in the development of specialized knowledge and competence. Ivarsson has studied work carried out in science education, medicine, computer gaming, and architecture.

Elin Johansson is a PhD student in Education at University of Gothenburg, Sweden. Her PhD project focuses on how video can be used for feedback and reflection on simulated team training scenarios.

Oskar Juhlin is Professor at the Department of Computer and Systems Sciences, Stockholm University, and founder of Mobile Life Centre. He conducts design-oriented research in the area of human computer interaction. Ethnographic study has been a prominent method throughout his entire career covering areas such as engineering work, car driving, deer hunting, and TV production.

Eric Laurier is Senior Lecturer in Geography and Interaction at the University of Edinburgh. He has written on the uses of video in social research and video cultures more widely.

Christian Licoppe is Professor of Sociology at Telecom Paristech, France. Trained in the history and sociology of science and technology, he is interested in conversation analysis and multimodal interaction analysis, and more generally ethnographic studies of multiparticipant interaction in mobile and institutional settings.

Oskar Lindwall is an Associate Professor at the Department of Education, Communication and Learning at the University of Gothenburg. His general research interest concerns the social, practical, and instructional organization of educational activities. He has conducted studies of lab work in science education, critique sessions in architectural education, demonstrations in dentist education, and the teaching and learning of crafts.

Lorenza Mondada is Full Professor in General Linguistics and French Linguistics at the University of Basel, Switzerland. She has researched on language, embodiment, and social interaction in a diversity of institutional, professional, and ordinary settings and has publisshed extensively in the major journals in the field.

Julien Morel is Associate Professor SES, TelecomParisTech, France. He studies the natural organization of face-to-face and mediated interactions (mobile conversations, videocommunication, location-aware communities, and augmented reality games). He also creates new video methodologies to study the uses of ICT in the situation of mobility.

Mark Perry is Reader in Interactive Systems at Brunel University, researching social and ubiquitous computing systems and publishing on embodied conduct around video, mobility, and systems of exchange.

Stuart Reeves is EPSRC Senior Research Fellow in Computer Science at the University of Nottingham, UK. He explores the design of interactive systems and has conducted research primarily on interactions with technology in public settings, particularly in cultural and performance spaces.

Claes Reit is Professor Emeritus at the Institute of Odontology, the Sahlgrenska Academy at the University of Gothenburg. He has published widely in the areas of endodontology, clinical decision making, and ethics.

Hans Rystedt received his PhD in Educational Science in 2002. He is Associate Professor at the Department of Education, Communication and Learning at University of Gothenburg. His current research is concerned with how shifts in visual technologies challenge the nature of disciplinary/expert knowledge and what role the possibility of sharing a visual field plays in developing professional competence.

Philippe Sormani is a Post-Doc Researcher at the Department of Science and Technology Studies at the University of Vienna. His main research interests are at the intersection of ethnomethodology, practice-based video analysis, and science studies. He is the author of *Respecifying Lab Ethnography* (2014).

Cédric Terzi is Associate Professor in information and communication at the University of Lille 3, where he led the undergraduate program "Culture and Media". His main areas of research include the analysis of public experience in an ethnomethodological perspective and ethnographic fieldwork on the public protests in Maghreb.

Index

An environmentally friendly book printed and bound in England by www.printondemand-worldwide.com

PEFC Certified

This product is
from sustainably
managed forests
and controlled
sources

PEFC™
PEFC/16-33-415

www.pefc.org

This book is made of chain-of-custody materials; FSC materials for the cover and PEFC materials for the text pages.

#0087 - 260416 - C0 - 229/152/16 [18] - CB - 9780415728393